counter-
terrorism
after 9/11

JUSTICE, SECURITY AND ETHICS RECONSIDERED

JOHN P. CRANK
Florida Atlantic University

PATRICIA E. GREGOR

 LexisNexis®

 anderson publishing
A member of the LexisNexis Group

Counter-Terrorism After 9/11: Justice, Security and Ethics Reconsidered

Copyright © 2005
Matthew Bender & Company, Inc., a member of the LexisNexis Group

Phone 877-374-2919
Web Site www.lexisnexis.com/anderson/criminaljustice

Crank, John P.
    Counter-terrorism after 9/11: justice, security and ethics reconsidered / John P. Crank, Patricia E. Gregor
    Includes index.
    ISBN 1-59345-957-2 (paperback)

Cover design by Tin Box Studio, Inc./Cincinnati, Ohio

EDITOR Janice Eccleston
ACQUISITIONS EDITOR Michael C. Braswell

Table of Contents

Introduction

A Catechism of Terror and Counter-Terrorism?

At the annual meetings of the Academy of Criminal Justice Sciences in 1996, Dr. Lawrence Travis of the University of Cincinnati sat on a panel with one of the authors of this book and discussed the history of policing. The papers on this panel described technologies used by the police and how the police were able to apply them with various degrees of success. Much of the discussion centered on the ability of the police to make use of technology to better enable them to suppress crime.

At the end of the presentations, Dr. Travis observed that the speakers viewed police as if there were a "catechism of policing." There was, he noted, no "immaculate conception of policing." To understand the police, one had to appreciate the settings from which they emerged and in which they acted. Central to his observation was that police operated within broader environments, social structures, and political cultures, and the way in which the police did their work was highly dependent on these broader contexts.

The daily fare of terrorism and counter-terrorism today has a similar stamp of catechism. Its form is most likely presented as, "Terrorism has reached American shores and we must do something about it." Individuals who question whether it is right to use the military in counter-terrorism find their patriotism challenged for not "supporting our troops," and those who suggest that past or current U.S. foreign policy stimulates terrorism or undermines counter-terrorism are accused of being flat-out anti-American. In-depth analyses of the contexts in which terrorism and counter-terrorism emerge are seldom presented in mainstream media, and when they are they tend to fade against the stony logic of the "need to do something about terrorism."

Treating terrorism and counter-terrorism as if they were a catechism, detached from broader political, religious, and cultural currents both in the U.S. and in the world, may be adequate for tactical security practices but provides no insight into the larger issues in which terrorism and counter-terrorism are embedded. At the strategic level, where policy is fleshed out, such views are limiting and can be counterproductive. At a minimum, students of terrorism should recognize that terrorism occurs within a broad climate of world violence, and some understanding of the dynamics of that violence is needed. Counter-terrorism occurs within a polity whose citizens care about the relationship between liberty and security, and cannot be adequately discussed without recognizing the importance of both.

This book is about the aftermath of a watershed event in U.S. internal and international security, the terrorist attacks on the World Trade Center and the Pentagon, and the aborted attack against the White House on September 11, 2001. This event will be referred to throughout this book as 9/11, consistent with the popular shorthand for the broader description of the attacks. The book is intended to provide many different insights and controversies concerning 9/11. It is about the domestic war on terrorism, what the U.S. is doing in the war, why it is doing what it is doing, and controversies associated with it. Accordingly, it covers general theories of nation-state conflict and looks at their implications for U.S. counter-terrorism policy, the development of the Department of Homeland Security, changes in treatment of immigrants and visa holders and the impact of those changes on immigrant communities, the treatment of prisoners, ethical issues in the war on terrorism, and critiques of the war.

Counter-Terrorism versus Liberty?

This book focuses on counter-terror issues, policy and practice in the U.S. and attempts to explore their dynamics. Controversy, in many instances, is central to these dynamics. This book focuses on the post-9/11 era, the changing security dynamics of public and private life, and the issues related to them.

When we began writing this book, our intent was to look at alternatives to the debate—a debate we took to be superficial—that the war on terrorism being carried out in the United States was enacted as a conflict between issues of civil rights and due process versus security and citizen safety. Yet, the more deeply we explored the way in which the war was being carried out, the more we realized that the principal weapons used by the government were constructed around restrictions in civil rights. Moreover, many of these restrictions, particularly during the early phase of the war, were carried out in such enveloping secrecy that nongovernmental actors could not even find out if civil rights were being violated. In the third year following the declaration of the war, as government audits and reports begin to assess the behavior of the government, we are beginning to learn of the extent to which civil rights were disregarded and physical abuse was carried out against suspects, many of whom were later freed without charges, while others continue to be secretly held in the U.S. and in other locations around the world. Hence, the focus of this book took its current form, that the conflict in the U.S. is, in fact, carried out as a conflict between civil liberties and security. A complex series of crime control legislative decisions and expansions of the power of the Attorney General limit access to U.S. courts. The underlying logic is universally crime control oriented—restrict civil liberties, expand surveillance, seize and interrogate anyone with suspected terrorist connections, and act aggressively against threats or symbols of terrorism.

Importantly and contrary to public opinion, the conflict between liberty and security in the war on terror does not have its roots in the government's response to 9/11. If one were to use a flower metaphor, one would better say that it bloomed post-9/11. Processes of governmental surveillance expanded throughout the twentieth century (Marx, 2002). The federalization of crime control has grown sharply since the Reagan presidency of the 1980s, and the coupling of aggressive crime control, extensive recordkeeping, and surveillance became pronounced in the 1980s (Gordon, 1991). If any one particular piece of legislation was particularly influential in the government's response to 9/11, it was the 1996 Antiterrorism Act, signed by President Clinton. Without the groundwork established by that legislation and its sister legislation, the 1996 Immigration Act, the government would not have the legal capacity it has today to act so forcefully against civil liberties.

Certainly, the response to 9/11 has been marked by a fervor of disrespect for civil liberties within U.S. jurisdictions and for international treaty obligations. In all aspects of the war on terrorism, one senses the war on crime writ large, acted out under a vision of civil liberties as complicating, unnecessary, and antagonistic to the needs of the new security environment. Yet, because the war on terrorism has taken this particular turn, it has become immensely controversial. Both within the U.S. and in the international setting, the war on terror is challenged. By looking at the many different facets of the war on terrorism, we attempt to provide the reader with a sense of the breadth of governmental activity, its nature, and the surrounding controversies.

Chapter Overviews

Chapters 1 and 2 are overview chapters. They assess general issues about terrorism and counter-terrorism.

Chapter 1 focuses on the contexts of terrorism and the definitions used to identify and respond to terrorism efforts in the United States. Part 1 of this chapter presents terrorism as a contested concept, which means that its core meaning is disputable. Because it is a contested concept, its meanings lie in the views of different people who are affected by them. A narrative style of description, we suggest, is appropriate for writing about contested concepts.

Part 2 of Chapter 1 presents terrorism as a criminal justice concept. Counter-terrorism as practiced in the "war on terrorism" is strongly crime control, and Packer's (1968) Crime Control-Due Process models of justice are used to conceptualize the war. This chapter closes with a discussion of the popular post-9/11 phrase, "connecting the dots." This phrase, it is argued, provides the force behind much of the thinking that drives the crime control elements of the war on terrorism.

Chapter 2 frames the core terms "terrorism" and "counter-terrorism." This chapter considers many different definitions of terrorism. In these varied definitions we can see the different arenas through which terrorism and counter-terrorism are contested. Many government agencies, for instance, define terrorism in ways that expand or justify their own mandate. One of the consequences of this is that a hodgepodge of public definitions of terrorism exist with little thought for their overall congruency.

This chapter also looks at what may be the central issue in defining terrorism, which is whether it should be thought of as a crime or as an act of war. If it is treated as a crime, a broad array of democratic values affect how we respond to it. If it is treated as an act of war, our response is fundamentally different. It would be convenient if we could legally frame counter-terrorism as a balance between police action and war. However, this does not work. Either democratic protections are available and afforded to suspects or they are not. Citizens are afforded an array of constitutional protections even when suspected of wrongdoing. Suspected enemy combatants are shot on sight.

The chapter concludes with a definition of counter-terrorism as a historical narrative: Counter-terrorism is the sum of the various practices currently being used against perceived terrorist activities or threats. The remainder of the book will discuss those various practices, and the issues and controversies surrounding them.

Chapters 3 and 4 look at the sources of terrorism and foundations of counter-terrorism practices in the U.S. These two chapters blend international issues (perspectives on world violence) with U.S. criminal justice issues (history of surveillance and justice system growth) to provide a comprehensive background to the events leading to the U.S. governmental response to 9/11.

In Chapter 3, terrorism is described as a form of world violence, comprehensible in terms of patterns of violence and the conditions that produce violence. Accordingly, perspectives on world violence are presented and discussed, and views on terrorism are derived from the broader images and views of violence. Only through a recognition of the extent of violence and war at the beginning of the twenty-first century can we make sense of terrorism and its place in those many conflicts. Various perspectives on international conflict are presented in this chapter, organized in terms of culture/religion based theories, theories of resource conflict and competition, and reciprocal causation (or "blowback") views of conflict and terrorism.

Chapter 4 looks at surveillance issues. Citizen and immigrant surveillance have expanded since the 9/11 attacks, raising concerns for privacy advocates. This chapter looks at the history of surveillance in American society. Surveillance is presented as a Tayloristic good, a way to control and increase the efficiency of the working class. We examine the ways in which surveillance has expanded throughout the twentieth century, giving rise to a "new surveillance" adapted to mass society and tracking virtually all aspects of American life. Surveillant strategies associated with post-9/11 have their roots in the development of surveillant strategies in the wars on drugs and on crime. This chapter also discusses surveillance dimensions of the 1996 Antiterrorism Act, the 2001 USA PATRIOT Act, the Domestic Security Enhancement Act of 2003, and the FISA court.

Chapters 5 through 9 look at 9/11 and its aftermath. Chapter 5 examines various ways in which counter-terrorism has affected the daily lives of American citizens. This chapter begins with a discussion of the history, structure, and practices of the Department of Homeland Security (DHS). Two of the most publicly visible components of the DHS, airline security and color-coded terror alerts, are discussed in detail. This chapter concludes with a discussion of the newly founded Northern Command (Northcom), the military equivalent of the DHS. Northcom is the first Department of Defense command to take military responsibility for the United States and its neighbors. The structure of Northcom and corresponding concerns related to *posse comitatus* are discussed.

Chapters 6 and 7 focus on immigrants in the post-9/11 era. No group has been more affected by the war on terror than aliens, particularly Middle-Eastern immigrants and visa holders. Programs focusing specifically on immigrants are both abundant and complex; a variety of programs aim at detainment, others at tracking and surveillance, and yet others at visa tracking. These chapters attempt to disentangle these programs and elucidate the controversies that are associated with them.

Chapter 6 focuses on the detainment and seizure of immigrants since 9/11, and describes the sweeping effects of changes in law for immigrants in the U.S. Part 1 of this chapter locates Middle-Eastern immigration in overall processes of immigration, to provide perspective. It then overviews current constitutional law regarding immigrants in the U.S., and rejects a commonly held view that immigrants and visitors on visa have no constitutional rights. This chapter also examines the 1996 Immigration Act, a corollary and less frequently noted companion act to the 1996 Antiterrorism Act. Part 2 looks at legal changes in the lives of immigrants. The increased legal flexibility in detaining and jailing of immigrants, chronicled extensively by the Migration Policy Institute (2002), is discussed. This chapter also discusses various interim rules implemented during the post-9/11 era, particularly the Alien Absconder Initiative, sometimes associated with the S-visa (or "snitch" visa to its detractors), used to gain leverage over immigrants during interrogation procedures.

Chapter 7 continues the focus on immigrants, this time looking at programs and laws that increase alien registration and surveillance. Again working with the Migration Policy Institute (2002) chronology, this chapter looks at several categories of post-9/11 counter-terrorism activity. It examines the National Security Entry-Exit Registration System, aimed at visitors and immigrants from countries that, according to the government, sponsor terrorism. The Enhanced Border Security and Visa Entry Program, which affects visitors, is also discussed. Of particular interest in this chapter are expansions in surveillance, which have been a hodgepodge of programs that envelop the tracking and observation of immigrants and visitors. Importantly, many of these new surveillance programs also apply equally to U.S. born citizens. This chapter also considers the Student and Exchange Visitor program (SEVIS) and discusses the "voluntariness" of the voluntary interview program.

Chapter 8 looks at the way in which foreign prisoners are treated in the war on terrorism. This chapter considers the prison at Guantanamo Bay and the complex issues surrounding the use of the Cuban base for detainees accused of terrorism. A history and the conditions of confinement are discussed. Many observers have raised questions about the terms of confinement of prisoners at Guantanamo, and their lack of POW status continues to be internationally controversial. Equally controversial is the provision of quasi-military tribunals, an issue explored in depth in this chapter. This chapter closes with a discussion of one of the most contentious elements of the war on terror, the use and justifications for aggressive interrogations and torture in efforts to uncover potential terrorist activity.

Chapter 9 summarizes critiques of the war on terrorism. Section I looks at three reports, an Amnesty International report, a report by the Inspector General of the Department of Justice, and the Migration Policy Institute report. The critiques presented in this section all were published in 2003, after the programs critiqued had been in place for a period and evidence could begin to accumulate regarding their effectiveness. Each report assesses a different aspect of the counter-terrorism effort, and each charts unexpected or unanticipated consequences of the war on terrorism. A critique of governmental access associated with the war on terrorism by Paul McMasters (2003), Freedom Forum Ombudsman, is presented in Section II. Section III takes an ethical look at the war on terrorism. Two ethical perspectives are presented. The first considers means/ends conflicts in the war, and the second looks at the war in terms of "just war" theory.

The conclusion examines the way the U.S. has adapted to the war on terror. Considering the second anniversary of 9/11, it notes those aspects of the war that have endured. We have learned to imagine terror, and our fears have led us to deal with those different from ourselves in ways that are not democratic. Yet democratic institutions endure, and moral-ideological conflicts between security and democracy show no indication of abating. Sharp contestations between security and democracy are likely to be permanent features of the war on terror for its duration, however long that will be. The controversies that emerged shortly after 9/11 have intensified and show no indication of abatement. Both within the U.S. and between the U.S. and its allies, conflicts are increasingly crystalline and polarizing. These conflicts do not stem from the 9/11 attacks. They stem from the U.S. government's response to 9/11.

Author Perspectives

The authors bring the following perspectives to this book. First, a background in police research provides insight into many issues dealt with in counter-terror efforts. Many of the issues in the war on terrorism and internal security (a euphemism for police work) are similar, and the two areas overlap considerably. Both are committed to security and both try to suppress dangerous behavior. The field of international security, however, is generally unavailable for research, and many operatives and government leaders openly resist—usually in the name of security—any release of information on their activities and organizations. Police research provides insight into ongoing practices, their likelihood of effectiveness and efficiency, and their problems.

Second, many issues in the war on terror have been framed in terms of the polar criminal justice positions of crime control versus due process. Today there seems to be an almost blind acceptance of the idea that if some strategy or tactic undermines due process, it must be effective. This idea must be challenged.

For example, controversies over profiling of individuals from Islamic countries have focused on whether due process considerations should be permitted to disrupt governmental efforts to identify potential terrorists. Rarely considered is whether profiling works. However, preliminary research on profiling among the police has been carried out, and it appears to be ineffective and even counter-effective. Even in cases where the profile is only one of a variety of techniques employed to identify drug couriers, a concern has been raised that individuals use that which comes most readily to hand, namely the race of the target, and end up lowering effectiveness, while the heightened number of stops creates the false impression that members of the group profiled are more likely to be drug couriers. What is needed is a hard look at the potential effectiveness of the weapons advocated in the war against terror, and efficient thinking about the implications of their use.

Third, U.S. crime control and security in the war on terror are politically framed in contradictory relations with human rights and due process. For example, on February 11, 2003, Afghanistan became the eighty-ninth country to join the International Criminal Court (ICC). The ICC, created in 1998, is a U.N. body whose purpose is to adjudicate crimes of genocide, crimes against humanity, and serious war crimes. Afghanistan joined over the objections of the U.S., which has refused to join. The U.S. has expressed concerns that its own citizens or military personnel might be charged with human rights violations by the court (Baker, 2003). We argue herein that issues in human and legal rights are complex, and that students of the war on terror should recognize that understanding the world around them is hindered by unyielding beliefs in absolute standards of justice. There are instead many people in different places and under different circumstances trying to do that which is right and just.

All social science investigation carries the biases of the investigator, whether acknowledged or not (Crank, 2003a). Put differently, we all construct the world around us through the cultural dispositions that we carry. Those dispositions both enable our social participation and limit the alternatives we find morally acceptable. In the world of social facts, knowledge is supremely relative and always value-laden. Accordingly, we bring the disposition to this book that government should be transparent. This parallels our perception that criminal justice is in large part a social science and, as such, moves forward through the willing participation of criminal justice agencies to open their records to research in order to improve their performance and understand the many contingencies and implications of the work they do. Only in exceptional circumstances should government restrict citizens' access to information, and in all cases that restriction should be legislatively limited in duration and later reviewed in a public forum, so that citizens can later decide whether the government was factual about the reasons for the restriction. This view also reflects the practical recognition that any governmental secrecy will inevitably become the subject of media debate, and it is better that citizens can analyze and participate in that debate in an informed way rather than having their sources of knowledge limited to the ratings-seeking and book-selling ambitions of popular pundits.

One of the most difficult aspects of writing this book is assessing the quality of information available on terrorism and counter-terrorism. Those who conduct research on the police in the United States have found a great deal of openness and willingness to share information. Comparable openness is simply unavailable in many areas of national security. Consequently, many of the references used in this book are drawn from mainstream media sources such as books, newspapers, and the Internet. This is always perilous, as anyone who has done similar research knows. One can encounter on the Internet large volumes of information, meticulously cited, clearly written, and simply wrong or so badly "spun" that it is no more than political rhetoric. Traditionally trustworthy newspapers, facing competition from their Internet rivals, are increasingly vulnerable to premature presentation of information as if it were factual before all the facts are known. This is an unsolvable problem; yet we believe it is better to accept and acknowledge the limitations, suspecting that there is unlikely to be a time in the future when access to national security data will improve.

CHAPTER 1

A Criminal Justice of Terrorism

Terrorism and counter-terrorism are about good and bad. Acknowledging this enormously complicated statement is the first step in the study of issues in terrorism and counter-terrorism.

We have a reason for describing the opening statement as "enormously complicated." Once we acknowledge that good and bad are important for understanding terrorism, we are in the realm of making value judgments about terrorist violence and counter-terror government practice. And this is complicated, because our values about the rightness of government practices may be quite different from someone else's. For the same reason, my sense of who and what is terrorism may also be quite different from yours. To understand this, try to have a peaceful discussion among 10 friends about whether anti-abortion efforts to restrict entry into so-called "abortion" clinics are a form of terrorism.

The complications of good and bad are central to this book. We do not take a descriptive position in this book, citing a laundry-list of groups that are terrorist, actions that constitute terrorism, and efforts by the government against these groups and actions. Terrorism and counter-terrorism do not stand alone, but are embedded in contexts. These contexts are moral, political, cultural, and international. They involve conflicts among peoples and the way in which those conflicts tend to endure. Oftentimes, groups have sharply different notions of good and bad, right and wrong. And these different notions extend to what constitutes terrorism and what the government should do in the way of counter-terrorism. Beginning in this chapter and throughout this book, we present terrorism and counter-terrorism as contested terms, meaning that there are profound problems embedded in any attempt to define them. Consequently, counter-terrorism will always be controversial. This book hopes to convey some of that controversy.

Chapter 1 is a framing chapter. In it, we frame three central issues in terrorism and counter-terrorism, focusing primarily on issues related to counter-terrorism. The first is the idea that terrorism and counter-terrorism are contested concepts whose definitions vary in time and place. By recognizing their contestedness, we recognize that there are limitations to which objective statements can be made about them, even at the most basic definitional level. In the second section, we present counter-terrorism as a form of criminal justice study. We try to locate it in the broad view of contemporary criminal justice, which is about the study of the behavior of justice organizations. The third issue is related to the second; it looks at an emergent 9/11 way of thinking about security, commonly called "connecting the dots." This way of thinking emerged after 9/11 in response to the widely held view that adequate information was available to anticipate 9/11 but was fragmented among different agencies. This section argues that the notion of "connecting the dots" has become a general way of thinking about counter-terrorism, but that it also has its own problems thus far unaddressed and generally unrecognized.

Terrorism, Counter-Terrorism, and Contested Concepts

How many of us have heard the phrase "One man's terrorist is another man's freedom fighter?" It is a phrase that carries the weight of insight for some people and arouses anger in others. Certainly, it is a phrase that has been bandied about as if it explained a great deal. However, its meanings bear scrutiny, both for what they say and for what they don't. To equate a terrorist and a freedom fighter is to suggest that something that is very bad for some people (terrorism) is very good for others (fighting for freedom). American revolutionaries in 1776 are sometimes cited as examples of terrorists whom we celebrate as freedom fighters. In 1991 President Reagan described militant Afghan Islamists as "freedom fighters;" some of them later participated in terrorist activities against the U.S.

The phrase is uncomfortable for a particular reason. It means that something that is recognized by some group as "good"—fighting for freedom—cannot be defined absolutely, but is relative to time and place. In other contexts, it is an evil that we call terrorism. It all depends on when some act was carried out, who did it, who they did it to, who observed it, and most importantly, who gives meaning to it.

Terrorism has been called an "essentially contested concept" (Gallie, 1956; see National Research Council, 2001). This, according to the National Research Council (2001:15), means that "some concepts are inherently incomplete, without being totally incoherent, and are filled out differently by individuals and groups who bring different backgrounds, beliefs, and political convictions to bear on them."

To understand a contested concept, we can compare it to a theoretical concept. The application of research to theory generally is based on the notion that a particular theoretical concept has many different real-world applications. For instance, "the law" is a theoretical concept. There are many different forms of the law, from the English Common Law to the Code of Hammurabi. But each is considered a real world example of a more general theoretical concept—the law. When social scientists test concepts, they are actually testing real-world applications of those more theoretical concepts. The idea of a theoretical concept means that there is some degree of agreement on what it means theoretically, and real-world or empirical instances are simply different forms that the theoretical concept takes.

With a contested concept, there are no rules of agreement on the meaning of the concept either theoretically or in any particular real-world setting. In fact, there is significant disagreement, either across groups or within the same group over time. Moreover, definitions of terrorism tend to reflect interests rather than some commonly shared notion. Consider the group Hamas, designated as a terrorist group by the U.S. State Department. The definition of terrorist groups for U.S. citizens depends on which groups are so designated by the State Department at any time, and Hamas is listed among those groups. However, there will be Palestinians who view Hamas as a group of freedom fighters. They will contest the U.S. definition of Hamas as terrorist. Moreover, Ariel Sharon was once listed as a terrorist by the U.S. State Department but in the current era, as head of state in Israel, he is one of our closest allies. Until 2003, Muammar al-Qadaffi, head of state of Libya, was viewed as one of the world's leading terrorists, blamed for the downing of Flight 103 over Lockerbie, Scotland, and subject to an assassination attempt by the United States by the Clinton administration. However, in December of 2003, after extensive secret diplomacy carried out principally by Great Britain, Qadaffi opened Libya to full inspections for weapons of mass destruction. Today he is widely seen as having moved his country on the path to nation-state rehabilitation.

The notion of "contestation" complicates efforts to develop definitions of terrorism and freedom fighting. By creating definitions that distinguish between the two, we make an artificial distinction that removes us from the real world where conflict between Israel and Palestine is acted out. Our definitions are not objective. They tend to reflect and reinforce our international alliances, organizational missions, or political and cultural preferences. Because of this, our definitions of terrorism can act as blinders, obscuring the human problems that drive terrorist activity.

Current criminal justice offerings do not tend to view terrorism and counter-terrorism as contested concepts. They view terrorism and counter-terrorism as normative concepts, which means that they view terrorism as wrong and as evil, and consider counter-terrorism specifically in terms of its ability to suppress terrorism. A scant literature also considers other issues related to terrorism, such as terrorism's relationship to economic, religious, and social factors (Griset & Mahan, 2003) or recognizes the way some tactics blow back and create more violence in the long term (Johnson, 2000). These concerns are secondary to the normative focus of the bulk of the literature, which is a discussion of the history, groups, and practices of terrorist groups and how counter-terrorism can suppress the behavior of such groups.

The problem with a normative focus is not that it is wrong-minded but rather that it is limited. What is absent is a sense of contested issues related to terrorism and counter-terrorism. Terrorism does not emerge in a cultural vacuum but is associated with particular groups' religious, ethnic, and economic circumstances, their conflicts with other groups, the geography of those conflicts, and resource access and availability. Studying terrorism without some attention to its cultural and geographical setting is like inquiring into crime in the U.S. by looking at the Uniform Crime Reports, absent studying the large volume of criminological writings that have emerged over the past 50 years.

A narrow normative focus for counter-terrorism fails to understand its impact on the broad social institutions in which it is carried out. It is comparable to thinking about criminal justice only in terms of its ability to contribute to crime suppression. Certainly an important part of criminal justice is crime suppression. Yet the criminal justice field has expanded considerably in scope since the 1960s, as we have begun to recognize that criminal justice practice has social, psychological, economic, and cultural dimensions, is embedded in and made coherent by its moral-political environment, and that it exists in a highly complex relationship with crime. Similarly, counter-terrorism has emerged from historic justice practices and should be considered in these terms.

This book is about terrorism and counter-terrorism as contested concepts. It undertakes the preliminary work of assessing some of the broader dimensions of counter-terrorism. It takes as a central principle that counter-terrorism practices in the U.S. since 9/11 occur in contested legal, moral, and political arenas; groups in these arenas conflict with each other, and the views of groups in these arenas must be considered in order to resolve these conflicts. Accordingly, the comprehension of terrorism and the study of counter-terrorism should take into account how both are contested in their many arenas.

The broadest arena of contest is that between nation-states and/or between states and sub-national groups. Students of terrorism should not be naïve about the sheer quantity of violence that exists in the world. To develop perspective on terrorism and thus develop meaningful counter-terrorism strategy, what is needed at an intellectual policy level is some sense of why world violence is occurring at the scale it is, and how the U.S. is implicated or directly involved in some of the violence.

The terrorism we deal with today emerged against the backdrop of what has been described as the most violent century in the history of the human race, what Brzezinski (1993) referred to as the century of "megadeath." Terrorism is one of the many kinds of wars, revolutions, coups-d'état, and minor conflicts that were ubiquitous on planet Earth at the beginning of the twenty-first century. Terrorism emerges from the same forces that give birth to these other conflicts, and it often accompanies these other kinds of conflicts. At the strategic level, these factors need to be addressed in order to provide long-term solutions to terrorism. Students consequently need some knowledge of world conflict in order to develop a sense of what terrorism is all about. That terrorism has migrated to the U.S. from the Middle East, for instance, is not accidental. It resulted from powerful forces already in play, and in which the U.S. was one of the players.

A second source of contestation is terrorism's core justice identity. If it is recognized as a term pertinent to the realm of criminal justice, as many argue, then the language we should use to talk about it is that of criminal law. This law is about due process and crime control, and deals with terrorism in terms of its criminal morphology. However, if it is a term whose meaning should be sought in the military language of international security and national defense, then a different legal sensibility applies, one conceived in terms of just war, self-defense, military deployment, and international treaties regarding the treatment of prisoners.

A third area of contestation lies in the expansion of surveillance under the war on terror. One of the central contests faced today is that between privacy and surveillance. The argument put forward herein is that surveillance under 9/11 is not something new, but is the product of a trend that has characterized the practice of criminal justice in the United States and was documented in the excellent book *The Justice Juggernaut* by Diana Gordon (1991). The growth of surveillance in public and private life in the U.S. is far more pervasive than most people realize, tapping activities from grocery purchases to cell phone use (Marx, 2002). The terrorist attacks of 9/11 accelerated the growth of surveillance technologies already in place or being developed. For example, airlines industries are beginning to do passenger background screenings, incorporating into the screening process such items as credit history.

A fourth area of contestation lies in conflicting views of the consequences of counter-terrorism practices between the justice department and its advocates, who use a variety of recently enacted laws to develop information about terrorist threats, and the lives of immigrants and foreigners caught up in the war on terror. In a series of programs such as the National Security Entry-Exit Registration System, the Alien Absconder Initiative and the Voluntary Interview Program, the government has sought to increase its ability to track aliens to find out if terrorists might be hidden among them. These programs are aimed at addressing the security vulnerabilities and lapses that resulted in 9/11. Another narrative has emerged from these programs, that of immigrants and visitors to the U.S. who were disenfranchised of many of their historical and constitutionally guaranteed due process and civil rights protections. This narrative is that of their individual stories, about what actually happened to them, and about the lives that were disrupted and sometimes lost in the war on terror.

By treating terrorism and counter-terrorism as contested concepts, we gain a strength. We become less naïve and, therefore, less vulnerable. We don't simply assume that our ideas of what constitute terror and counter-terrorism have some absolute quality of rightness. We recognize instead that they reflect cultural, moral, and legal preferences.

To say that our views are balanced by those of others who disagree does not trivialize our beliefs. Certainly, we must believe in what we do in order to protect ourselves and those we care about, and this belief need not be complicated. But we would be foolish to think that the terrorist who uses his or her body as a bomb in order to carry out a killing has any less conviction that they are right. Their acts demonstrate their conviction. The challenge lies in finding ways to protect ourselves that do not inadvertently lead to further conflict and terrorism in the future, and that also preserve those central governmental institutions which provide the core cultural and legal identity of Americans.

The study of terrorism and counter-terrorism as contested concepts places an obligation on us. By studying them as contested concepts we are obligated to understand the breadth of the effects of what we do and what is done to us, the meanings of our actions to others as well as to ourselves. If a concept is contested, it is contested by people. This means that, in order to understand the meanings of terrorism and counter-terrorism, we must recognize the different voices that contribute to their meaning. This may be an uncomfortable way of thinking about terrorism and counter-terrorism, but it is the nature of the creature we study.

Counter-Terrorism as Narrative

How does one set about studying contested concepts? Social science notions of empirical analysis do not seem particularly suited for it, because such notions make the assumption that there is some agreement on how to define concepts. Social science also is facilitated by the availability of empirical data on its field of study, and data on government counter-terror efforts has generally not been forthcoming. The government may keep information restricted for the quite sensible and official reason that terrorists might use such information in planning attacks. However, the government may also keep information restricted so that critical assessment of its true and possibly disreputable behavior cannot be carried out. Whichever of these is true (and certainly both can be true at the same time), information is not forthcoming. This book, consequently, takes a narrative approach to the study of counter-terrorism.

Narrative, put simply, is story-telling. Viewing counter-terrorism as a "story" removes the notion of "privilege" from counter-terrorism efforts and relocates those efforts in the saga of human history. The narrative notion is an explicit rejection of the "catechism" of counter-terrorism mentioned at the outset of this book. Counter-terrorism is viewed as a human process, full of historical particularity, sometimes successful and sometimes tragic, inevitably error filled, and full of the panoply of emotions that mark human stories.

Narrative is a perspective. Binder and Weisburg's (2000:22) description of the law as narrative applies equally to the study of counter-terrorism. Narrative "tends to connote particularity rather than abstraction, emotional involvement rather than detached rationality, creativity rather than technicality, and fluidity rather than rigidity." When we look at counter-terrorism as narrative we ask questions such as "Does it reveal or distort? Is it reliable? Does it lull us into repression or awaken us to resistance? Does it promote self-deception or self-understanding?" By asking these sorts of questions, we are looking at the human dimensions of counter-terrorism, its particular effects, its emotional costs and profits, how the war on terrorism is one current in the flow of the human experience.

When we view counter-terrorism as narrative, we are not trying to come up with a specific, abstract or universal definition of it. We accept its contestedness. Counter-terrorism as narrative is the variety of the ways in which the U.S. currently carries out counter-terrorism efforts, and the success or failure of those efforts is weighed in terms of how they affect us individually and generally.

A part of the narrative function is to identify the historical trends that characterize current counter-terror issues and practices. We seek comprehension; we hope to recognize the wide panoply of issues that counter-terror efforts touch. This is a substantial task, because counter-terrorism touches many different aspects of the American experience.

Counter-terrorism, viewed through the lens of narrative, tells us about events not simply as "factual overviews" typical of textbooks, but as stories of people, those making the law and those on the receiving end of those laws. In unanticipated ways, the object of our research—government counter-terrorism—compels us in this research direction.

When we look at the way in which the government dealt with immigrants in the early days after 9/11, we find that much of what the government did was carried out in secret. The numbers of immigrants held, the basis of their charges, the length of their detention, their identity, their location, and other aspects of detention, were kept secret. When the government carries out its activity in secret, fundamental challenges to the field of criminal justice are raised. Research in this field is typically empirical and quantitative, and the ability of the field of criminal justice research to contribute to the public depends on access to information about the behavior of government. When information is not forthcoming, either alternatives to empirical data analysis must be found or the field must be abandoned. We can choose two paths. On the one hand, field researchers can become advocates of open government, recognizing that only through the full availability of information can the field of criminal justice maintain its viability as an empirical science. Or we can use other methodologies to assess the work in our field.

The work carried out in this book accepts the secrecy of the government as a historical fact and takes a narrative and descriptive approach. By coupling a description of governmental decisions as they are actually acted out in the public domain with a discussion of the impact of those decisions on various American peoples, we begin to understand the reach and meanings of counter-terrorism in the U.S. since 9/11.

The Criminal Justice of Terrorism

In this book we focus on counter-terrorism perspective, practices, and issues, rather than on terrorism per se. The distinction between terrorism and counter-terrorism used here is intended to mirror the common distinction between the study of criminology and the study of criminal justice. The common distinction is that the study of criminology focuses on crime, particularly its etiology or causes. In parallel fashion, the study of terrorism is about the terrorist act and actors, and tends to assess terrorist criminology. The study of criminal justice aims at an understanding of the behavior of governmental institutions responsible for crime control, and is commonly separated into theory of crime, the police, courts, corrections, and juvenile justice. Counter-terrorism study, from this perspective, looks at the agencies and laws that deal with terrorism and seeks to understand their behavior.

In Part 1, we noted that books on terrorism tend to be normative. This also characterizes a great deal of research in criminal justice. This book recognizes counter-terrorism as a proper area of justice study. Counter-terrorism is located in a variety of justice-related contexts, including the way in which current practices relate to the historical context of crime control expansion in the U.S., the expansion of surveillance practices, the immigration context in which much of the counter-terrorist effort has been carried out, and ethical context concerning some practices advocated by counter-terror specialists. Studying these contexts in which criminal justice intersects with terrorism helps us to understand the consequences, intended and unintended alike, of counter-terrorism efforts.

To compare and contrast the studies of criminal justice and counter-terrorism, consider interrogations. Interrogations are a central weapon in the *armamentarium* of prosecutorial tools in the United States. From a normative perspective, interrogations serve several purposes. They seek additional information about a crime. They help police seek evidence of the guilt of the person interviewed. And they enhance the ability of the prosecutor to make a legal case against a suspect.

In counter-terrorism, interrogations serve all of these purposes and one more: They seek information about terrorist acts likely to be committed. In these interrogations, the interrogator is not simply building a legal case but may also be under the pressure of time to prevent casualties resulting from a terrorist act. Under these circumstances, the normative question is, "How can we make interrogation more effective for finding information quickly to prevent loss of life?" Many television pundits, and not a few federal investigators, argue that coercive interrogation—a euphemism for torture—is justified when potential loss of life is imminent or an anticipated act of terrorism may produce many casualties.

We take an issue-oriented approach to coercive interrogation as a counter-terrorism tool. We ask three overlapping questions: (1) What are current practices? (2) What are the moral issues associated with the use of coercive interrogation? and (3) What evidence bears on the efficiency and effectiveness of coercive interrogation? In the current era, in which torture is bandied about as a remedy for dealing with hardened terrorists and the only counter-arguments are stated in terms of broader concerns over civil liberties, we think that a broad-ranging assessment of the actual practice of torture will shed some light on the history and current use of torture as an interrogative tool.

Security versus Fair Play

This book argues that issues in counter-terrorism in the U.S. are framed by the conflict between the competing justice perspectives of crime control and due process, each characterized by central organizing values. This may or may not be the best way to develop counter-terrorism tactics and strategies (see, e.g., Gilmore, 2003). It, however, is the way selected by the government to combat terrorism within the U.S. and its many extra-national jurisdictions following the events of 9/11. The crime control perspective is based on the value of security, the due process on the value of fair play. These value perspectives are not new to students of justice system processes; they represent a central divide in debates over justice system practices. According to the security perspective, the primary purpose of the justice system is the efficient use of state resources to prosecute and punish wrongdoers. According to the fair play perspective, the primary purpose of the justice system is the maximization of information so that guilt or innocence can be accurately determined. Rules of procedure should guide the prosecution of wrongdoers.

Security and fair play are acted out in court processes in terms of a structured presentation that seeks to balance the influence of a crime control oriented prosecutor and a due process oriented defense counsel. The prosecution, representing the government's case, seeks a finding of guilt for those brought before the court. Findings of guilt are facilitated by plea-bargaining (which guarantees a finding of guilt), by presenting evidence held by the government, and by suppressing defense efforts to acquire information. Defense counsel presents evidence on behalf of the accused, and seeks to demonstrate that the government's evidence is inadequate for a finding of guilt. The balance of the forces of prosecution and defense can be described as an effort to balance the competing interests of efficiency in bringing cases to a reasonably quick conclusion, and the maximization of information through due process so that the findings of the court bear some resemblance to the actual facts of the case.

Packer's crime control model allows us to look at security and fair play with regard to the conduct of the war on terrorism. The model is presented in Figure 1.1.

Figure 1.1
Packer's Model of Crime Control and Due Process Forms of Justice

Packer argued that the practice of justice in the U.S. could be characterized as the tension between two competing models of justice, each characterized by different values. The crime control model has the following characteristics (Packer, 1968):

1. Repression of criminal conduct is the most important function performed by the criminal justice process.

2. A failure of law enforcement means a breakdown of order, necessary for freedom.

3. Criminal process is the positive guarantor of social freedom.

4. Efficiency is the top priority of the model. By efficiency is meant the ability to apprehend, try, and convict high numbers of criminals whose offenses become known.

5. There is an emphasis on speed and finality. Facts can be provided more quickly through interrogation than through courtroom examination and cross-examination.

6. The conveyor belt is the model for the system. This is a steady stream of cases from arrest through conviction.

7. A presumption of guilt makes it possible for the system to deal efficiently with large numbers of felons.

The Due Process Model has the following characteristics.

1. The reliability of the criminal justice process is closely examined. The model focuses on the possibility of error. It is particularly concerned with the third degree and coercive tactics.

2. The outcome is in question as long as there is a factual challenge. Finality is not a priority.

Figure 1.1, *continued*

---

3. There is an insistence on prevention and elimination of mistakes in factual assessments of culpability.

4. If efficiency demands shortcuts around reliability, then efficiency is to be rejected as a system goal. The aim of the process is as much the protection of innocents as punishment of the guilty.

5. The combination of stigma and deprivation that government inflicts is the end goal.

6. The coercive power of the state is always subject to abuse. Maximum efficiency means maximum tyranny.

7. A person is to be found guilty if and only if a factual finding of guilt is accompanied with procedural rigor in the criminal justice process.

Source: Packer, Herbert (1968). *The Limits of the Criminal Sanction.* California: Stanford University Press.

According to Figure 1.1 above, the due process model of justice emphasizes that individuals have rights that supersede the authority of the government. Inherent in this perspective is the idea that the power of the state is subject to abuse, and that an over-concern for efficiency, at the sacrifice of individual rights, can lead to tyranny. In order to prevent governmental abuse of authority, any guilt-finding process must be accompanied by procedural rigor. This means that the government must follow clearly stated guidelines for the demonstration of guilt, and that the behavior of the government is always "transparent," open and subject to review by citizens.

The crime control model is about the repression of criminal conduct, typically described as specific or general deterrence. Efficiency is the primary goal of the system, by which is meant that the justice system seeks to apprehend, try and convict large numbers of those whose offenses become known. Justice proceedings should focus on efficiency, speed and finality; and those arrested are generally presumed to be guilty. Interrogation, rather than courtroom procedure, produces efficient crime control.

Over the past three decades, there has been a decided shift in public and political support for crime control, accompanied by steadily eroding support for due process. In criminal justice practice, the relationship between crime control and due process is sometimes combative. Yet the most likely outcome of a court case is a plea arrangement, often mistakenly called a "bargain," which properly understood is a finding of guilt determined after an individual gives up his or her constitutional rights in preliminary court hearing. The widespread practice of plea bargaining dramatically increases efficiency of the courtroom process, and is evidence of the extent to which crime control values dominate court process today.

Crime Control and Due Process in the War on Terrorism

The conduct of the war on terrorism is similar ideologically to the crime-oriented model of justice. In many aspects of crime control, the legislation produced during the 2000-2004 Bush presidency does not differ noticeably from that of his predecessor. The USA PATRIOT Act, widely criticized as an assault on due process, is probably not as far-reaching in its invasion of citizen privacy as was the 1996 Antiterrorism Act signed by President Clinton (see Cole & Dempsey, 2002). And like his predecessor, President Bush has expanded the role of government in counter-terrorism in ways consistent with the conservative crime control model.

Elements of the due process model are generally limited in the administration's prosecution of the war on terror. For instance, the military tribunals established to try detainees at Guantanamo Bay are widely recognized as more friendly to the government's case and hostile to the use of civilian courts. Elements of due process have been added to the tribunals, but only after the administration faced repeated challenges, both domestically and from its international allies. Furthermore, much of the government's case has been conducted in secret. For example, the government continues to refuse to release the names of individuals held in its roundup of foreigners after 9/11. Indeed, if we review elements of the crime control model, we see that many aspects of the war on terrorism are consistent with the model. Figure 1.2 presents examples representing the seven elements of the crime control model presented in Figure 1.1.

Figure 1.2
Seven Elements of Crime-Control Applied to Counter-Terrorism, Post-9/11

1. **Repression of criminal conduct.** The conduct of foreign policy under the Bush presidency has been re-organized to facilitate the war against terrorism. The first large foreign policy act of this policy, the invasion of Afghanistan and military operations against Al-Qaeda and the Taliban, was a clear effort to repress terrorism.

2. **Order as precondition for freedom.** Since 9/11, President Bush has reinterpreted his principal responsibility as protecting the security of the United States, which he has often described as a war of freedom against terror. The existing security apparatus had broken down, as was apparent on two fronts. Terrorists had been able to board and seize commercial aircraft, and surveillance had failed to uncover the plot beforehand. The response was to increase airport security and infrastructure security in general, and to beef up surveillance at all levels of American life.

3. **Criminal process guarantees freedom.** Many elements of the war are characterized by the beefing up of the federal law enforcement role in American life. For example, under the USA PATRIOT Act, many areas of

Figure 1.2, *continued*

immigration law traditionally resolved in the courts were reinterpreted as Immigration and Naturalization Services functions and hence relocated from the courts to the executive branch of government. Some of these were later turned over to the Federal Bureau of Investigation.

4. **Efficiency.** The efficient application of government practices is seen in many counter-terrorism programs. For example, under the NSEERS program, all immigrants from designated countries were required to submit to government designated centers for a special registration. During the registration, all those who had any sort of visa violation were arrested by INS agents. Most were subsequently deported. The INS made efficient use of the NSEERS program to deport aliens it considered illegal. It should be also noted that the determination of illegality was made as an administrative decision by the INS, and individuals picked up in the sweep were not permitted the use of the courts to appeal their cases. In this sense, efficiency is obtained by (a) using NSEERS to screen and trap aliens with questionable papers, and (b) excluding the courts from executive decision-making processes.

5. **Speed, finality, and interrogation.** Under executive order from the President, prisoners from the Afghanistan war, as well as many from Saudi Arabia and Yemen, were sent to Guantanamo Bay in Cuba, where they were imprisoned. The government was clear on the reason for locating them there—they were not on U.S. soil and hence were beyond the jurisdiction of American courts. Moreover, they were not to be granted POW status. These two decisions permit the unimpeded interrogation of all prisoners there held, which could not occur in such fashion if (a) they were on U.S. soil or (b) they were protected by Geneva Convention rights, which prohibits interrogation of prisoners of war.

6. **Conveyor belt.** The conveyor belt is witnessed by the government's efforts to build a streamlined courtroom procedure, referred to by the President as a military tribunal, for the trial of prisoners at Guantanamo Bay. The proliferation of secretive CIA detention centers around the world, combined with rendition practices in which captives are turned over to third world countries to extract information, are about holding war on terror suspects and obtaining intelligence unhindered by notions of individual rights or international treaty protections.

7. **Presumption of guilt.** Finally, a presumption of guilt is evident in many incidents. Many of the individuals in Guantanamo Bay, an estimated 10 percent of the prisoners held there, are there because they were at the wrong place at the wrong time, not because they pose a threat to the U.S. Yet the government has steadfastly refused to consider the likelihood of their innocence. Moreover, in all areas, procedural rigor associated with due process has been almost completely replaced with bureaucratic rigor determined by the executive branch of government. Indeed, due process has largely become irrelevant because the executive branch has effectively avoided the use of the court system in most cases.

Many organizations and countries have argued that the U.S. should be more sympathetic to some standard of fair play for individuals arrested after 9/11. Officials in the Netherlands, including the Dutch Foreign Affairs Minister, have contended that detainees in Guantanamo Bay should be afforded the rights available under the Geneva Convention (Serrano & Hendren, 2002). The Red Cross has made similar requests. The Human Rights Watch has expressed concerns about the repatriation policy from Guantanamo Bay, and about the failure to accord Taliban soldiers Geneva Convention protections (Roth, 2002). The Inter-American Commission for Human Rights, an agency of the Organization of American States, has requested that a competent tribunal be convened to resolve the question of the detainees at Guantanamo Bay, a request the U.S. has rejected (Malinowski, 2002). These groups are influential in many quarters, but their efforts to introduce some notion of detainee rights has been consistently rejected by the U.S. government.

Eighty years ago, New York State Supreme Court Justice Benjamin Cardoza famously observed that it was better that 10 guilty men go free than one innocent man be imprisoned. This observation, a restatement from the common law, is at the heart of the due process view of the practice of justice. Yet in the war on terror the relationship between due process and crime control is sharply tilted in the direction of crime control. When asked why the military continued holding at Guantanamo Bay detainees that it knew to be innocent, one officer replied, "No one wanted to be the guy who released the twenty-first hijacker" (Miller, 2002). His comment shows a concern that a guilty person might be released inadvertently if policies permitted innocent individuals to be freed. It is a logic that reverses Cardoza's famous maxim.

The officer's statement typifies many of the decisions made by the government in the war on terror. The study of the war on terror is in large part a study of crime control writ large: Punitive crime control strategies have become the basis for counter-terrorism activity in the U.S. Whether they work has been the subject of heated debate, and is only of secondary importance in the national dialogue. They are used not because they work, but because they are consistent with crime control values that dominate the current era. They resonate with the way in which many U.S. citizens think about the world around them. Those who advocate more due process are certainly as reasoned and persuasive as are those who argue on behalf of crime control. And some are quite assertive. But they lack widespread political support, and have been powerless to slow down the relentless expansion of crime control practices that define counter-terrorist policy in the U.S. since 9/11, and crime policy generally since 1980.

Redefining the Relationship between Crime Control and Due Process

It is widely observed that water, on dropping to 32 degrees, turns to ice. This observation is sometimes used to make the metaphorical point that quantitative changes can lead to qualitative changes. Today a similar phenomenon is occurring with regard to the relationship between due process and crime control in the war on terrorism. A new model of the relationship between crime control and due process is emerging. The old model was that, in the practice of justice, crime control and due process were related in a combative or adversarial relationship. Though crime control tended to prevail, the justice system nevertheless maintained a belief in the importance of due process. In the new model, crime control issues take priority, and after they are satisfied, due process or fair play issues are addressed. That is, crime control is prioritized over due process. The driving force behind the change, the metaphorical cooling force that turns water to ice, is fear of crime and terrorism.

One might counter that the U.S. government is only placing security ahead of due process for a relatively narrow population of detainees from the war in Afghanistan and for immigrants who have violated their visas. How many of us have heard the pundits on television comment that immigrants who have illegal visas should be deported anyway, because they are here illegally? This argument, however, is flawed, and it is flawed in a way that undermines due process generally. What the argument fails to address is that immigrants, indeed, anyone on U.S. soil has been historically protected by a core body of rights. If they have been suspected of illegal behavior, traditionally they have been permitted to appeal their case within the American court system. However, under the USA PATRIOT Act and revised guidelines of an interim rule, the determination of their illegality has shifted to the Bureau of Immigration and Customs Enforcement (ICE) if their case in any way is suspected of involving terrorism. Complicity in terrorism is wholly determined by the Justice Department, and only after that determination is made are courts permitted to address suspected wrongdoing.

In other words, in the war on terrorism, the use of the courts has been replaced by administrative decisionmaking in the Justice Department, from which there is no appeal, and under which even detention and evidence (except in summary form) may be kept secret. In this way, many individuals who have been traditionally protected by the right to access American courts no longer have that right. The determination about whether they have that right is a Justice Department decision. Once terrorist concerns are resolved, the person may be released to return to their families, if they are in fact legally in the U.S. and have been uncontroversial. Or they may be turned over to the justice department for prosecution if an investigation into their activities has produced evidence of criminal wrongdoing. Or they may be deported to their country of origin. Or, for an unfortunate few, they may be held indefinitely, without charges. But first, the security issue is resolved to the satisfaction of the Justice Department.

In many aspects of the war on terrorism we see the shift to the resolution of security concerns, with due process rights subsequently permitted by the government only after security issues are satisfied. Because the government, under the USA PATRIOT Act, can keep its proceedings secret to all but the FISA court established under the 1996 Antiterrorism Act, and even there only need provide summary data, there is no effective oversight of the behavior of the government. Once identified by the justice department as a person of interest, an individual, citizen or not, has no recourse but to throw himself on the icy mercy of the state. Without access to the U.S. court system, a plea of guilty during interrogation may be the only opportunity a person has for justice, and that is very little opportunity at all.

Connecting the Dots versus Standards of Evidence

"Connecting the dots" became the buzz phrase of the post-9/11 era. The phrase refers to dot pictures in puzzle books enjoyed by children. By connecting the dots, children can outline a picture that the dots suggest. The dots are all there, but only by connecting them can we reveal the hidden picture.

In the post-9/11 era, "connecting the dots" became a metaphor central to understanding the shortcomings of American intelligence. To say that intelligence agencies had failed to "connect the dots" meant that they had failed to understand the patterns in the information they had collected regarding terrorism. To connect the dots, the agencies needed increased information sharing to better understand the patterns that made information meaningful. However, in a more general and public sense, connecting the dots became a justification for government intrusiveness in order to find out about potential terrorism. It justified that way of thinking in the public mind as well, generating hope that more effectively connecting the dots might help identify future terrorist acts.

The connect-the-dots way of thinking carries an important downside that tends to be overlooked in efforts to anticipate a formidable threat. Sometimes the dots are not true dots. Sometimes the information is bad. Sometimes the pictures drawn by connecting the dots are simply wrong pictures.

There are also many dots to connect. Think of dots as individual communications. As Berkowitz (2003) noted, at one time individual communications were relatively straightforward to intercept. Law enforcement officers could simply tap a phone directly, with the consent of judges and assistance of the phone company. That has changed in recent years. Digital messages are sent on the Internet or cell phone and can follow multiple routing directions from point to point.

Under the USA PATRIOT Act, law enforcement can now monitor individuals across multiple phone lines. However, terrorists have adapted to this by replacing cell phones every week or so and by using Internet cafés with e-mail accounts changed frequently (Berkowitz, 2003). Moreover, modern encryption software is widely available and of a quality equal to government encryption products. Berkowitz likened intercepting terrorist communications to eavesdropping in a crowded restaurant: "Which table? Which conversation? And just what are they talking about?" (Berkowitz, 2003:1).

Yet, this kind of intelligence plays a strong role in the government's decisions about the importance of terror threats. An agent for the National Security Council referred to most information so received as "snippets and threads of information" (Priest & Schmidt, 2003). The plot must be inferred by the interpreter from these snippets and threads. And that is always guesswork, as one of Priest and Schmidt's (2003) interviewee's put it, more of an art than a science. Consider the following description of one such snippet:

> The CIA received one such scrap of information from a detainee now imprisoned overseas, whose prior confessions about terrorist colleagues had turned out to be accurate, according to senior government officials. Several weeks ago, a man told his interrogators that a Jewish gathering scheduled in Virginia Beach over this weekend was a target. The date matched information that had been collected in previous weeks indicating that attacks could occur right after the conclusion of the Haj, the annual Muslim pilgrimage to Mecca. The dates Feb. 13, 14, and 15 were specifically mentioned.
>
> It took two squads of FBI agents three weeks to run down the tip. When the FBI finally conducted a polygraph on the detainee, it concluded Feb. 9 that he had fabricated the information, perhaps to please his interrogators (Priest & Schmidt, 2003:2).

The connecting-the-dots way of thinking is mobilized by a central principle: The level of threat from terrorism is so great that conventional protections of privacy and citizens' rights must be reconsidered. Consider the attitude of Secretary of Defense Donald Rumsfeld:

> Rumsfeld contended that the greater the threat, the less the evidence that should be required before attacking.
>
> Focusing on the danger of nuclear and biological weapons falling into the hands of groups that want to attack the United States, Rumsfeld said "I would submit that the hurdle, the bar that one must go over, changes depending on the potential lethality of the act" (Ricks & Slevin, 2003).

The "threat" argument is a powerful one that carries weight in how the U.S. government practices counter-terrorism. However, the emergent picture of potential terrorism depends on the quality of the dots being connected. Sometimes that quality is unknowable. And the connecting-the-dots way of thinking always carries the possibility that the picture assembled is only in the imagination of the assembler. There is the possibility of outlining a nonexistent threat. Indeed, this is what happened in the example above presented by Priest and Schmidt (2003).

Connecting the dots is a fundamental shift away from the idea that investigation tempered by the rigor of evidentiary standards should guide the intercession of the government in citizens' affairs and in the collection of information. It allows error to creep into the government's counter-terrorism practices. Furthermore, because the government's decisions can be made with evidence of unknown quality and without court hearings to assess its quality, the validity of the entire prosecution of counter-terrorism becomes suspect.

Historically in American criminal courts, criminal liability involves three standards of evidence, each more demanding because the potential outcome is more severe: *Reasonable suspicion* is an articulable belief by a reasonable officer that a specific person committed or was about to commit a crime. This is required for a police officer to approach a suspect, ask some preliminary questions, and carry out a superficial search. *Probable cause* is a set of facts and circumstances that would induce a reasonably intelligent and prudent person to believe that a particular person had committed a specific crime. This is required for arrest. Finally, *proof beyond a reasonable doubt*, required for conviction, is the moral certitude that a specific person committed a crime. It is not absolute proof, which is not demanded by law.

Military courts have standards of evidence similar to civilian courts, namely *clear and convincing evidence*. This can be defined as a high probability that a claim is true. It is a heavier standard than a preponderance of evidence, but less than proof beyond a reasonable doubt. Arrests require *probable cause*. Similarly, a standard of guilt *beyond a reasonable doubt* is required for conviction.

These standards might seem cumbersome and confusing. Yet their importance cannot be underestimated in understanding how American justice works. Central to justice is that the government should prove, by some sort of standard reasonable to ordinary people, that a law was violated or was going to be violated if the government did not intercede. Evidence must tie a specific person to a specific crime, and that evidence must satisfy one of the standards above, depending on the jurisdiction. By establishing evidentiary standards, both civilian and military courts introduce validity into their legal proceedings. These standards are intended to prohibit the government from acting arbitrarily or with impunity against those within its jurisdiction.

"Connecting-the-dots" ways of thinking, seemingly justified by terrorist threat, can upend these traditional standards and lead to erroneous decisionmaking. Consider two examples. The first has to do with a terror alert based on erroneous information obtained during an interrogation. On

December 29, 2002, the FBI issued a national alert for five men, together with their names, ages, and photographs. The alert was broadcast on all media, indicating that the men were suspected terrorists who had slipped into the United States illegally. A national manhunt was initiated for the five men.

There were fundamental problems with the alert from the outset. The FBI noted that they were never certain that the men had actually entered the U.S., nor did immigration have records of the men entering the country. And one of the men, a jeweler in Pakistan named Mohammed Asghar, stated that one of the photos circulated by the FBI was of him but carrying the name Mustafa Owasi.

The alert was a hoax. The information concerning the terrorists was passed to the FBI by Michael Hamdani, an accused immigrant smuggler in custody. He had been arrested in Toronto, Canada, for trafficking in stolen traveler's checks and running a counterfeit passport ring. He had given the information to the FBI in order to avoid deportation to the United States (Mintz, 2003a).

What we see in this example is how information, gathered by the FBI but untested for its quality, was used to mobilize a national manhunt. It was, in retrospect, clearly erroneous information. Evidence gathered from a police interrogation, in and of itself, is of unknown quality. It can easily be tainted by the suspect, who wants to avoid or mitigate prosecution, and by the police, who want to produce results.

A second example, below, shows how information of unknown quality can easily lead to errors and unintended consequences.

On September 6, 2002, a waitress at a Shoney's restaurant in Calhoun, Georgia, reported hearing three men, who appeared to be Middle Eastern, discussing a terrorist attack. One of them was reported to have said "we do not have enough to bring it down." She reported the men's descriptions and license plate numbers to Georgia State police, who in turn relayed the information to Florida State Police. A regional manhunt was initiated for the men. Later, a tollbooth operator stated that the men "blew a toll plaza at the beginning of Alligator Alley at around midnight" (Click10.com, 2003). A long strip of road in Florida, known as "Alligator Alley," was subsequently closed down.

The three men were stopped and held for 14 hours. Their vehicles were searched. Specialized equipment was used in the search, including a bomb-detection robot. One container from the vehicle was blasted with a water cannon. According to the Sheriff, the men were uncooperative. However no explosives or illegal contraband were found in either car. Alligator Alley was reopened later that evening.

As the facts were uncovered, it was learned that the three men had received medical training at Ross University on the Caribbean Island of Dominica and were on their way to Miami for additional training at Larkin Community Hospital in South Miami. There was no evidence of terrorist activity by the men, and background checks uncovered nothing suspicious. However, because of the publicity surrounding the event, the hospital ultimately decided to remove the three men from the program. The hospital chief's executive officer stated that the hospital had received more than 2,000 communications about the incident and that some were threatening to the students and to the hospital (Sutton, 2002).

The story was broadcast across the media. After it was found that the men were not terrorists, many pundits on national TV noted that the men had probably joked with the waitress, and had received what they deserved. However, no evidence subsequently emerged that the men had joked or intimidated the waitress in any way were substantiated, and the men denied both charges. A tollbooth surveillance video substantiated the men's story that they had paid the toll.

The Director of the Georgia Department of Public Safety later stated, "The message I would like to relay . . . is that the system we have relayed to the public in Georgia to be alert, to be aware, and report—has worked—the system has worked." The system did not work. The erroneous identification of terror suspects and mobilization of the state police in two states was a system failure. The technical term for the failure is that the men were "false positives" or individuals who seem to have characteristics of some particular group of interest, but in fact do not belong to that group. The men were mistakenly arrested, received negative press, were harangued on television talk shows, and their career opportunities were curtailed. Again, in this example, information of unknown quality was allowed to determine the behavior of the justice system. Indeed, one can trace a string of erroneous information that played to public fears, beginning with the waitress's report of terrorist talk, followed by the tollbooth operator's allegation of toll-dodging, and culminating with the accusations of a "sick joke" by national pundits.

In both of these cases, "connecting the dots," driven by a fear of terrorism, became an alternative for the substantiation of danger through evidentiary quality. In the examples above, the terrorist threat was nonexistent. The "connect the dots" perspective, driven by public fear and legitimated by a connecting the dots way of thinking, permitted incorrect threat assessments. In the short term, the "connect the dots" approach to threat assessment can lead to erroneous and wasteful government action. In the long term, it delegitimizes government counter-terrorism efforts.

Conclusion

This chapter presented two concepts integral to this book. First, terrorism is presented as a contested concept. That it is contested affects virtually all aspects of the war on terrorism. They tend to become controversial. This is one of the central problems with a contested concept—all issues related to the concept tend to become politically controversial. Thus, whether we consider whether terrorism should properly be thought of as an act of war or as a crime, how we treat immigrants and visitors to the U.S., what our constitutional protections should be in the war, who we should fight against, how we should balance surveillance and privacy, all these issues become controversial.

The second theme that runs through this book is that, in the conduct of the war on terrorism, crime control issues are resolved administratively before due process and constitutional rights are acknowledged. Crime control, in a word, is elevated over due process. Importantly, this is not a dramatic change that results from the war on terrorism, but represents trends already existing in U.S. criminal justice practice.

It is widely believed that counter-terrorism can become more effective by "connecting the dots." This way of thinking was fostered by concerns that information about the impending terrorist attacks might have been present prior to 9/11, and that lack of communication across different agencies prevented critical knowledge sharing. Indeed, criminal justice agencies have a long history of competition in their efforts to solve cases, and the idea of connecting the dots is long overdue. Moreover, intelligence must work with the materials available to it, and frequently those materials are no more than mere communications scraps.

The problem with "connecting the dots" is the elevation in importance we have given it. Connecting the dots is a useful way to think about systematizing intelligence, but it is a bad way to think about the collection of evidence for criminal prosecution during the war on terrorism, and it is a poor basis for the construction of policy. The problem with "connecting the dots" ways of thinking is that it justifies the use of a wide body of highly interpretive and sometimes erroneous information, to provide a basis for counter-terrorism policy and actions. Because some of the intelligence data so collected is the basis for the war on terrorism, the crime control part of the war on terrorism has lost crucial validity. This is not a criticism of intelligence agencies who do the best they can with the information at hand, but a recognition that there is an upper limit to the quality of a great deal of what passes for intelligence. The idea that it should become the cornerstone of crime control in the war on terrorism is to place a great deal of trust in quite fallible information, and ultimately, to permit a great deal of error to enter the practice of crime control.

CHAPTER 2

What Is Terrorism? Counter-Terrorism?

This chapter is a definitional overview of terrorism and counter-terrorism. It continues the framing of issues begun in Chapter 1. One of these issues is that terrorism, because it is a contested concept, seems to defy all efforts to define it. Defining terrorism is a bit like defining obscenity—as a famous jurist noted, "I know it when I see it." 9/11 was clearly a terrorist action. But the clarity and intensity of this act obscures important general questions: (1) What is terrorism? and (2) Should counter-terrorism be treated as war or crime control? It is not that terrorism cannot be defined, but that any definition immediately runs into problems. We review several definitions and discuss their problems.

Part 2 considers counter-terrorism. The principle issue discussed here is whether counter-terrorism should be carried out as police activity or as military activity. That is, is it best to deal with terrorism in the courts or deal with it militarily and through international treaty obligations? This chapter concludes with an approach to counter-terrorism grounded in a narrative logic. This logic asserts that counter-terrorism is best understood neither as an objective study nor as something detached from other facets of social life. We can best understand counter-terrorism through a discussion of the way in which it is acted out, its good and its bad, its emotional impacts and consequences, and its complex interactions with citizens in American society.

Defining Terrorism

Definitions of terrorism are diverse. There is not a commonly agreed upon definition of terrorism. Instead, definitions reflect the particular interests of the groups united by a common interest in terrorism. Consider the FBI definition of terrorism:

> . . the unlawful use of force or violence against persons or property to intimidate or coerce a government, the civilian population, or any segment thereof, in furtherance of political or social objectives (Dyson, 2005:21).

This definition serves an important purpose. By referring to the "unlawful" use of force, terrorism is associated with criminal activity and falls within the FBI's jurisdiction (Dyson, 2005). It should also be noted that the defined objectives of terrorism are political and social. This definition hence justifies the gathering of data on the political and social behavior of individuals as part of the FBI's anti-terror responsibilities.

The *Dictionary of Criminal Justice* (Rush, 1994:333) has a four-part definition of terrorism. The four elements are:

1. The calculated use of violence to obtain political goals through instilling fear, intimidation, or coercion.

2. A climate of fear or intimidation created by means of threats or violent actions, causing sustained fear for personal safety, in order to achieve social or political goals.

3. An organized pattern of violent behavior designed to influence government policy or intimidate the population.

4. Violent criminal behavior designed primarily to generate fear in the community . . . for political purposes.

This definition has several notable elements. First, unlike the FBI definition, elements 1, 2, and 3 do not necessarily refer to criminal behavior. Only element 4 is pertinent to criminal codes. Second, all the behaviors are tied to a political purpose. One would conclude from all four elements that a behavior is terrorist depending on the political intent of the person carrying out the violent or intimidating activity. Third, all elements carry some notion of the creation of fear among the population. This is a subjective notion; it suggests that an activity is terrorist only as long as someone is fearful. If there is no fear, is an act then terrorist? Moreover, how does one legally assess a legal standard such as "intent to create fear?" Amid this complexity, one can fashion a three-pronged legal standard developed from these elements: (1) was there violence, (2) was the violence carried out for political purposes, (3) did the population where the act took place feel fear or was there a deliberate effort to make them fearful?

Mueller (2002), former Chief of the United Nations Crime Prevention and Criminal Justice Branch, suggests that the concept of terrorism is a criminological one. To distinguish between terrorism and other kinds of crime, he considers six elements.

1   Who is the potential perpetrator? Generally, terrorists are non-governmental agents.

2. Who is the victim? Terrorists differ from freedom fighters in that terrorists target innocent populations, and freedom fighters do not.

3. What is the target selection? Terrorists focus on symbolic targets.

4. What is the purpose? The purpose is to instill fear and terror.

5. What is the goal? It is usually to force a change in governmental policy.

6. What is the motive? It is usually to create an aura of invincibility and capacity to strike anywhere.

Mueller's definition, it should be noted, does not include the legal element of a crime. All the criminal things that terrorists do, he observes, are already against the law. He focuses only on the *mens rea*, the intent of the actor. Though he does not suggest it, these elements, when treated as criminological, would serve as enhancements for guilty findings in a court of law.

A leading scholar of terrorism, Hoffman (2003), observes that terrorism needs to be carefully distinguished from other, similar kinds of phenomena. For example, terrorists are distinct from guerillas: Guerillas are armed individuals who operate in the open as military units, seize and hold territory, and engage military forces, none of which terrorists do.

Hoffman also distinguishes between terrorists and criminals. The violent acts committed by both are similar, but the motivations are different. Criminals typically use violence for selfish ends, and repercussions are usually not intended to extend beyond the act itself. Nor does the violence intentionally convey any message. The terrorist, on the other hand, seeks political or ideological ends, the consequences are intended to extend beyond the act to the target population, and the message is one of fear.

Finally, terrorists are distinct from lone assassins. Both may be politically motivated and use the same tactics. However, the lone assassin's goal is typically idiosyncratic and deeply personal. Terrorists' goals are never egocentric.

From this, Hoffman (2003:23-24) develops the following definition of terrorism, as "the deliberate creation and exploitation of fear through violence or threat of violence in the pursuit of political change." This recognizes that terrorism is:

1. Political in aims and motives.

2. Violent, or threatens violence.

3. Intended to have a psychological impact beyond the immediate victim or target.

4. Carried out by an organization with a chain of command or consistorial cell structure.

5. Perpetuated by a sub-national group or non-state entity.

Hoffman's distinctions, on close inspection, are not always clear. (For example, in the widely cited book *Inside Terrorism* the author cites "lone wolves"—individuals who act wholly without contact with others—as a particular kind of terrorist, whose strength is that, because he acts alone, he does not face the group problem of infiltration by government agents. And guerrilla groups and terrorist units may exist under the same organizational umbrella.) However, his definition of terrorism provides an important degree of specificity needed for a term whose use and meanings sometimes seem to be ubiquitous. Figure 2.1 is a discussion of the "lone wolf" element of terrorism.

Pillar (2003a:25) provides a definition of terrorism whose dimensions are similar to Hoffman's. Terrorism is "premeditated, politically motivated violence against non-combatant targets by sub-national groups or clandestine agents, usually intended to influence an audience." This definition has four elements.

1. Premeditation. There is an intent to commit an act that qualifies as terrorism. It is not momentary rage or impulse, nor accident.

2. Political motivation. This excludes acts for monetary gain or personal vengeance. There is a claim to be serving some greater good.

3. Noncombatant targets. This means that targets cannot defend themselves. Hence, this definition includes military personnel who are unarmed or off duty as well as civilians.

4. Perpetrators are either subnational groups or clandestine agents. On this point Pillar disagrees with Hoffman. Mir Aimal Kansi's attack on the CIA was a lone act, but was nevertheless politically motivated and best considered an act of terrorism.

Pillar recognizes that any definition of terrorism is "blurry." Terrorism is a kind of behavior that exists along a continuum of political behaviors expressed by people who oppose the status quo.

One of the most difficult aspects of Pillar's definition of terrorism is that, once something is identified as terrorism, a particular kind of response is appropriate for it that differs from the response to criminal behavior. The problem with this aspect of a definition of terrorism is that we end up defining terrorism not by acts themselves, but in terms of our inferences about their motivations. Given the broad definition of terrorism provided by the USA PATRIOT Act, terrorism can refer to almost anything that is interpreted by the government as a potential threat to the government. Terrorism becomes whatever we want it to be.

Figure 2.1
Lone Wolves and Terrorism

How important is the inclusion of "lone wolves" in a definition of terrorism? The FBI, during a code orange alert in February, 2003, warned that "lone extremists" could become enraged by current events and launch an attack against U.S. targets. They noted that "Lone extremists may operate independently or on the fringes of established extremist groups either alone or with one or two accomplices."

The FBI cited Hesham Mohammed Hadayet as an example of such lone extremist terrorism. Hadayet was an Egyptian immigrant who killed two individuals at the El Al airline ticket counter at the Los Angeles Airport in 2002. He was subsequently shot to death by a security guard. He had killed, authorities concluded, because of hatred for Israelis, and had also suffered recent personal problems.

Hadayet carried out his attack on July 4, a period of heightened terrorist alert. Israeli officials and Jewish community leaders declared that his attack was terrorist. However, the FBI probe into the incident concluded that "Hadayet was a devout Muslim who was angered by Israel's policies toward the Palestinians, but also had Jewish friends in the United States and had never associated with any known Muslim extremists" (United Press International, 2002).

The FBI distinguished between lone extremists and terrorist group members. They are driven by "psychological abnormalities and, even when members of groups, may act without the group's approval or knowledge." Often, the FBI suggested, they lack the social skills to participate in an organized terrorist group or conclude it is insufficiently radical.

That the FBI decided to raise this concern suggests that, from a security perspective, it is unwise to view terrorism only in terms of organized groups. However, the inclusion of lone wolves into a notion of terrorism changes the counter-terrorism dynamic considerably. One cannot bring Rico statutes against terrorists who are not members of any particular group. And one cannot infiltrate a group of one. Counter-terrorism against lone wolves is nearly impossible, and the inclusion of lone wolves in any official definition of terrorism will consequently create the impression that counter-terror efforts are not particularly effective. Indeed, it is difficult to see how any proactive strategy would be effective against lone wolves. Nevertheless, the inclusion of lone wolves in a definition of terrorism seems realistic, if for no other reason than a great deal of terrorism has in fact been carried out by lone wolves.

Source: Adapted from Mintz (2003b). "FBI Worries about Revenge Terrorist Attacks." *The Idaho Statesman*, February 24:4A ; United Press International (2002), "Report: No Terror Link in LAX Shootings." Sept. 5.

There is a practical danger in creating legal definitions of terrorism based on the imputation of religious, ideological, or political intent, then developing a specialized "terrorist" response. The danger is that it may encourage a "normalization" of counter-terror practices by the police. Kraska and Kappeler (1997) remind us that police paramilitary units, more commonly known as SWAT (special weapons and tactics) teams, emerged as a highly specialized unit to deal with hostage situations. These units, however, rapidly normalized, which means that they became general use units, and have become especially popular for routine police drug operations. The same could happen with emerging police counter-terror units, but with the label "terror" permitting much broader police intrusion into people's affairs. This is not to suggest that the police should be oblivious to counter-terrorist needs. It is to say that, if history is to be a guide, they will quickly become used for operations that may have little to do with terror but are facilitated by the lower evidentiary standards available in counter-terror law.

Is there no way to provide an "objective" definition of terrorism that we can count on, that will be useful regardless of circumstances? Ganor (2002) frames the issue of objectiveness as follows: Most observers think that the determination of who is a terrorist is wholly a subjective matter; that "one man's terrorist is another man's freedom fighter." He states that an objective definition of terrorism is necessary for any serious attempt to counter terrorism, and presents such a definition.

A correct definition of terrorism can be based on accepted international laws and principles of conventional war between nations. These laws are already set out in the Geneva and Hague conventions. These laws, he argues, can be extended straightforwardly to conflicts between non-governmental organizations and states. Under this notion, terrorism is uniquely identified in terms of deliberate violence against civilians. This distinguishes terrorism from guerrilla war, which has as its focus military targets. Hence, an objective definition of terrorism has three components:

1. The activity is the use of or threat to use violence. This excludes tax revolts and other forms of nonviolent protest.

2. The aims are always political, which includes religious and ideological motives. This distinguishes it from common street crime, which is violent but lacks a political goal. Ideological and religious aims can be included under the rubric "political."

3. The targets of terrorism are civilians. This distinguishes terrorism from other forms of political violence such as guerrilla warfare and civil insurrections. However, it does not include the inadvertent killing of human shields or accidental injuries inflicted on civilians. And it does not include the killing of civilians who may be working inside a military target.

This objective definition, Ganor contends, serves several purposes. It provides security forces with a legal tool to use in combating terrorism. If accepted internationally, it will strengthen cooperation in countries combating terrorism. It enables and clarifies offensive action against terrorism. And, by distinguishing between terrorism and other forms of violence, it undermines the legitimacy of terrorist action.

The definition offered by Ganor has the advantages of simplicity and distinctness, and it focuses on a criminal act. It carries the essential elements of crime—behavior and intent. In many ways, it may be the best definition possible. However, like similar definitions, it carries four problems. First, it includes threats to use violence. A threat to commit a harm, under the criminal law in most states, is typically categorized as an assault and is a misdemeanor crime handled locally. If I were to tell a civil servant that I was going to get even with the government for charging me too much money for some service, I have threatened a public figure who is also a civilian, and the context is political—she was carrying out her duties. It is difficult to imagine that I have committed an act that justifies federal investigation as a terrorist crime. Yet failure to include threats into a definition of terrorism excludes one of the most potent terrorist tools, the creation of fear in a population.

Second, the actual distinction between civilians and military figures is not always clear. What about internal security forces? Are police officers who carry out counter-terror activities considered military or civilian? How about police who are actively working with military units in counter-terror activities? How about civilians employed by police? How does private security fit into this? Certainly, many of the security forces used in the current era to police Iraq are private companies hired by the U.S. to carry out internal security. Is an act against them a terrorist act? How about an off-duty police officer, or a military officer on leave? The point is that civilian and military identities overlap in many and complex ways.

Third, the moral distinction between civilian and military targets is even muddier than the occupational distinction. In democracies, civilians elect representatives who make decisions about military interventions and are responsible for the behavior of the government, even if not directly involved in counter-terror activities. Many civilians are strong supporters of the military. And emphasizing civilians over military personnel somehow suggests that civilian lives are more important than military lives.

Fourth, definitions of terrorism tend to be vague and easily manipulated by governments, if they so desire. The notion that motives can be religious or ideological avails almost any value-based crime to be considered a terrorist act if the government can impute a religious or moral connection to it. Further, in a country like the U.S. where the notion of a free economy is itself seen as central to the American way of life, isn't any economically based street crime or crime against a business an ideological crime?

All this does not mean that Ganor's definition is a poor one; to the contrary, given the inherent problems with the term "terrorism," it may be the best we can do. We have challenged it, not because it is a weak definition but because it is among the best we have encountered. In the end, the difference between a terrorist and a freedom fighter requires some distinctions that are less than perfect in real-world settings.

Real-world examples show the difficulty in defining terrorism and then applying that definition to some entity. The National Research Council offers the following examples: Jesse and Frank James, Waco, Palestinian bombings in Israel, Israel killings of Palestinian civilians. One could use Ganor's definition and happily pigeonhole these into different categories. However, many people in the United States would look at Waco and argue that terrorism occurred when the FBI acted against the civilians, not vice versa. And any discussion of the Palestinian question will immediately divide Western and Middle Eastern countries. In other words, even trying to employ Ganor's quite reasonable definition, we quickly run into foundational cultural differences. The contestedness of this "essentially contested concept" is cultural, religious, and ideological through and through.

In all of these examples, we see how terrorism is a contested term. The core cultural contestedness of "terrorism" can be seen in Ahmad's definition of the term. In Figure 2.2 Ahmad (1998) challenges the way in which terrorism is commonly defined. The effort to label groups as terrorist, he observes, is not a rational, fact-finding process but reveals the security and economic interests of particular states. His discussion is a moral counterbalance to efforts to define that which is always, to a degree, political and hence relative to particular state interests.

Figure 2.2
Ahmad's Critique of Terrorist Definitions

Any attempted definition of terrorism must recognize that it is a challenge to some territorially bounded state. Hence, any definition is political. Ahmad's (1998) six-point critique of terrorist definitions shows his recognition of its embeddedness in politics. He noted that:

1. The terrorist of yesterday is the hero of today and vice versa. We live in a constantly changing world of images.

2. The official approach is a "posture of inconsistency." Definitions require a commitment to consistency. Definitions in official documents are designed to arouse our emotions, not exercise our intelligence.

3. Officials are globalistic about terrorism, even in the absence of a definition of it.

    They may not define terrorism, but they can call it a menace to good order, a menace to the moral values of Western civilization, a menace to humankind. . . . Anti-terror policies must therefore be global.

4. Official approaches claim some omniscient knowledge. We claim to know where terrorists are, and therefore, where to attack them.

Figure 2.2, *continued*

---

5. The causes of terrorism are unimportant in official approaches The author relates a story from the *New York Times*, in which then Secretary of State George Schultz was asked to consider the sources of Palestinian terrorism by the foreign minister of Yugoslavia.

> He (the secretary of state) pounded the table and told the visiting foreign minister, "There is no connection with any cause. Period."

6. Official accounts selectively create a need for moral revulsion. This is so that we can applaud the behavior of terror groups officially sanctioned by the government. This is particularly important with regard to the terrorism of friendly governments. The United States has sponsored terrorist regimes like Somoza in Nicaragua, Bautista in Cuba, the contras in Nicaragua, and the mujahideen in Afghanistan.

Ahmad offered three recommendations to official approaches to terrorism

1   Avoid double standards A superpower cannot promote terror in one place and expect to discourage it in another.

2. Do not condone the terror of allies. Low-intensity warfare and covert activities are breeding grounds for terrorism and drugs

3. Reinforce and strengthen the framework of international law Support the UN and the international court of justice. Go to the international courts to obtain warrants before seeking out terrorists.

Source: Adapted from Ahmad, Eqbal (1998). "Terrorism: Theirs and Ours." In R. Howard and R Sawyer (eds) *Terrorism and Counter-Terrorism*. Guilford, CT: McGraw-Hill.

Ahmad's critique of terrorism serves an important point. It reminds us to avoid being uncritical about uses of the term terrorism. His critique may be rejected by some as anti-U.S.; on the other hand, it also reflects a pragmatic recognition that the foreign policies of nation-states can be self-serving, sometimes obscuring other motives, and may not necessarily be in the best self-interest of their citizens.

Counter-Terrorism: War or Crime?

One of the most difficult and enduring issues in current counter-terrorism is whether terrorism should be thought of as criminal activity or as an act of war. The notion of counter-terrorism as law enforcement or as war is a definitional issue with substantial policy implications. The distinction between war and policing involves all the issues associated with democracy under conditions of threats to internal and international security. Whether we define it as war or terrorism may well determine the future of democracy in the Untied States.

The simplest way to determine whether terrorism is war or crime is by looking at the dangerousness of the threat posed by some terrorist group. Normatively, the distinction between war or crime is tied to the extent of the terrorist threat. If the threat is relatively localized or contained, then it can be treated as a crime and prosecuted accordingly. However, if it is too extensive and dangerous to be suppressed by the police, then a limited military response involving the National Guard may be necessary. If the National Guard lacks the power to deal with the threat, or if the threat has an out-of-country military component, a full-fledged military response may be required. This is a normative conception of the war versus crime issue, because it views the decision to treat terrorism as a war or crime as directly determined by the threat posed by a terrorist group. The response is "normed" to the threat.

This straightforward distinction between war and crime is complicated by several factors. White (2002:277) notes four problems commonly associated with using the military in a counter-terrorist role:

1. Western democracies carry an aversion to military forces used to deal with domestic problems. The use of the military in a police role in the U.S. is a violation of federal law.

2. The use of military power to deal with terrorism has frequently been associated with the rise of repressive regimes, particularly across the Americas. Often, the repressive regimes linger long after the terrorist threat has subsided.

3. Military units may employ specialized tactical units who engage in anticipatory and retaliatory strikes. Yet, many argue that such strikes lead to a cycle of violence, in which terror is meted out by both sides in never-ending conflict.

4. The debate over the proper use of the military in civilian affairs is often rancorous. The debate particularly focuses on the use of unconventional military tactics aimed at terrorist groups, and the "fair play" implications of those tactics (see Chapter 1).

White's concerns do not amount to a rejection of the use of military forces in counter-terrorism efforts, but rather suggest that military forces should not be deployed indiscriminately or in haste. His concerns are cautionary, suggesting that the military has a role to play, but that these four issues should be carefully and thoroughly considered when a decision regarding the use of military forces must be made.

Turk (2002) takes a position supportive of the use of military forces in counter-terrorism. He frames the war-crime debate in terms of the "limitations of individualized justice" characteristic of democratic process. Democracies make use of an individualized notion of justice. Each individual has worth, and the law ensures that individual worth, commonly conceived as life, liberty, and the pursuit of happiness, is protected. The state, to strip an individual of rights, must establish the criminality of that individual's behavior, usually "beyond a reasonable doubt."

Individualized justice, however, becomes ineffective when faced with threats from criminal organizations and conspiracies. The issue we face in the war against individual terrorism is how we can limit individualized justice without loss of citizen rights. Turk suggests that we have three options:

1. Continue to apply standards of individual justice against global enemy networks.

2. Treat the enemy network as if it were a nation and apply internationally recognized rules of war.

3. Recognize the enemy as a special case requiring "exceptional non legal and extralegal measures" (2002:281).

Turk favors the third option. The enemy is different from what we face with ordinary crime:

> This is not an enemy intent on material gain or political dominance; this foe is dedicated to our cultural extermination and willing to kill all of us unless those of us who survive accept rule by a barbarous regime of alien and theologically primitive religious absolutists." (2002:281).

Turk emphasizes the substantial dangers posed by terrorists. He recognizes that terrorism has many roots, social as well as economic, and states that those roots should be addressed by international policy. But the sheer dangerousness posed by terrorism must be addressed as a central element of any discussion of counter-terror measures. Only exceptional measures can deal with the immediacy of the terrorist threat.

There are problems with his justification for "exceptional measures." In the quote above, he locates the terrorist mind-set in cultural and religious differences. One can as easily imagine a Moslem in Saudi Arabia making the same comments in response to the presence of American military bases on Saudi and Iraqi soil. Terrorism becomes a highly relative notion, in part defined by the moral predisposition's of those with whom we disagree.

One might respond that we could put exceptional measures into place but require their periodic renewal. Great Britain, for example, has put into place a variety of exceptional measures to deal with terrorism and attached sunset provisions to them, requiring re-approval after five years for their sustenance. However, human rights do not lend themselves to an on-again, off-again legal interpretation. If we curtail some of those rights in a "war" of lengthy duration against terrorism, those exceptional circumstances become melded into daily life. This brings us back to Turk's opening query: How far can we stretch limitations on individual justice and still have citizens' rights? The answer to that question may be a fourth option not identified by Turk: Democracy will be sustained, but it will be something different from what it was before 9/11 and the security-oriented administrations of Clinton and Bush. It will be a democracy thinner in citizens' rights and denser in surveillance, and in which legal rights to privacy will be sharply diminished. It may be a democracy in which due process is secondary to security. And, as has become the case for immigrants legal and otherwise, there may be no democracy at all.

More difficult is the notion that we can recognize an enemy as a special legal case, while carrying on a war against a "shadowy" enemy that, by all accounts, is likely to engage us indefinitely. Pillar (2003b) observes that terrorism is an enemy that can never be defeated. "If there is a war against terrorism," he notes, "it can never be won" (2003b:295). If we cannot defeat the enemy, the most we can hope for is to control it.

Consequently, counter-terrorist strategies should not be implemented in some sort of all out effort, but should be blended in with other national interests, in a way to be as unobtrusive to those other interests as possible. Pillar notes that:

> . . . counter-terrorism constantly and inevitably impinges on other important U.S. interests, and so counter-terrorist policy must be judged according not only to how many lives it saves but to how little damage it does to those other interests (Pillar, 2003b 297).

Other interests include such policy arenas as foreign relations and civil rights. According to Pillar, it is important to recognize that, if we are in this "war" for the long haul, we don't make critical sacrifices in other venues that prove to be costly to national identity and economic vitality.

Certainly one can reasonably take the position that, if the nation-state faces a grave threat that has international bases, the use of a military reaction force may be the most reasonable security option. This question may be phrased more specifically: Did the 9/11 attacks justify a declaration of war by the president, or should it have been treated as a police action? Soros (2003) argued for the latter.

> The terrorist attack on the U.S. should have been treated as a crime against humanity rather than an act of war. Treating it as a crime would have been more appropriate. Crime requires police work, not military action. Protection against terrorism requires precautionary measures, awareness, and intelligence gathering—all of which ultimately depend on the support of the populations among which terrorists operate (Soros, 2003:4).

Soros continues that, had the attacks been treated as crimes, the U.S. response would have been directed only at Al Qaeda, Iraq would not have been invaded, and loss of life on both sides would have been avoided. Moreover, war is inherently an action of states against states, and declaring war against a non-state actor is likely to lead to a permanent state of war. This state of war produces victims, victims produce more terrorists, and the war becomes self-perpetuating.

As we note in Chapter 3, a characteristic feature of inter- and intra-state relations in the world today is conflict. Leaders use whatever forces are available to them, whether military or police, according to pragmatic considerations of self-defense, survival, and victory. Soros cautions us that the use of the military is wrong, not in principle, but in the current instance of the war on terror. The U.S. may be in a position of over-commitment of troops in a non-winnable war. That over-commitment may lead us in directions far from the causal agent of 9/11, Al Qaeda.

The exchange presented in Figure 2.3 shows how the distinction between war and crime in the legal construction of terrorism carries into many different areas. The discussion is excerpted from an American Bar Association panel at the ABA annual meetings in 2002 (American Bar Association, 2002), and captures many of implications of a war-conception of counter-terrorism.

Figure 2.3
Debating the Distinction Between War and Crime

Angela Davis: [Commenting that 314,000 immigrants are "so-called absconders" because of visa violations but that Attorney General Ashcroft had sent a memo to Assistant Attorney General Thompson to pick up the roughly 5,000 Middle-Easterners, not deport them but arrest them and offer S-visas (commonly called snitch visas) in exchange for information.]

They're just going after the Middle-Easterners. A lot of those folks, you're saying that they're Al-Qaeda, are you saying the majority are? The vast majority are people who we're now finding out, after some of them have been released after six or seven months of not seeing their families or not having lawyers, are hard-working people.

Yeah, maybe they're here illegally, but so are a lot of other people here illegally because their visa papers are not in order. They're hard-working in this country for years and years. They're construction workers, they're parking lot attendants, they're people who are doing the hard work of building this country like other people, and yet we're singling these people out and there's not one iota of evidence that they're involved in terrorist activity, and yet they're being held.

And so if you've got the evidence, and let me tell you something as a former public defender, it doesn't take much for a government to make out probable cause, it doesn't take much at all; so if they can't make out probable cause to show that they're involved in that sort of behavior then they're innocent. It doesn't take much, so if you've got the evidence, put it on. If you don't, let these people go.

Figure 2.2, *continued*

Rodney Smolla: Angela, you're using the language of lawyers in the way that courts know law But one of the tricky things, I think, about September 11 is that it's put us into a world of ambivalence about whether this is law and crime and enforcement by law enforcement officials, or whether this is war. In war we don't think in terms of guilt or innocence. We, in fact, profile. If you're wearing the wrong color uniform, you can be shot at. You can be captured It's a different paradigm, different morally and, in a sense, different legally.

Jane Kirtley: Rod, are you taking the position that it *is* war? I mean, it has not been declared to be war.

Rodney Smolla: That's just it. I'm asking the question.

Jane Kirtley: Well, I'm asking you. Is it, in your view? I mean, you've used the term "war" before in this panel . . . I mean, do you buy into this view that this is war, this is different, this is not crime, this is war and the rules are different? Because Congress has not so stated.

Rodney Smolla: Yeah. I think that, um, I think that the reason I'm conflicted is that a part of me wants to be on your side and say, "This isn't the war." This is no more a "war" than the war on drugs is a "war." The war on drugs is law enforcement. The word "war" when we say "the war on drugs," is used metaphorically. I'm not entirely convinced, though, that I believe that any more with regard to Al Qaeda. Al Qaeda's not Germany during World War II, it's not Hanoi during the Vietnam War. But it's not quite, for me, the Colombian drug cartel, either It is an ambiguous thing, and I don't know the right answer But I think that some of the elements of how a society deals with a foreign enemy are fair here, are appropriate here given what we've been through.

Angela Davis: A lot of these people are not foreign enemies, though. That's my point. We look at them and they look a certain way, and we assume they're foreign enemies. And a lot of them aren't. They've lived in this country 15, 20 years.

Rodney Smolla I don't make that assumption, Angela. I don't make that assumption, but I do make the assumption that there is something loosely out there, Al-Qaeda or Hamas or something, some shifting group of organized elements . . .

Angela Davis: Or Timothy McVeigh's people?

Rodney Smolla . . who wants to destroy this society I think that's a reality and that has some of the aspects of a war, as opposed to routine crime.

Andrew Napolitano: But the war on terror as the Justice Department is waging it is itself destructive of this society because of the civil liberties that, if unchecked by federal judges, it will knowingly and intentionally trample.

Source: General Practice and Small Firm Section (2002). "September 11 and the Constitution." American Bar Association annual meetings. Panel discussion, telecast on C-SPAN.

Call it war or call it law enforcement, the choice of label has profound implications for the way in which we live. Davis's opening rebut to Ashcroft's memo, which was aimed at acquiring intelligence from Middle-Eastern nationals through the threat of deportation, is framed in terms of legal notions of the way in which democracy is acted out. Smolla's initial response to her, "you're using the language of lawyers in the way that courts know law" contextualizes her argument by locating it inside democratic process. From here he frames a position outside of democratic process, suggesting that democratic notions of fair play can only be preserved by acting militarily against an enemy of democracy. Democracy, as described by Smolla, can be thought of using the metaphor of a *container*, the container being the constitution that protects citizen rights and affords individual security. Actions outside of the container can be distinguished from actions inside the container. This is a central justification for thinking about terrorism as war: if it is a war, then we can act outside the container, which includes acting outside the limitations of democratic due process. Outside the container, we can presume the guilt of suspected enemies, even though inside the container we are responsible for the protection of their rights vis-à-vis due process.

Davis brings a different perspective to bear on the discussion. She is arguing from a moral position, and central to that morality is the notion of *fair play*. Due process is not simply a practice located inside a metaphorical container that we can act outside of, but invokes a set of universal principles that are to be observed in all cases. Fair play is acted out in the United States as the law of substantive due process, but it is only one form that fair play can take; what is important is that we have democratic notions of fair play clearly in place, and there is no evidence that their abandonment would somehow better enhance counter-terror efforts. From this perspective, fair play does not fit inside a container, but is a universal principle that should always be followed. Further, she argues that the particular strategy used by the Justice Department is destructive of fair play principles, a view echoed at the end of the dialogue by Andrew Napolitano.

This exchange shows that the distinction of counter-terrorism as policing or as war carries a great deal of moral heft. In the conflict between the two notions lies the way in which democracy will be acted out by the U.S. government for many years to come. If democracy is viewed as a universal set of principles that guide and constrain the behavior of the government, then notions of fair play must be formalized into counter-terrorism activity both internally and internationally, be it through the Geneva Convention or substantive due process. However, as this book argues and as Smolla inferred, the U.S. increasingly acts as if democracy is something that has to be protected by a powerful security force, and in which notions of fairness, due process, and citizen rights are secondary to security interests.

Conclusion

This chapter provided an overview of definitions of terrorism, and dealt with the question of whether counter-terrorism against Al Qaeda should be carried out in terms of principles of war or of crime control. That acts of terrorism represent a threat to citizens and to weak nation-states is not debatable. But beyond that simple idea, defining in an actionable way what constitutes terrorism becomes difficult and controversial. Perhaps in a more harmonious world consensus might be achieved regarding the definition of terrorism. But this is not the world in which we live, and practicing definitions of terrorism will always carry an "us versus them" element, supporting some ethnic or religious groups and condemning others.

The problems in defining terrorism are passed on to efforts to determine counter-terrorism. Even the most central concerns of counter-terrorism—what works—are complicated by concerns that aggressive short-term solutions might be effective but can backfire, antagonizing some peoples and lead to increased terrorist recruitment. The issue of backfiring, and other issues related to world conflict and the roots of terrorism, are discussed in Chapter 3.

World Violence: The Stage for 9/11

> "We have just seen the first war of
> the twenty-first century."
> —President George W. Bush

Overview: Why Context Is Important

Two days after the 9/11 attacks, President George W. Bush announced that the U.S. would lead the world to victory: "We have just seen the first war of the twenty-first century," he observed (Associated Press, 2001a). Again, on December 10, meeting with Kenyan and Ethiopian leaders, the President noted that, "We welcome two strong friends of America here . . . two people that the American people can count on when it comes to winning the first war of the twenty-first century" (International Information Programs, 2001:1).

The rhetorical strengths of calling the terrorist attacks of the first war of the century are clear. The president sought to rally the American people around a common cause, a cause that would come to be known as the "war on terrorism." However, the attacks did not in fact represent the opening volley in the first war of the twenty-first century. To the contrary, the world was awash in conflict of every kind and intensity at the time of the attacks.

Lee (2002) identified 20 major world conflicts that had been ongoing prior to 2001 and current to 2003. He defined major world conflicts as "wars and conflicts in which more than a thousand people have died, involve more than one nation (for internal conflicts) or more than two nations (for international conflicts), and/or have the near-term potential to turn into a multinational regional conflict" (Lee, 2002:2). He also identified 56 minor conflicts, defined as "wars or conflicts which have relatively small impact on the world or the region in which they occur"(Lee, 2002:5).

Another source, the National Defense Council Foundation (2001) (NDCF), identified 59 "conflict zones" in the world, and also placed 121 countries on its "watch list" as areas that carried potential to become conflict zones. Eleven countries were added to the 2001 tallies, including the United States because of the terrorist attacks on 9/11. Twenty countries were removed the same year, suggesting that the overall level of world conflict had declined from the previous year, though the level continued to be substantially higher than the Cold War era average of 35. Criteria for inclusion "is the level of political, social, economic, and military disruption caused by a relevant conflict." The report noted that the final decision to include a country was subjective because hard measures fail to account for real differences in state economies and population sizes.

The most conflict-intensive area in the world is the Middle East. Regehr (2001), counting 37 armed conflicts, observed that:

> The Middle East region continues to be the most conflict-intensive area of the planet, with more than one-third of the states (5 of 14) in the region experiencing armed conflict. In Africa and Asia about one-quarter and one-fifth of the states respectively were at war, and together these two regions were the site of almost 80 percent of the world's wars at the end of 2001" (Regehr, 2001:1).

Regehr's definition of armed conflict was "a political conflict in which armed combat involves the armed forces of at least one state (or one or more armed factions seeking to gain control of all or part of the state), and in which at least 1,000 people have been killed by the fighting during the course of the conflict (Regehr, 2001:2).

The issue in this discussion is not to remonstrate against the commander-in-chief for being factually wrong. Rhetoric has its place in politics, and definitions of war tend to be highly subjective and self-serving to the state engaged in conflict.

The issue we are concerned with is context, by which we mean the geographical, resource, ethnic, and religious settings in which conflict occurs. Context is important for two reasons. First, the terrorist attacks of 9/11 occurred within a context of regional violence and are a subtext to conflicts occurring across the world. If we want to comprehend conflicts, ours and ones similar to it, we must move beyond a "good guy-bad guy" explanation. We begin by recognizing that regional and interstate conflict, of which terrorism is a part, is a pervasive feature of the world political landscape. A consideration of factors associated with such conflicts is an appropriate beginning for considerations of terrorism, for those factors will provide critical information on how to develop strategy to prevent terrorism's reoccurrence.

Context is important for the long view, and is consequently an integral part of counter-terrorism. Anti-terrorist strategy should contain two elements. One element is a short-term and highly focused effort, carried out in the name of immediate security interests, to remove an articulable terrorist threat; such effort ends with the removal of that threat. This element of anti-terrorism is a calculus of action intended to remove a security threat. The second element is the recognition of the conditions that give rise to terrorism and the implementation of policy aimed at the amelioration of those conditions. This is the moral element of counter-terror efforts, aimed at addressing, on a world stage and through the policy tools of diplomacy and economics, the conditions associated with the rise of populations vulnerable to terrorist recruitment.

Describing the 9/11 terrorist attacks as "the first war of the twenty-first century" permitted the American people the luxury of ignoring how terrorism is embedded in conditions throughout the world, which brings us to the second reason context is so important. The United States played a role in producing some of those conditions. To state that the U.S. contributed to conditions that produced terrorism does not mean that the U.S. is responsible for terrorism. An act of terrorism is the proximate responsibility of those who carry out such acts. However, it does mean that the U.S. should recognize how its international actions sometimes have unanticipated consequences, and that its leaders and citizens bear a responsibility to make themselves familiar with those consequences. Only by doing so can future occurrences of terrorist actions be prevented, unless we imagine that we can build an impermeable barrier around our country and protect our citizens wherever they travel.

The argument that the U.S. is in any way implicated in the "root causes" of terrorism is not widely accepted. Steve Cox for example, argues that:

> The question of whether, and to what degree, American policies "provoked" the events of September 11 is interesting in certain respects, but it is not interesting in regards to our plans for the future. Adolf Hitler may have come to power because of the injustices of the Treaty of Versailles, but once he came to power, abrogation of the treaty by Britain and France would not have kept him out of war. In fact, the treaty was dead as soon as he marched his troops into the demilitarized zone of Western Germany, three and a half years before the beginning of World War II (Cox, 2003:135).

This view is correct, but only to a point. It correctly recognizes that a nation-state has a legitimate security interest in protecting its citizens from extra-national threats. This security interest focuses on the command staff and active cadre of terrorist groups. It fails to account for active supporters and for passive supporters (Fraser & Fulton, 1984). Passive support can be large, and is made larger when its cause is consistent within local or regional politics and grievances. Passive supporters are locals who provide the base for recruitment (White, 2002). Polls carried out across the countries of the Middle East consistently show large numbers of Muslims sharply dissatisfied with the policies of the United States. The high level of dissatisfaction is congruent with regional politics, and dissatisfied Muslims provide a large base for passive terrorist support. Active supporters and operatives are drawn from this group.

Dissatisfaction has two sources, described by Pillar (2003a) as antecedent conditions for the emergence of terrorism. First, the socioeconomic conditions and living standards of peoples can become the breeding ground for terrorism. For example, the Palestinian Islamic Jihad does its most successful recruiting in the bleak neighborhoods and refugee camps of the Gaza Strip. Addressing economic concerns for such populations undercuts recruitment prospects. Second, as Pillar notes, recruiters find fallow ground where people are angry about social or political issues, such as political repression, a lack of self-determination, or the depravity of their rulers. America's responsibility in such cases is to ensure that its policies do not inadvertently (or intentionally) support repressive governments.

If the U.S. wishes to prevent future recurrences of terrorism it will have to mitigate the conditions that generate terrorist support. This cannot be addressed only through the application of military force, but instead must be approached through thoughtful foreign policy and international diplomacy that in some way addresses the grievances. Hence, in response to Cox's observation that future counter-terrorism plans are unaffected by whether or not American policies provoked terrorism, the correct response is that they should be affected. Whether we capture Bin Laden will certainly affect the leadership of Al Qaeda, but will have no regional impact on the formation of new terrorist organizations that spring from the disaffected Muslim masses in the Middle East. Security should aim at the short-term solution to immediate security threats, but wise foreign policy must also recognize long-term factors that mitigate or intensify the formation of anti-American terrorist groups.

Moreover, the world did indeed learn a great deal from the injustices of the Treaty of Versailles. The loyalty Hitler was able to obtain from his troops stemmed in part from the sense of persecution the German people felt from the conditions set by the treaty and the loyalty to the homeland those conditions fostered. After the fall of the Soviet Union, many observers noted the necessity of avoiding foreign policy that would foster conditions in Russia such as those Germany faced under the Versailles Treaty. This was an important lesson of international relations learned the hard way. Let us not forget it in the war on terrorism, as we carry out military occupations of Iraq and Afghanistan.

The remainder of this chapter provides an overview of perspectives on world conflict. Perspectives included here are selected because they resonate with concepts of terror and because they are pertinent to international policy aimed at the long-term development of effective counter-terror strategy.

Religion and Culture

Several views of contemporary world conflict look at religion and culture as prime movers of conflict. They are included under the same rubric here because some authors, Huntington (1996) for example, view religion as one of the defining elements of culture. Each is discussed below.

Huntington – *The Clash of Civilizations and the Remaking of World Order*

Samuel Huntington's thesis is that, in the post-Cold War world, the most important world conflicts will arise between peoples belonging to different cultures. These conflicts will occur "along the fault lines between different civilizations" (1996:28).

For 40 years, Huntington argues, practitioners of international relations acted in terms of a "Cold War paradigm of world affairs" (1996:30). The Cold War paradigm was useful because it accounted for a great deal of activity in the arena of world politics. However, with the dismemberment of the Soviet Union this paradigm lost its utility. If we are to understand international relations, what paradigm might meaningfully enable us to think about international relations in the current era? After reviewing a variety of alternatives, Huntington concludes that the best model is what he calls a "civilizational paradigm."

Civilizations are defined in terms of six elements. First, civilizations are plural, an idea different from the old notion of civilization versus barbarism. What many Westerners call "barbarism" he recognizes as another form of civilization, a logic that similarly applies to the U.S. when others call us "barbaric." Second, civilizations are cultural entities. Both civilization and culture refer to ways of lives of peoples, and civilization is "culture writ large." Third, civilizations are comprehensive. A civilization is a totality with a certain degree of integration. It is superordinate over the lives of its members, occurring at a broader level than villages and regions. Fourth, civilizations are mortal but very long-lived. They evolve, adapt, and endure. As a narrative, civilization is the "longest story of all." Fifth, they are not political entities. All civilizations are generally made up of more than one nation-state, and their identity is separate from, though perhaps coincidental with, political boundaries. Sixth, scholars tend to agree on the boundaries and identity of modern civilizations.

The modern world is characterized by seven major civilizations. They are:

Sinic. This is the common culture of China and Chinese communities across Southeast Asia, Vietnam, and Korea.

Japanese. Japan is a distinct civilization, an offspring of China between A.D. 100 and 400.

Hindu. This refers to the Indian subcontinent, and Hinduism is the core of Indian civilization.

Orthodox. This is centered in Russia and separate from Western Christendom as a result of its Byzantine parentage.

Western. This is what used to be called Western Christendom. It refers to Europe, North America, and European settler countries such as Australia and New Zealand.

Latin America. Although it has roots in European civilization, it has developed along more corporatist, authoritarian lines.

African. Africa is not normally seen as a distinct civilization. However, Africans are increasingly developing a sense of African identity. It is, Huntington notes, conceivable that sub-Saharan Africa could cohere into a civilizational identity.

Civilizations tend to be characterized by core states, member states, and culturally similar minority groupings in neighboring states. The core states of the European Union, for example, are circled most closely by Belgium, Luxembourg, and the Netherlands, then more loosely by Spain, Portugal, Denmark, Ireland, Great Britain, and Greece, the 1995 additions of Austria, Finland, and Sweden, and the associate members of that era.

Islam, of all the civilizations, does not have a core state. This is in part because, historically, national identities did not exist in Central Asia but were superimposed by the West. Consequently, loyalties are "hollowed out" at the nation state level. The hierarchy of loyalty is to the extended family, tribe, and clan, then to Islam generally as a powerful uniting force. Six states are potential contenders for the Muslim core: Indonesia, Iran, Pakistan, Saudi Arabia, and Turkey.

The central thesis of *The Clash of Civilizations* is that future conflicts are most likely to occur and intensify along the perimeters of civilizations. These "fault line wars" are defined as "communal conflicts between states or groups from different civilizations" (1996:252). Frequently, the goal is the acquisition of territory and expelling of members of the other side of the conflict. Ethnic cleansing is common in such conflicts. The territory at stake, the author notes, tends to have historical and religious significance. It is a source of cultural and religious identity. Moreover, since religion is the defining characteristic of civilizations, fault line wars are almost always between peoples of different religions.

The Soviet-Afghan war of 1979-1989 was a fault line war. The Soviet Union sought to control a satellite country. It quickly became a civilizational war, because "Muslims everywhere saw it as such and rallied against the Soviet Union" (1996:247). The (first) Gulf War was also a civilizational war, because

Muslims opposed the military intervention of the West into what was seen as a Muslim affair. A paradox of democracy was noted by one observer: Those countries where freedom of expression was most relaxed were those where support for Saddam Hussein was the strongest (Khouri, 1991).

The West occupies a front-stage role in the clash among civilizations. Like all civilizations, it actively promotes its values, which it views as the best, and which it tends to see as universal. Western values of democracy, free markets, limited government, human rights, individualism, and the rule of law are actively promoted by the U.S. The problem, Huntington states, is that "What is universalism to the West is imperialism to the rest" (1996:184). Huntington identifies three areas where the West is most likely to conflict with other civilizations:

1. Efforts to maintain superiority through nonproliferation treaties concerning nuclear, biological, and chemical weapons.

2. Promotion of Western political values and institutions by pressing other societies to adopt human rights and Western-style democracy.

3. Protection of social, cultural, and ethnic identity of Western societies by restricting immigrants and refugees.

In sum, the future of the world's conflicts will be marked by conflict along civilizational fault lines. And because of its international policies, the United States is likely to be increasingly involved in these conflicts.

The multi-polar civilizational perspective presented by Huntington has an important strength: It requires that we familiarize ourselves with the world around us if we wish to understand and do something about terrorism. His perspective is also a challenge to the idea that conflicts are caused buy bad people. Indeed, some leaders may be cruel and brutal, but such leaders cannot in and of themselves mobilize armies and gain recruits. They must have a cause. And few causes are as mobilizing as a sense of religious persecution.

It should also be noted that not all religious terrorism is civilizational conflict. In Figure 3.1 we see an example of terrorism that is acted out, not across civilizational divides, but within one of Huntington's civilizations. This is the conflict between Sunni and Shiite Muslims in Afghanistan.

What we see in Figure 3.1 is that one should not underestimate intra-civilizational religious conflict. Indeed, one of the central problems faced in the current U.S. occupation of Iraq is that the country might splinter from conflicts involving Shiite and Sunni Muslims.

Figure 3.1
Religion and Civilizations

> In Pakistan, sectarian violence between Sunni and Shiite Muslims is centuries old, dating to a seventh-century disagreement over who the heir to Mohammed should be. The population of 140 million is predominately Sunni. Most co-exist with the Shiites without conflict; however, a small number are committed to violence against the Shiites and particularly against their places of worship. Fighting between Sunnis and Shiites has become important to the United States because it counts on Pakistan as its ally, and sectarian violence reveals the fragility of the alliance and of Pakistan itself.
>
> On February 22, 2003, a group of attackers patiently waited at a tea shop close to the mosque. Shortly after the bell for evening prayers sounded, four people on two motorcycles rode up to the gate. They then "stormed into a Shiite mosque in southern Pakistan and sprayed worshipers with automatic weapons fire, killing at least nine people . . ." Nine additional victims were injured. No group claimed responsibility; however, the area had a history of violent sectarian attacks.
>
> Of concern to the United States was that these attacks had recently expanded to Westerners and minority Christian groups. A suicide bombing on June 14, 2002, had killed 12 and injured 50 outside the U.S. consulate in Karachi, and a May 8 bombing at the Sheraton hotel killed 11 French engineers and three others. These incidents are associated with the Sipah-e-Sahaba Pakistan (SSP), an extremist group outlawed in Pakistan. A faction of the SSP, the Lashkar-e-Jhangvei, also is associated with the attacks. So were the attacks against the West, or were they the outgrowth of sectarian violence? Or, with the arrival of Americans in the region, is the nature of sectarian violence itself changing?
>
> This incident shows how contemporary terrorism, conceived by most Westerners in terms of a West-East conflict, is embedded in regional conflict with deep historical roots. As the U.S. deploys its forces into these areas, it is increasingly likely to be pulled into these conflicts. It may become difficult to distinguish East-West conflict and East-East conflict, leaving Westerners to conclude—perhaps reasonably—that everyone is against them.

Source: Adapted from Nadeem (2003). "Gunmen Open Fire on Shiite Mosque in Pakistan, Killing 9." *The Idaho Statesman*, February 23: A13.

Benjamin and Simon – *The Age of Sacred Terror*

Daniel Benjamin and Steven Simon (2002) also address religious terrorism. However, they focus specifically on the religious roots of Islamic fundamentalist terrorism. They argue that the terrorist attacks of 9/11, and indeed a great deal of modern day terrorist violence, can only be understood in a religious context. Their work is consistent with Huntington's *Clash*, in

its premise that modern Islamic terror stems from a religious tradition pit-
ting religious values of Islam against the "far enemy" of the West, particularly the United States.

> The motivation for the attack was neither political calculation,
> strategic advantage, nor wanton bloodlust. It was to humiliate and
> slaughter those who defied the hegemony of God; it was to
> please Him by reasserting His primacy. It was an act of cosmic war.
> What appeared to be an act of senseless violence actually made
> a great deal of sense to the terrorists and their sympathizers, for
> whom this killing was an act of redemption (Benjamin & Simon,
> 2002:40).

To understand the world views of Al Qaeda and its followers, Benjamin and Simon argue, one must begin with Ibn Taymiyya. Ibn Taymiyya was
born in 1269 in what is today Turkey, and wrote extensively on Islamic law
and public policy. Embittered at an early age after witnessing the destruction perpetrated by the Mongols, he became committed to a view of Islam
unsullied by impure or external influences. He displayed academic genius
and became an "uncompromising religious authority" at an early age. As he
matured, he argued for a reconception of the roles of religion and the
state. The relationship between the rulers and subjects should be in the form
of a contract. The sultan would receive obedience from the people in
exchange for just rule under Islamic law. Day-to-day guidance would be provided by the Ulema, the religious establishment. Religion should never be
subordinated to the state. A fatwa issued by Ibn Taymiyya, accusing the Mongols of apostasy, was instrumental in a successful jihad against the Mongols.

Ibn Taymiyya and his followers carried a messianic vision of jihad and
of the apostasy of secular rulers. Their views combine today in a fundamentalism that sees a world in crisis, a battle waged simultaneously in
heaven and on earth, and a need to hasten divine intervention to reassert
the authority of the Ulema.

That Ibn Taymiyya's messianic vision is alive today was evidenced in the
Soviet Afghanistan war. The Soviet-Afghanistan war was, for the Islamic fun-
damentalists, a conflict waged both on heaven and earth. Clerics and governments across the Muslim world encouraged young men to fight against
the Soviet invader. Osama bin Laden's reputation was made during this war.
He was one of the few Arab Muslims to attain fame as a fighter, in combat
at Ali Khel in Patkia province.

Muslims did not see the conflict as a proxy war of the U.S. and the Soviet
Union, but as a "call to neglected religious duty, jihad in the name of God"
(al-Zawahiri, Ayman, 2001). Bin Laden claimed that he perceived at this early
time that the ultimate enemy was the United States. Al Qaeda was formed
at this time, and its goals were similar to those spelled out by Ibn Taymiyya;
jihad would be used to defeat existing Muslim governments and a new order
would be established under a religious caliphate.

The assassination of Egyptian ruler Anwar Sadat is an example of this fundamentalist tradition. Following Nasser, Sadat initiated a program of economic liberalization in Egypt in the 1970s. His policies were strongly resisted among traditional Islamic groups and university students, who described him as "pharaoh" who represented the "far enemy," the United States.

A radical group calling itself al-Jihad formed in opposition to Sadat's program of modernization. Interestingly, members of al-Jihad were as likely to be middle- as lower-class. They generally could not be considered the "downtrodden rising up." However there was enormous disparity between education attainment and opportunity, giving rise to a sense of class frustration. Frustration coalesced around fundamentalist Islam, and al-Jihad drew on religious interpretation to guide their actions.

On October 6, 1981, one of the co-conspirators learned that he was to be assigned to participate in a military parade commemorating the 1973 war against Israel. He arranged to be in a truck with others that would pass in front of the reviewing stand where President Sadat was located. At the critical moment, he and two others sprayed the reviewing stand with automatic rifle fire, killing Sadat. The assassin "jumped up and down, shouting 'my name is Khalid Islambouli, I have slain Pharaoh, and I do not fear death'."

Jihadist Islam, and Al Qaeda in particular, have consistently focused on the revival of Islam in the Arab countries. However, Islamic fundamentalism is not currently as strong as it has been, and the various secular regimes in the region—the "near enemy"—have generally been effective in controlling fundamentalist terror. The authors identify four reasons why, in spite of the influence of these regimes, Jihadic fundamentalism may gain strength.

1. Radicals generally have won the debate at the theological level. They may encounter state resistance, but radicals have the "hearts and minds" of the populace. Governments are increasingly described as apostate and illegitimate. In their efforts to maintain control, the governments themselves are increasingly "burnishing their Islamic credentials." The game, the authors state, is now played by "Ibn Taymiyya rules" (2001:174).

2. Many of the Islamic Jihadists have relocated to Europe, Southeast Asia, Central Asia, East Africa, and America. They are in the land of "dar al-harb," the realm of war. European Muslims increasingly see themselves as Muslim first, and sense themselves alienated from European society.

3. In many of the Middle East countries, the secular governments are not as strong as they appear. The authors remind us that, in spite of our open access to Iran in the 1970s, the Iranian revolution in 1979 resulted in the formation of a state devoted to Jihadic Islamism.

4. The Middle East faces massive socioeconomic problems. Population is growing at breakneck pace, and within this growth are particular trouble signs. In many countries, 50 percent or more of the population is under 20 years old. Such numbers have historically correlated with war and violence. Education has been growing, and an increasing number of citizens are well educated. However, job opportunities have not grown, and the population is increasingly educated and unemployed, a politically explosive mix. Living conditions in the major cities, aggravated by chronic water shortages, make life difficult.

Because of these factors, no easy solutions can be found to the problems created by Islamic Jihadism. If anything, one predicts that problems for secular governments will intensify. Benjamin and Simon have provided a sobering assessment of the way in which religion can interact with violence in the modern world.

Figure 3.2
Osama bin Laden and the Far Enemy

The following are excerpts from a statement made by Osama bin Laden, received by Al Jazeera satellite network in the last week of January, 2002. The context of these statements is the anticipated assault of U.S. forces on Iraq. His observations display all the elements of Islamic Jihadism described by Benjamin and Simon (2002).

We are following with great interest and utmost concern the preparations by the crusaders to occupy the capital of Islam formally and to rob the wealth of Muslims and to appoint over you an agent government that follows Washington and Tel Aviv, like all other treacherous and spy Arab governments, in preparation for the founding of the greater Israel. So may Allah help us.

Second, we remind that victory comes from Allah Almighty alone, and we only have to do our best through preparations and incitement and jihad. Allah Almighty said, all you who believe, if you fight for the sake of Allah, he will give you victory and strengthen your feet . . .

The conclusion of the (Tora Tora mountain) battle was the great and miserable failure of the forces of evil over a small group of mujahideen, a group of 300 in the trenches inside one square mile, at a temperature that was 10 degrees below zero . . . So if all the international forces of evil could not achieve its goals over one square mile and a small number of mujahideen with very humble capabilities, how can these evil forces achieve victory over the Islamic world? This is impossible, Allah willing, if the people held fast to their religion and insisted on fighting for his sake.

So, our brothers in Iraq, do not be scared by what Americans promote about the greatness of its forces and their smart bombs and laser-guided bombs, for smart bombs have no mentionable effect in the

Figure 3.2, *continued*

middle of mountains and trenches and plains and forests. They must have an obvious target.

What the enemy fears most is the war of cities and streets, that war that the enemy expects tremendous, grave losses in. So we also stress the importance of suicide operations against the enemy in the U.S. and Israel and they have never seen anything like them in their history, thanks be to Allah.

We also stress that Muslims have to move and incite and organize the nation into armies to face these great events and harsh conditions, and to liberate themselves from the slavery of these unjust and infidel regimes enslaved by the U.S. From among the most ready for liberation are Jordan, Morocco, Nigeria and Pakistan, Saudi Arabia and Yemen.

It's also not hidden that this crusader war targets first and foremost Islam, irrespective of whether the Ba'ath party and Saddam were deposed or not.

And it doesn't harm in these conditions the interests of Muslims to agree with those of the socialists in fighting against the crusaders, even though we believe the socialists are infidels. For the socialists and the rulers have lost their legitimacy a long time ago, and the socialists are infidels regardless of where they are, whether in Baghdad or in Aden.

Oh Allah, the sender of the book, and the mover of the clouds and the defeater of the enemy, defeat them. Let us be victorious and let us be victorious over them . . . And as Allah said, "Make us do good things on Earth and good things in eternity, and protect us against the tortures of Hell." And may Allah have peace upon his prophet, Mohammed.

Source: Excerpts taken from Washingtonpost.com (2003). "Osama bin Laden Urges Attacks on the U.S."

Figure 3.2 is notable for several reasons. First, one can see that bin Laden distinguishes between the Iraqi political leadership, which is described as "socialist" and viewed as apostate or godless, and the Islamic faithful of the country. Secondly, bin Laden argued that different groups were justified in uniting against a common enemy, the U.S. in this missive. This suggests that the increased military activity of the U.S. in the region carries potent back-firing capacity, mobilizing traditionally disparate Muslim groups to unite against an outside enemy. Third, his words are steeped in religious perspective. His is a powerful statement consistent with the notion that religious belief is at the core of cultural identity, cultural identities are civilizational, and the conflict the U.S. is engaged in could become a civilizational one.

It is uncomfortable to think that the war on terror is a civilizational war instead of a "good guy/bad guy war." Yet the message in Figure 3.2 is stated in civilizational terms, and its target audience reacts in terms of these religious values. What must be recognized is that, whether or not military action is justified in the Middle East region, such action may carry consequences substantially beyond the rooting out of the leadership of a particular terrorist group such as Al Qaeda or an apostate country such as Iraq. It has the capacity to strengthen the boundaries that separate "them" from "us," and to harden religious and cultural differences into conflict and violence.

Brzezinski – *Out of Control: Global Turmoil on the Eve of the Twenty-First Century*

Out of Control was written by Leonid Brzezinski, the foreign security advisor under President Carter. It is an assessment and a warning. Brzezinski's (1993) book is about values, and his concern is that Western societies, particularly the United States, have not developed morally in a way that matches either their democratic system or their world power. Without a guiding set of moral values, the U.S. faces moral decline and loss of legitimacy in the world.

The twentieth century, he begins, was an astonishingly violent period in human history. Its wars accounted for the deaths of approximately 87 million people, making it the bloodiest century in history. It was also the age of mass totalitarian movements, described by Brzezinski as "coercive utopias." These movements, carried out by Hitler, Stalin, and Mao, had been defeated by the beginning of the twenty-first century. However, a dangerous vacuum has been left in their passing. This vacuum is the absence of an international moral leadership.

At the beginning of the twenty-first century, the United States has become the peerless global power. Its position is characterized by four dimensions of global power: (1) its global military reach, (2) its economic impact, (3) cultural-ideological appeal, and (4) political muscle. The international problem faced by the U.S. is translating global power into legitimacy, authority, and relevance.

Compliance of other states with American authority, Brzezinski argues, depends on perceptions of American moral legitimacy. America offers the appeal of liberty, and freedom is a product of democratic processes. However, perhaps more important than democratic process is content, which refers to the things we hold important and the goods with which we surround ourselves. And here, the United States comes up short.

America today is perceived as a "permissive cornucopia." A permissive cornucopia refers to a society with a heightened concern with material-gratification and the immediate satisfaction of individual desires, where hedonism is the motive for behavior. The guiding ethos is that "greed is good." The central political danger is that "self-gratification is becoming an end in itself in the West at a time when much of the rest of the world is still struggling with existential needs" (1993:73).

The notion of the good life seen by the rest of the world is carried by television. Television in itself removes barriers of time and space. Anyone anywhere can see what is going on in America by turning on the tube. Television carries an image of artificially stimulated desires for the latest fashions, fads, gimmicks, and toys (1993:72). These images do not satisfy basic needs, but instead play to one's indulgence for consumption. It is this—self gratification and stimulated desires—that the rest of the world sees as the content of Western democracy.

The world is a politically awakened place. The collapse of the coercive utopias has contributed to the emergence of many states within their previous boundaries. Many of these new states are poor and have limited resources. They tend to be undergoing rapid and chaotic urbanization. They have massive poverty and high infant mortality. For these, the contrast between the image of the West and their own living conditions could not be greater. The West is consumed with self-gratification and much of the rest of the world is dealing with fundamental issues of daily survival. For many of these people, the moral definition of the American good life is corrupt.

The process of political awakening is particularly intense in the Eurasian political vacuum left in the wake of the collapse of the Soviet Union. That vacuum is in danger of becoming a whirlpool for America. The United States is increasingly asserting its influence in the Middle East, and is engaged in what has been called the "Great Game II" with Russia in the Caspian Sea basin. Islamic identity is increasingly asserting itself throughout the region. Brzezinski notes that:

> Islam is becoming a motivating force for the rejection of inequality through its repudiation of Western-type modernity. Viewing that modernity as fundamentally corrupt and driven by a cultural capitulation to the most basic sensate impulses, Islam thinkers are attempting to develop the concept of an Islamic modernity that would permit Muslim societies to enjoy the technological fruits of modernity minus its cultural handicaps (Brzezinski, 1993:190).

Islam's current success in reaching new members is driven both by its repudiation of Western morality, and by its offer of a comprehensive alternative vision. If the United States fails to comprehend and adapt to that vision, it is in danger of being caught militarily in a whirlpool of Mideast conflict from which it will be unable to withdraw.

America's notion of the good life, located in consumerism, cannot be replicated in the Middle East or in the remainder of the world. The resources are simply unavailable. What is essential for long-term global stability is an American notion of the good life that is morally meaningful to the rest of the world. Until it achieves such a notion of morality, America will find itself unable to maintain legitimacy and world authority.

Conflict, Democracy, and the Problem of Values

Brzezinski's critique of American moral leadership is a challenge to core notions of Western democracy. Moral codes are legally embodied in standards of justice. A core element in the constitution and bill of rights is that individuals are the bearers of rights (Habermas, 1994). The political identity of individuals is carried in the idea that citizens have a right to life, liberty, and the pursuit of happiness.

Individual pursuit of happiness is the core Western rationality. This means that I make decisions about what to do or what is important to me, or what I want out of life. My choices in all these things are individually made, and I am the one who makes them. Individuals determine their preferences by first asking, "What do I want?" and then attempting to achieve desires or goals according to financial or political means. We face a bewildering variety of choices—what church we attend, what school, what kind of camping equipment, who our friends are, what color we want our hair to be—and we select that which we want the most (MacIntyre, 1988). This rationality is called "interests and passions" by MacIntyre, which means that what I choose is driven by my interests and passions.

Other ways of thinking, MacIntyre observes, are different and may be termed "first principle" rationalities. In these ways of thinking, instead of asking "What do I want?" I first ask "What are the acceptable moral or religious standards?" My self-worth is determined by the extent to which I am able to meet those standards. They are not standards that I select. I do not choose who to marry, what church to attend, or how to follow religious scripture. These are selected for me, and how well I do them is the measure of my worth. My "interest and passions" are not of my own choosing.

Western democracy is a neutral playing field. It permits citizens to select their interests and passions according broad rules of legal justice (Walzer, 1994). Because of this, democracy is always, to an extent, morally "hollow." Its moral commitment is to the governing principles of democracy themselves, to process, procedure, and equality. The actual content of individual values is simply irrelevant to democratic process, within the condition that those values do not actively subvert the pursuit of happiness of another person.

Islamic states tend to be ordered by "first principles." Saudi Arabia, for example, is governed by a Council of Senior Ulema, a ranking body of religious figures charged with providing religious guidance to the citizenry (Benjamin & Simon, 2003). In these states, the mantle of statehood rests lightly and has little moral value. Citizens are loyal first to clans and next to religions. The concept of "individual desires and preferences" as a guiding moral principle lacks state sponsorship and is fundamentally inconsistent with religious doctrine.

Hence, at a fundamental level, the differences between American and Islamic states are profound. The value systems are starkly different. For the

West to reach across this moral chasm to receive legitimacy in the Middle East, it has to somehow accept a value system that, in many cases, rejects outright Western liberalism. An effort to instill a religiously neutral democracy is likely to be rejected out of hand, or where it is established, as was the case in Iran, it is likely to quickly vote in an Islamic state.

Resource-Based Theories of World Violence

According to resource-based theories, to understand world conflict we should look at the distribution of resources. Resource-based theories begin with a simple, brutish idea: If nation-states or powerful groups need a resource and have sufficient strength, they will take the resource, by force if necessary. States may have an abundance of resources and weak security, or multiple states may seek a common resource so valuable they are willing to fight over it. Below, three resource theories of conflict are considered.

Homer-Dixon – *Environmental Scarcities and Violent Conflict*

Thomas Homer-Dixon (1994,1999) observed that environmental scarcities contributed to violence in many parts of the developing world. He defined environmental scarcity as "scarcity of renewable resources, such as crop-land, forests, river water, and fish stocks" (1999:8). Violence resulted from these scarcities, which Homer-Dixon described as subnational, persistent, and diffuse.

Three processes describe the development of scarcity. They are:

1. *Supply-induced scarcity*, a process that occurs when a particular resource is depleted or degraded. It is a human-induced decline in a renewable resource that outpaces its rate of renewal. Fish stocks in the Atlantic, for example, are a supply induced scarcity and have resulted from over-fishing many prime Atlantic areas.

2. *Demand-induced scarcity* occurs when the per-capita availability of resources is reduced and divided among more people, and is a consequence of population growth or increased consumption. Water scarcity in the Western U.S. is increasingly a problem because of the large in-migration of people to the region.

3. *Structural scarcity* occurs when resources are unevenly distributed. This scarcity is grounded in local institutions and in class and ethnic relations. African-Americans suffered structural scarcities in the South from post-Civil War through the 1930s because of laws permitting contractual servitude and limiting property ownership.

Scarcity sets several processes in motion. Powerful groups, anticipating or recognizing that resource availability is changing, shift resource access in their favor. And disadvantaged peoples are forced into areas that are already ecologically fragile, further degrading available resources such as fresh water and wood for heating, or spurring desertification and creating additional hardships for these groups. Consequently, scarcity can intensify class, ethnic, or economic stresses in which the "haves" increase their advantage over the "have nots."

Scarcity can undermine the viability of nation-states in two ways: On the one hand, it increases the financial and political demands on governments, both from resource loss and from relocation of migrants or refugees in urban areas. Scarcity also expands the number of people who need help from government, because rural residents are displaced to cities where they require food, transport, shelter, energy, and employment (1994:25). On the other hand, revenues to local and national governments are diminished.

Scarcity thus increases a variety of demands on countries, while it simultaneously reduces their capacity to meet those demands. States in turn can become enfeebled or can harden. If states became enfeebled from conflict and economic stress, they fragment and/or lose control over their outer territories. Homer-Dixon found that fragmentation inevitably led to the outflow of refugees and contributed to the destabilization of surrounding countries receiving refugee populations.

Some countries respond to scarcity by beefing up internal security, militarizing police, and becoming more authoritarian. These are "hard regimes" (1994:36). A state became a "hard regime" if (1) it had the economic capacity to mobilize or seize resources for its own ends, and (2) sufficient surplus wealth remained for the state to pursue its militarized course.

Ultimately, scarcity and its consequences result in conflict. Ethnic identity can emerge or intensify after migration and relocation (Eller, 1999). Hence, the processes that lead to migration can also result in increasing group identity formation and provide a basis for we-them group polarizations and conflict (see also Coser, 1956). And migration carries the potential to trigger xenophobic backlash (Homer-Dixon, 1999:142).

The model developed by Homer-Dixon (1999) is an economic model, according to which increasing environmental problems interact with human social and economic arrangements to destabilize local governments and create the conditions for conflict. The model carries clear neo-Malthusian implications. It views hardening and/or collapse of regional economies and nation states as potential consequences of environmental degradation if problems are not addressed through social interventions.

Homer-Dixon's resource model is useful for the study of U.S. conflicts and associated terrorism. Terrorism, for example, has been widely associated with the Christian Identity Movement, whose members are drawn from economically deteriorating rural areas (Audsley, 1985). The process of resource capture by growing metropolitan areas has depressed surrounding rural areas, both by bleeding off their most talented individuals and youth, and by taking valued resources such as water for their growing populations. Conflict over water rights in the Klamath Valley in Oregon, Crank (2003) noted, was associated with decreases in renewable resources. In old city urban areas, conflict between groups, stimulated by in-migration of economically competitive minorities, has led to hostilities and violence (Rieder, 1985).

Processes of resource capture by elites can be seen in the increasing numbers of disaffected in Muslim countries such as Saudi Arabia. Rising unemployment has given rise to a class called the "educated poor," people who are well-educated, and who historically are members of the middle class, but who have witnessed a relative deterioration of opportunity against a backdrop of increasing wealth among the ruling Saud family (Sachs, 2001). Virulent strains of anti-Americanism and Jihadic Islam have found this to be fertile breeding ground for terrorist recruits.

Klare – *Resource Wars: The New Landscape of Global Conflict*

"Resource wars will become, in the years ahead, the most distinctive feature of the global security environment" (Klare, 2001:213). This is the central premise of Michael Klare's (2001) analysis of global politics, national security, and conflict. Within this general view of future conflict lie two sub-themes: (1) Security interests worldwide are being determined by increasingly scarce resource assess, and (2) American security interests, since the Cold War, are determined by economic considerations.

Since the end of the Cold War, America's strategic security interests have undergone a fundamental shift. Formerly based on the presence of a powerful arsenal and extended alliances, global security in the current era is associated with economic dynamism. The economic-security linkage was made explicit in the Carter Doctrine of 1980, which stated that "An attempt by an outside force to gain control of the Persian Gulf region will be regarded as an assault on the vital interests of the United States" (2001:4). American strategy today, Klare notes, depends on "oil-field protection, the defense of maritime trade outs, and other aspects of resource scarcity." (2001:6) Caspian Sea oil became a security concern during the Clinton presidency, due to concerns that the political environment of Persian Gulf oil was too unstable and a secondary source of oil needed to be identified.

The refocusing of security on economic interests is not unique to the United States, but characterizes international relations generally. Russia and the United States today, for example, are in what has been called the Great Game II, vying for control of Caspian Sea oil and the pipelines for moving the oil out of the region and into friendly ports.

Three factors have elevated the importance of resources to a security concern (2001:6).

1. **Insatiable demand.** The demand for critical resources is growing at an unsustainable rate, precipitated by two influences. First, population is growing, and it is growing most rapidly in those countries where resources are already scarce. The world's population has increased from three billion in 1950 to about 6 billion today. Second, industrialization has increased both the desire for goods and the ability to manufacture them. From 1950 to 1999, the Gross World Product has increased 583 percent. The most spectacular growth is the Asian rim. China alone grew by 93 percent from 1990 to 1996, and is currently growing at a rate twice that of the United States.

2. **Looming risk of shortages.** Human usage of oil and water is increasing at an unsustainable rate. Significant shortages of oil are likely by the third decade of this century. Water usage will approach the available supply by the middle of the century. Forests are also dwindling. Currently, 70 percent of the tropical dry forest, 60 percent of temperate forest, and 45 percent of tropical moist forests are gone.

3. **Contested resources.** Resource supplies often lie in contested areas, across or under borders, or in offshore economic zones. The Rumalia oil field, for example, sits below Iraq and Kuwait, and was one of the stimuli for the Iraqi invasion of Kuwait in 1991. Some resources extend through several international boundaries. The Nile River, for example, is contested by Egypt and its upriver riparians, all of whom have growing water needs. And offshore claims can be contested. Iran and Russia claim that the Caspian Sea is a "lake," which invokes their older 1921 and 1940 treaty arrangements. The other Caspian Sea states of Azerbaijan, Turkmenistan, and Kazakhstan claim that it is a "sea," which brings it within 1959 United Nations Convention on the Law of the Sea (UNSCLOS) jurisdiction of offshore access boundaries more favorable to them.

Market forces and technology can mitigate the effects of some of these resource conflicts. Increasingly efficient automobiles, for example, can postpone oil shortages for a considerable time. However, globalization can also intensify conflicts. If none of the countries demanding a limited resource are willing to accept a smaller share, then conflict becomes more likely.

In many of these countries there is an increasing divide between rich and poor, which itself can be a consequence of globalization. This gap provides opportunities for recruitment to terrorist organizations; as the poor find themselves in desperate situations, they become vulnerable to radicalization and fundamentalist influences.

Chua – *World on Fire*

Amy Chua's (2003) book is about the dark side of free market democracy. She is not against free market policies. But under some circumstances free markets can have harsh consequences. Chua argues that, to understand much violence in the world, we should look at the nexus between three of the most powerful forces in the world today—free markets, democracy, and ethnic hatred.

> This book is about a phenomenon—pervasive outside the West yet rarely acknowledged, indeed often viewed as taboo—that turns free market democracy into an engine of ethnic conflagration. The phenomenon I refer to is that of *market-dominant minorities*: ethnic minorities who, for widely varying reasons, tend under market conditions to dominate economically, often to a startling extent, the "indigenous" majorities around them (2003:6).

She presents a detailed description of market-dominant minorities around the world and their relationships with the majorities in their countries. The Chinese, for example, are such a minority in Indonesia. They constitute three percent of the population but control about 70 percent of Indonesia's private economy. These minorities, she states, are the "Achilles' heel" of free market democracy. Free markets concentrate wealth in the hands of market-dominant minorities, often "spectacularly." Democracy, on the other hand, increases the political power of minorities who often live in abject poverty. Foreign policies that push free market democracy end up becoming engines of "catastrophic nationalism." Markets continue to consolidate wealth for dominant minorities, while the poor, often with the promotion of nationalist politicians, use democracy to assert their new-found political power. The result can be devastating, as indicated by the mass genocide in Rwanda. This kind of conflict is widespread around the world today, occurring in Burma and across Southeast Asia, Russia, Southern Africa and across Africa generally, Mexico, Latin America, and the Middle East.

Chua challenges the notion, widespread in policy debates and foreign policy, that globalization of free markets is a curative for economic problems facing the word today (see Friedman, 2000). According to this notion, capitalism and democracy are the most efficient and fairest systems the world has known. By promoting them together, the world will change into a "community of prosperous, war shunning nations, and individuals into liberal, civic-minded citizens and consumers" (Chua, 2003:8-9). She takes an opposing position—that globalization is a "principal, aggravating cause of group hatred and ethnic violence throughout the non-Western world. Democracy and market economies do not reinforce each other in that world. When market democracy is developed in the presence of a market dominant ethnic minority and indigenous peoples are poor, the result is explosive and violent.

The United States has unwittingly been a part of the collision of markets and democracy. Through foreign policy initiatives, and through the policies of the World Bank, the Western world and the U.S. in particular have promoted the simultaneous development of markets and democracy. However, Chua notes, the kinds of markets and types of democracy promoted are quite different from those in practice in the Untied States. The U.S. has a market system that is embedded in social institutions that emerged historically and gradually, and that cushioned the most severe excesses of market economics. The U.S. experienced gradual suffrage, and capitalism was softened by the welfare state. In many foreign markets, however, we have tied loans and other forms of financial support with privatization policies, destroying the same kinds of institutions that have enabled the free market to work in the U.S. without great social upheaval. And we have promoted instantaneous suffrage abroad, instead of gradually developing democratic institutions.

The result, in many countries around the world, is backlash against simultaneous market/democratic reforms. Backlash takes one of three forms. Backlash may be against markets, as occurred with the land seizures in Zimbabwe, Pakistan, and Bolivia. Or the market-dominant minority may fight democratic reforms, as occurred under General Suharto in Indonesia. The third form of backlash, ethnic cleansing and other forms of majority violence, is the most savage. This is what occurred in the 1990s in Yugoslavia under Milosevic and in Rwanda.

The U.S. has been the recipient of this backlash. The U.S. cannot be characterized as a country with a market-dominated minority. However, on the world stage, the U.S. is seen as such a dominant minority. This view is particularly acute in the Middle East, where the influence of the U.S. is widely felt and where the U.S. uses its market position to acquire great wealth, yet poverty is endemic throughout the region. We are, Chua emphasizes, the world's market-dominant minority. World bank statistics show that, throughout the developing world, the numbers of poor are increasing steadily through the current period of globalization. As a consequence, we are indeed hated in many developing countries of the world, Chua concludes.

World on Fire has been accused of being neo-socialist in its orientation. It is not. Chua is not promoting universal suffrage or other democratic reforms at the expense of economic development. Her writing is a hard dose of realism, written to describe a world rife with conflict, and she attributes conflict to the "haves" and "have-nots" in full and equal measure. Critical of liberal and conservative alike, she recognizes that solutions to the problems faced by many countries will be hard-won, if they can be won at all. Pessimistically, if she is right, it is unlikely that many economic problems are solvable; more likely, conflict will become a constant feature of the international setting. The historical instant that characterized the emergence of the West is past, and there is no good reason to believe that we can replay our past in other countries.

One can see the play of some of the dynamics of Chua's *World on Fire* in efforts to rebuild Iraq after the second Gulf War. L. Paul Bremer III, the occupation administrator of Iraq, arrived in Baghdad on May 12, 2003. The country at that point was in disarray; the government was wholly collapsed; the ministries were burned out; significant looting had stripped universities, commercial centers, and hospitals. Security forces and police had abandoned their posts. Only the oil industry was protected from looting by American soldiers.

Bremer brought with him an extensive conservative pedigree, having worked under Henry Kissinger and as counter-terrorism chief in the Reagan administration. When he arrived in Iraq he had clear ideas that the economy of Iraq should be rebuilt around free-market ideas. Surprisingly, however, these views changed. Tyler of the *New York Times* reports the following conversation between Bremer and Bahram Salih:

> Bahram Salih, a senior aide to another Kurdish leader, Jalal Talababi, said: "He came with some very definite ideas on what needed to be done," adding that Mr. Bremer "believed that Iraq needed to be rebuilt along free-market principles. "I told him that Iraq is a welfare state and its government is dependent on oil revenues and the people have gotten used to being given handouts," Mr. Salih said. "I told him it would be a disastrous policy if he is thinking of ending the welfare state overnight."

> Mr. Bremer accepted part of this advice. He protected the food aid operation on which 60 percent of Iraqis rely for sustenance, and he accelerated the distribution of subsidies and salaries to Iraqi civil servants, most of whom are still sitting at home (Tyler, 2003).

Tyler also noted that Bremer at first "took a meat cleaver"to the salaries of the Iraqi military, many of whom had put down their arms after receiving air-dropped U.S. leaflets urging them not to fight. This enraged many military men. With the onset of guerrilla-style attacks Bremer reconsidered the salary issue, and decided to pay back-wages and re-institute salary payments to officers. National Public Radio also reported that Bremer was considering a national oil subsidy payment to all Iraqi citizens, to provide them with a dividend payment linked to the sales of their oil.

We see in Bremer's policy changes in Iraq what appears to be a growing recognition that the emplacement of a free market economy without welfare protections for the resident population has the potential for significant blowback. Indeed, the suggestion above is that, at least in part, the violence directed against U.S. military personnel is associated with the collapse of the welfare state in Iraq and that Bremer recognizes a need to reestablish that state. Whether some sort of reorganization of the state incorporating both welfare and free market ideas actually occurs remains to be seen. However, the issues described by Chua are vital in Iraq in the post-war era.

Perspectives of Reciprocal Causation

Reciprocal causation is not so much a theory as it is a perspective on foreign policy. It is rooted in the notion that international action on the part of a government is reciprocated by an action on the part of another government. Notions of reciprocal causation embody the idea that a nation's behavior, as it affects foreign countries, has consequences in the international community. Like all complex social phenomena, some of the consequences will be intentional and some will be unintentional.

The dark side of reciprocal causation is revealed in anti-terror activities that have the backfiring effect of causing more violence. The behavior of the British Army, for example, may have played a central role in the rebirth of the Irish Revolutionary Army (IRA). White (2002) describes an example of blowback with the arrival of the British Army in Ulster, Ireland, in 1969. The British identified the presence of two groups when they arrived; one who "flew the Irish tricolor and spoke with a deep seated hatred of the British," and the other, the Oranges, who "flew the Union Jack" and viewed themselves as British patriots (2002:88). The mistake the British made was to align themselves with the seemingly favorable group instead of remaining neutral in the conflict.

The British acted as agents of repression, siding with the unionists. Catholics and republicans, seeking protection from the British, turned to the IRA. The IRA in turn reorganized and turned its attention to the elimination of British troops. However, as the ranks of the IRA grew, the Orange extremist organizations also expanded. Hence, violence by one side was reciprocated by violence on the other. White concluded that "The policies of the police and the British Army had done much to set these hostile forces in motion." We can see in this example how suppressive activities by the British Army led to increased hostilities by the IRA, and these in turn led to increases in Orange violence. In all cases, violence backfired producing more, rather than less, opposition violence.

"Blowback" was a term first developed by the CIA, and it has slipped into the language of international relations. In the section below, I review Johnson's and Weaver's discussion of *Blowback*.

Johnson – *Blowback: The Costs and Consequence of American Empire*

The United States is engaged in empire building, and many bad acts by totalitarian governments are carried out in the name of the United States. The only time the American people hear about these bad acts is when they blow back in the form of violent anti-American activity. This is the central theme of Chalmers Johnson's (2000) book, *Blowback*. Johnson defines blowback as the "unintended consequences of policies that were kept secret from the American people" (2000:8).

The downing of Pan Am 103 by Libya in 1989 was a blowback from military exchanges between Libya and the U.S., particularly an aerial raid on Libya that killed President Muammar al-Qadaffi's stepdaughter. After the bombing, then-President George H.W. Bush decided that retaliation was a futile strategy. As a consequence, the Bush administration shifted to a legal solution through the U.N., concluding that international pressure would be more effective (Benjamin & Simon, 2002).

The civil war in Afghanistan in the 1980s is another case of blowback. The Soviets intervened on the government's side during the war and the U.S. covertly aided the mujahideen, at one time referred to as "freedom fighters" by President Reagan. The eventual defeat of the Soviet Union was economically destabilizing, and has been associated with the Soviet Union's later collapse. It also brought to power the Taliban, a fundamentalist Islamic sect. The U.S. also armed and supported Osama bin Laden. In this example we see that the forces the U.S. put into play to subvert the Soviet Union had a broad range of effects, some of which can be linked to the 9/11 hijackings and bombings of the World Trade Center and Pentagon by bin Laden and Al Qaeda.

Johnson is not friendly to post-Cold War American policy. He argues that, since the end of the Cold War:

> . . . the United States largely abandoned a reliance on diplomacy, diplomatic aid, international law, and multilateral institutions in carrying out its foreign policies and resorted much of the time to bluster, military force, and manipulation. The world is not a safe place as a result (Johnson, 2000:217).

A "go-it-alone" attitude is witnessed in Secretary of State Madeleine Albright's comments on the use of cruise missiles against Iraq: "If we have to use force, it is because we are America. We are the indispensable nation. We stand tall. We see farther into the future" (2000:217). The Clinton administration refused to support either the ban on land mines or the establishment of the world court, a position also taken by the 2000 Bush administration.

Johnson is clearly staking out moral ground based on democratic notions of citizen participation in governmental decisionmaking. American government, he notes, has not been honest to its citizens about the reach and consequences of its imperial domain. He also makes an economic argument, that the consequences of imperial outreach could be economically destabilizing. We are moving into what he calls an "exploitative hegemony," attempting to homogenize the global economy through the use of military and economic force. Such force will generate increasing blowback, and will prove too expensive to sustain. Our future, he concludes, may be much like the former Soviet Union—an empire economically collapsing on itself.

Weaver – *"Blowback"*

Mary Anne Weaver (1996) provides a more specific discussion of reciprocal causation. In an article also titled "Blowback," she discusses the historical progression of terrorism from the Afghan-Soviet conflict. She opens with a discussion of three terrorist incidents: a bombing in Peshawar, Pakistan, in December, 1985, and two similar bombings in November, 1985, one outside the Riyadh headquarters of a U.S. military training center and the other outside the Egyptian embassy in Pakistan. These incidents, she observed, marked a fundamental change in the nature of terrorism since the Cold War. The new face of terrorism was a "proliferation of amorphous underground Islamic groups . . ." The common element of the attacks is that they were carried out by the Afghan Arabs, veterans of the war in Afghanistan.

That the Soviet-Afghanistan conflict was viewed as an Islamic Jihad is thoroughly documented by Weaver. She notes that:

> For more then a decade some 25,000 Islamic militants, from nearly thirty countries around the world, had streamed through Peshawar on their way to the Jihad . . . "Even today you can sit at the Khyber Pass and see every color, every creed, every nationality pass," a Western diplomat told me in Peshawar last spring. "These groups, in their wildest imagination, never would have met if there had been no Jihad. For a Moor to get a stinger missile! To make contacts with Islamists from North Africa! The United States created a Moscow Central in Peshawar for these groups, and the consequences for all of us are astronomical" (Weaver, 1996:4, 5).

The veterans of the Jihad have spread around the world. Weaver asserted they had set up cells and recruitment centers in the United States, the Persian Gulf, Germany, Switzerland, Scandinavia, Sudan, Pakistan, and Afghanistan. Peshawar was the nexus for the Pan-Islamic movement both during the conflict and after the end of the Soviet occupation.

Among those who fought in the Jihad, the Saudis were some of the most committed. They were, Weaver observed, different from the other Jihadists. They tended to come from wealthy families, and to be well educated. They were, a diplomat informed her, sent by their government, because it was the honorable thing to do. Though wealthy, they were underemployed and "frustrated, an accident waiting to happen"(1996:8). Among the disaffected Saudis was Osama bin Laden, blamed for the 9/11 terrorist attacks on the United States.

One might wonder why the Americans were not praised by the Afghans for their role in the Afghan jihad. Sheikh Omar Abdul-Rahman offers the following explanation.

> The Americans were there to punish the Soviet Union, and when they were sure that the Soviet Union had suffered and was about to collapse, they stopped everything—all the aid, all the equipment—just like that." He snapped his fingers and his voice began to rise. "They didn't care that there was still a communist government in power in Afghanistan. They simply turned their backs and walked away. And the Saudis, oh the Saudis and the Egyptians—they did precisely the same. It took three more years for the mujahideen to oust the Najibullah regime. Thousands of lives were lost; crops and livelihoods were destroyed. But not one life mattered to the Saudis, the Egyptians, or the United States (Weaver, 1996).

Weaver provides a more focused example of blowback than does Johnson, absent the explicit criticism of U.S. foreign policy that characterizes the latter's work. However, a powerful implication of her work is that contemporary terrorism in the Middle East owes a great deal to the Afghan-Soviet war, a conflict viewed as a jihad across the Islamic world. That conflict was a training ground that gave purpose to, and armed, Islamic Jihadists, and the United States has paid a stern price for its involvement since.

Understanding processes of blowback contributes to counter-terrorism perspective in several ways. First, in the development of foreign policy, large and bold decisions can have complex and far reaching results, including quite positive as well as negative effects. By studying the long-term impacts in a region where a policy was carried out, "backfiring" effects can be studied, mitigated, and perhaps prevented. By looking for blowbacks we will not be lulled into complacency by the good effects of policies.

Secondly, blowback effects are common to nation-state efforts to suppress terrorism. Where terrorists have ideological support among a large population, efforts to stamp out the terrorism with broad-based suppressive and intelligence strategies may backfire and increase their likelihood: organizations that sponsor terrorism will thrive and terrorism will increase. Indeed, this is the lesson of the British experience in Ireland in the 1960s and 1970s. This is a central concern that the U.S. faces in Iraq. If the insurgency against the American occupation is the result of the remnants of the Baath Party regime, formerly the Baath Arab Socialist Party, seeking to hold on to fading power, as some have claimed, then suppressive counter-terror techniques may be successful. However, if they stem from broad dissatisfaction and distaste for Americans across the region, then suppressive counter-terrorism is likely to blow back, fueling anti-American sentiment and increasing terrorism.

Conclusion: Perspective for a Violent World

Perspective is important, because it carries profound policy implications. Get the perspective wrong and terrorism spreads, people die. On February 4, 2002, Secretary of State Colin Powell presented evidence to the Security Council of the United Nations, arguing that the evidence demonstrated that Iraq had ties to Al Qaeda. As proof, he described the links between Abu Musab al-Zarqawi, a Jordananian extremist, to Osama bin Laden on the one hand and to Baghdad on the other. The active presence of al-Zarqawi in Iraq demonstrated the willingness of Baghdad to permit the operation of Al Qaeda on its territory.

Burke (2003) states that the notion that al-Zarqawi is a member of Al Qaeda stems from a fundamental misconception of Islamic terrorism. The U.S. is not fighting a terrorist war against an identifiable group or individual. It is fighting a war against a political religion.

The battle for Afghanistan, Burke notes, was a battle against a "Jihad International." In his travels through Afghanistan, he observed fighters from Chechnya, Yemen, Egypt, Algeria, and Iraq. All were militants, all hated the West and were committed to the holy struggle. They were not affiliated with bin Laden.

The war against the Soviets was a similar jihad. A number of fighters made names for themselves, among them bin Laden. Al-Zarqawi, with his band of Jordanians, also made his reputation there. And through the anti-Soviet jihad, they and many others planted the seeds of Islamic militancy that has increasingly enveloped the world with terrorism.

Many different Islamic groups made allegiances with the Taliban during their reign, each with their own goals and agendas. There was, Burke noted, a "temporary coalescing of different radical groups, (representing) the full range of modern Islamic militancy." With the start of the bombing in Afghanistan, some militants fought, and others fled. Al-Zarqawi was injured in March, 2002, and escaped to Iran, who later expelled him. From there he sought the nearest safe zone, which was in northern Iraq. Burke concludes:

> His (al-Zarqawi) story is the story of modern Islamic militancy. It is also the story of why the American-led "war on terror" risks backfiring badly   . Primarily, al-Zarqawi is part of a broad movement of Islamic militancy that extends well beyond the influences and activities of any one man. This is a movement that is rooted in broad trends in the Middle East, in the economic, social, and

political failure of governments, both locally and in the West, to fulfill the aspirations of hundreds of millions of people. Islamic militancy is a multivalent, diverse and complex phenomenon. Focusing on individuals, even bin Laden, is a ludicrous oversimplification. (Burke, 2003).

Burke presents an image of conflict that, correctly understood, is rooted in Islamic fundamentalism. By focusing on an individual or group, the enemy is misidentified. If Burke is right, any victory over Al Qaeda will be only a starting point in a war on terrorism. It could lead to the false conclusion that the war was conducted successfully. Worse, it could contribute to the spread of terrorism.

Others have come to similar conclusions. Van Natta and Johnson (2003) noted that al-Zarqawi is a dangerous man with extensive terrorist ties. He is known to have skills working with poisons and chemicals, and is suspected of working in training camps in Afghanistan. An American diplomat in Jordan, Lawrence Foley, was shot to death by associates of al-Zarqawi in October, 2002. The link between al-Zarqawi and Al Qaeda, however, is uncertain. German officials observed that they have investigated al-Zarqawi for a long time, but had found no link between him and Iraq. By mid 2004, al-Zarqawi had become increasingly prominent as a source of anti-American terrorism. He was the alleged mastermind of the Madrid train bombings on March 11, 2004, which killed more than 200 people. Yet, most of his alleged violence has been in Iraq. He has been accused of personally beheading an American contractor, Nicholas Berg, in May, 2004. In June, he was accused of coordinating a series of spectacular bombings that killed 92 Iraqis. And many consider him responsible for the assassination of the Shiite Cleric Ayatollah al-Hakim in 2003. Indeed, he is deemed so significant that the U.S. offered a $25 million reward for his capture.

Yet, al-Zarqawi remains poorly understood in important ways. It is not known if he has one leg or two; one may have been lost in 2001, after a U.S. missile strike on his Afghan base, after which he fled to Iraq. His death has been formally proclaimed by one Islamist terrorist organization in February, 2004, though that claim is generally discredited. And some have argued that his prominence in the world of terrorism is fictitious, a product of media efforts to put a human face on an illusive and growing anti-American Islamic resistance across the Middle East.

Al-Zarqawi's organizational identity is important. The U.S. continues to claim that he is the central link between Al Qaeda and Iraq, justifying the invasion of Iraq in the war on terrorism. German security forces that interrogated members of his organization make a different claim—al-Zarqawi's organization at that time was especially for Jordanians who did not want to join Al Qaeda. In the Iraq war, a similar counterclaim has been made that he sought to create an organization that is competitive with Al Qaeda, not affiliated with it.

If, as the U.S. government claims, al-Zarqawi is the personification of Al Qaeda in Iraq, not only will the invasion of Iraq be justified in the war on terrorism but his capture or killing will be a substantive victory against Al Qaeda. If the U.S. is wrong, al-Zarqawi's rise to power in Iraq must be understood in quite a different way. Al-Zarqawi's growing influence and lethality in Iraq (and elsewhere) in 2004 may be a consequence of our military invasion of Iraq, verification that the Iraq invasion has made the world a more dangerous place to live for Americans and their supporters worldwide. If the U.S. government has misunderstood him, then we may have fought the wrong war in the name of counter-terrorism.

What will the world be like for the children of the twenty-first century? The legacy received from their parents was, in many ways, bleak. The twentieth century was the first century of megadeath, with estimates of 250 wars and war-related deaths ranging as high as 187 million deaths worldwide (Hobsbwan, 1994). Land mines, a legacy of wars, continue to kill people long after a war has officially ended. Currently, about 25 countries are sown with in excess of one million land mines each. There continues to be a stock of about 250 million land mines in 16 countries. Of these, only about 13 million are in countries that have ratified the 1997 Ottawa Convention to ban land mines (IIMCR, 2001). In 2002, an estimated 11,700 people were killed by land mines, according to *International Campaign to Ban Land Mines*. Moreover, many deaths are not reported because they happen in small civilian populations in remote areas with no way to communicate.

Against a backdrop of world violence and megadeath, what is amazing is not that the United States should become the object of the violent attack now known as 9/11. It is not as if the United States were unengaged in the world prior to that date; all analyses of U.S. security and economic interests reveal a deep and continual expansion of its economic and security reach across the world. What is amazing is that the American people could have been so astonishingly unaware of their country's involvement in international issues, the unremitting violence of the world around them, and the inevitability that at some point that significant terrorist violence would migrate to the United States. The wrong lesson we can acquire from 9/11 is that we are engaged in the first war of the twenty-first century. The best lesson is that we live in a violent world, shaped in part by events and players beyond our control and in part by events of our own doing. We bear a moral responsibility, as well as a clear security need, to address proximate threats and to attend to the fundamental social and economic inequalities that metastasize into world violence.

CHAPTER 4

Surveillance: Toward Panopticon

One of the defining tensions in modern society is that between privacy and surveillance. Surveillance has expanded dramatically since the terrorist attacks on 9/11. However, current trends in surveillance occur within a historical context, a context that has witnessed and that justifies surveillance as a part of American life.

Surveillance in American Society

This chapter will first consider pre-9/11 perspectives on surveillance. This section looks at the history of surveillance and argues that surveillance post-9/11 is an extension of existing surveillant trends in U.S. civil society and in the criminal justice system.

Surveillance: A Tayloristic Good

One of the celebrated characteristics of American society is the development of efficiencies in the production of work. This is the Tayloristic vision of work, which views workplace efficiency as a form of technological development that facilitates and enhances the ability of businesses to harness the labor of workers in order to compete in the marketplace. Taylorism is tightly bound with notions of scientific development and progress, both of which are products of the Enlightenment.

When one imagines the stereotypical Tayloristic workplace, one thinks of a highly efficient factory setting in which each and every action made by a worker has been carefully researched, and represents the most efficient movement a person can make for the production of some particular product. Accompanying the idea of worker efficiency is surveillance, according to which a worker's movements are carefully examined for their relative contribution to the end product. Surveillance is an integral aspect of such efficiency, because workers cannot become more efficient unless their work behaviors are carefully examined. Surveillance brings "discipline," the capacity to guide and direct human behavior, to the workplace (Foucault, 1995).

Tayloristic efficiency has a darker edge, that workers are not to be fully trusted and their behaviors should be monitored. The Tayloristic notion is wedded to a class structural perspective, according to which the "working class" is generally lazy and uninterested in the welfare of the company. Workers need to be watched. In this way, surveillance weds notions of scientific progress to elite distrust of the working and dangerous classes, permitting the observation of workers in terms of scientific progress, and facilitating the extension of elite control over workers.

That Tayloristic surveillance was a way to control workers has been widely noted. The film *Modern Times* with Charlie Chaplin, filmed in 1936, carried both the themes of Taylorism and surveillance. In *Modern Times* Chaplin acts out the part of the average person struggling against the "dehumanizing machine in the Industrial Age." In one scene, he is a factory worker carrying out mindless tasks. He tightens nuts. Dirks (2003) observes that:

> The key to successful nut-tightening is to perform his movements and tasks with clock-like tempo and precision. This scene illustrates the American factory's obsession with time and automation. From his work station on the assembly line, he holds wrenches in both hands to tighten nuts on a long stream of steel plates carried on the conveyor belt production line (Dirks, 2003:1).

At one point Chaplin is caught in one machine and "fed" to another. The film shows him passing through various cogs in the machine, a human caught in the cogs of modern Tayloristic society. In a later scene, he encounters a "Big Brother" manager, who watches workers via a two-way TV screen. The manager uses the system to monitor workers, and orders foremen to "hurry production." At one point Chaplin is seen sneaking a "smoke" in a bathroom and is harangued by a foreman for wasting time. We can see in this comedy both aspects of surveillance, the notion of progress caught by the acute focus on efficient assembly-line production, and class control through secretive observation, even in the discrete setting of a bathroom.

The Chaplinesque notion of industry is antiquated in the current age, with its complex businesses and highly decentralized practices. The corresponding notion of surveillance as "Big Brother," exterior and visual, is similarly antiquated. Today, surveillance is not exterior to us, but envelops us and emanates from our actions. As Stalder (2003) notes:

> We live in a surveillance society. The creation, collection and processing of personal data is nearly a ubiquitous phenomenon. Every time we use a loyalty card at a retailer, our names are cor-

related with our purchases and entered into giant databases Every time we pass an electronic tollbooth on the highway, every time we use a cell phone or a credit card, our locations are being recorded, analyzed, and stored Every time we go see a doctor, submit an insurance claim, pay our utility bills, interact with the government, or go online, the picture gleaned from our actions and states grows finer and finer.

Our physical bodies are being shadowed by an increasingly comprehensive 'data body.' However, this shadow body does more than follow us It does also precede us. Before we arrive somewhere, we have already been measured and classified. Thus, on arrival, we're treated according to whatever criteria have been connected to the profile that represents us (Stalder, 2003:120).

Marx and the New Surveillance

The surveillance of today, Marx (2002) notes, is fundamentally different from surveillance as traditionally conceived. The traditional conception of surveillance is captured by a dictionary definition, as "close observation, especially of a suspected person." Today, however, much observation is neither close nor of a suspected person. He notes the following elements of the new surveillance:

1. Self-monitoring has emerged as a theme in the current surveillant age. Home tests for alcohol level, AIDS, and pregnancy are all forms of self-surveillance.

2 Observation is not always "close." It is often from a distance, as in satellite imagery.

3 Observation is not always visual. At times, the means of tracking is hearing, touching, or smelling.

From this, Marx offers a new definition of surveillance: "The use of technical means to create personal data." Data may be taken from individuals or contexts, such as particular settings habited by the individual, and enables the surveillant to look at "settings and patterns of relationships" (Marx, 2002:12). The new surveillance has several dimensions. These dimensions, and how they compare the new to the old surveillance, are presented in Figure 4.1.

We can see in Figure 4.1 that the new surveillance differs in many dimensions from the old. It infrequently involves direct coercion of individuals, but depends on manipulation. The data collection tends to be automatic, lowering the overall expense. The data is immediately processed, and its results are available in real time rather than in some future after they have been processed and interpreted. It is less affected by physical and social distance. Consider a scanned shopping card. One uses such a card after shopping to receive local discounts. It loads information about the buyer and the purchases into a distant computer, and immediately processes it. It is not particularly expensive per individual. Because shoppers voluntarily use the cards, self-monitoring is involved. And a profile of buying habits is gradually developed around aggregate buyer characteristics.

Figure 4.1
Surveillance Dimensions

Dimension	Traditional Surveillance	New Surveillance
Senses	Unaided senses	Extends senses
Visibility (of the actual collection of data)	Visible	Less visible or invisible
Consent	Tends not to be involuntary	Less likely to be voluntary
Cost	Expensive	Less expensive
Location of collectors/analyzers	On scene	Remote
Ethos	Harder (more coercive)	Softer (less coercive)
Integration in social life	Not integrated	Folded into routine activity
Data collector	Human, animal	Wholly or partly automated
Data location	Local, with collector	Migratory, with third party
Timing of data gathering	Data collected once	Continuous data stream
Time period	Present	Past, present, future
Data availability	After collected and processed	Real time availability
Technology availability	Mostly to elites	Democratized, some widely available
Object of data collection	Individual	Individuals and groups
Comprehensiveness	Less	More
Context	Contextual	Acontextual
Depth	Less intensive	More intensive
Breadth	Less extensive	More extensive
Surveillant/subject knowledge	What surveillant knows is what subject knows	Surveillant knows more than subject
Form	Single media (visual)	Multi media, including video and audio
Who collects data	Specialists	Self-monitoring
Data analysis	Difficult	Commonly available
Data communication	Difficult to send, receive	Easy to send, receive

Source: Marx, Gary T. (2002). "What's New about the 'New Surveillance'? Classifying for Change and Continuity." *Surveillance and Society*, 1(1):9-29.

Figure 4.1 shows us that, generally speaking, we are much more cocooned in information-gathering systems than suggested by traditional surveillance. They have become a routine part of our lives; ordinary citizens use them and often take them for granted. Citizens tend to accept the legitimacy of information so acquired as appropriate for their well-being and safety.

Marx concludes that the difference between the new and old surveillance is profound and fundamental. It is a technology that will have far-reaching implications for the way in which we relate to each other. However, what it means for personal liberty and freedom is not clear. He suggests that surveillance technologies exist in a dialectic relationship with rules and counter-technologies designed to limit their application. They do not "enter a neutral culture," but one with existing notions of propriety and privacy. And they interact with the social structure in unknown ways, ways that may result in fundamental changes in the social ambient. And we all may be changed as a result. What we know with certainty is that traditional notions of privacy have disappeared.

Surveillance and Criminal Justice

One of the central features of the new security environment is the enhancement of crime control surveillance, or as put by its critics, government spying on citizens. Proponents of enhanced surveillance argue that the expansion of information will help terrorism experts "connect the dots," that is, figure out when and where terrorists are next likely to strike. Critics counter that information technologies contribute little to counter terrorist efforts. In practice, they serve the interests of those who want to control the rights of citizens to express their disagreement with the government.

Current efforts to expand crime control surveillance did not emerge whole cloth following the terrorist strikes against the United States on 9/11/2001. The growth of crime control surveillance has a long history in the U.S., and can only be understood against the backdrop of that history. If we want to understand surveillance of civilian populations today, we must begin with a review of the surveillance of criminal populations prior to 9/11. The attacks occurred at a time when the war on crime was in its third decade of intensification and crime control was steadily expanding around the more recent "war on drugs." Surveillance, making use of a diversity of technologies, was advocated to do something about drug users and distributors. Surveillance practices and technologies were part and parcel of the dramatic expansion of the reach of the criminal justice system that had occurred through the 1970s to the end of the twentieth century. Gordon's discussion of the growth of surveillant technologies during this era is discussed below.

Gordon – *The Justice Juggernaut: Fighting Street Crime, Controlling Citizens*

Perhaps the strongest review of justice system crime control and surveillance through the 1970s and 1980s was carried out by Diana Gordon (1991). In an extensive documentation of the growth of surveillance systems and justice practices we witness the foundation of the expansive surveillance systems put in place under presidents Clinton and Bush in the period between 1996 and 2002 and justified in terms of counter-terrorism.

Criminal justice in the latter half of the twentieth century underwent a profound change. The way in which we thought about justice became politicized. Beginning with President Nixon in the late 1960s, the way in which America dealt with criminals became a political issue, and that issue was about punishment. Politicians of the political right and left alike argued for a "get tough on crime" approach. The politicization of crime control resulted in two trends with broad-reaching consequences. First, penalties were steadily increased while alternative sentencing practices, particularly those that did not look tough enough, declined. Second, and less widely recognized but equally far-reaching, were efforts to expand surveillance and information technologies to identify and catalogue people according to their criminal behavior and suspected intent. As Gordon observed, the two tracks of the justice juggernaut were to capture and confine, and to observe. State control of public (and increasingly, private) space through observation became a key strategy, leading to the current growth in surveillance ideology, practice, and technology.

The FBI had three primary repositories of information. One of these repositories was called the National Crime Information Center. It was a criminal justice information clearinghouse, readily providing information for officers trying to find out about someone's criminal background. By 1988, it contained about eight million records. These records were immediately accessible to about 60,000 criminal justice agencies nationally. Another information bank is the Identification Division, which contains fingerprint cards, increasingly computerized, for about 25 million people. Finally, the Interstate Identification Index, or "Triple-I," provides an electronic directory of about 12 million people in 20 states.

These data sources contain criminal histories. However, other kinds of information are maintained as well. Gordon notes that additional information is of two types, investigative records and intelligence records. Investigative records contain information on suspects, including identifiers such as date of birth and physical characteristics, associates, and activities. They represent what law enforcement learns about a suspect before he or she is arrested. Intelligence records reach into an even more "preliminary, and therefore ambiguous, stage of law enforcement activity" (1991:64). Gordon cites the California definition of criminal intelligence as:

stored information on the activities and associations of individuals or groups known or suspected to be involved in criminal acts or in the threatening, planning, organizing, or financing of criminal acts. [This includes groups that are] operated, controlled, financed, infiltrated, or illegally used by crime figures (Criminal Intelligence File Guidelines, p. 1, State of California Department of Justice, in Gordon, 1991:64).

Who has access to these records? California permits occupational screening checks for auto mechanics, barbers, cosmetologists, optometrists, liquor store owners, shorthand reporters, pest control employees, TV repair persons, real estate brokers, and notaries public. Under compelling circumstances records may be acquired by out of state prosecutors, Inspectors General of most regulatory agencies, Postal Service and Veterans Administration, and security officers for a variety of state and local agencies. In short, almost anyone with a bit of imagination can easily acquire a great deal of information on persons with criminal, investigative, or intelligence histories. Also, linkages enable local police to tap into the FBI record system to run routine background checks. To avoid problems with the illegal provision of Federal information to local authorities, the FBI "message-switches," running state records through its computers so local authorities from one state can find out about records that might exist in another state.

Gordon offers a four-part explanation for the Panopticon of contemporary surveillance. The first is the "crime problem" explanation: Surveillance increased at a time when crime was also increasing, and was straightforwardly justified as a way to track those who committed crime. This explanation is consistent with the "normative" notion of criminal justice described in Chapter 1. The problem with this explanation is that the surveillance Panopticon continued growing even through periods when crime wasn't growing in the early 1980s.

A second perspective is called "permissive consensus." According to this view, Americans generally think that their government does not do enough about crime and are willing to invest more in crime control strategies. The criminal justice system is seen as too easy on offenders. Hence, Americans are comfortable with criminal justice system expansion to address crime problems, even if it means increasing surveillance and expanded record keeping of suspects generally.

The third perspective is that processes of federalization are increasing the reach of justice activities into citizens' privacy. The U.S. has provided an increasing crime control role for the federal government throughout the twentieth century. In the first part of the century the FBI was founded and a national campaign against prostitution was begun. Growth of the sphere of influence of the FBI has continued steadily. In the late 1960s the federal government, under President Johnson, declared a "War on Crime," and a series of congressional acts expanded the federal responsibilities in criminal justice practice. The war on drugs, which began in the 1980s, has contributed to the expansion of the federal role, and today we witness its continued extension with the war on terrorism.

Fourth is called "elite influence," described by Gordon in her concluding chapter. This view argues that elites have had a pervasive influence on political decisionmaking over crime control policy. Elites have frequently served on blue ribbon commissions. Perhaps the most far-reaching blue-ribbon committee was the President's Commission on Law Enforcement and Administration of Justice, or simply, the Crime Commission of 1968, a group of criminal justice professionals and legislators. The Crime Commission produced a report, titled "The Challenge of Crime in a Free Society," that was a blueprint for comprehensive crime control strategy. It set a series of standards against which criminal justice practices continue to be measured today.

Historically, the greatest thrust for surveillance and crime control can be traced to the Commission's creation of the Law Enforcement Assistance Administration (LEAA, 1969-1980). Gordon makes the following observation regarding the LEAA:

> The final bill . . . was a grab-bag of hard-line provisions; millions of dollars were earmarked for riot control in the first year, expanded authorization was provided for wiretapping, and legislation was proposed to defeat the Supreme Court's position on confessions. In its early years LEAA always gave away at least 50 percent of its action grants to police, often for hardware like helicopters and tanks (even an armored personnel carrier for Louisiana) (Gordon, 1991:200).

The LEAA contributed to the growth of surveillance and recordkeeping in two ways.

1. It seemed to promise the development of technologies that would conquer crime, much as space had been conquered. Academicians and liberals were as enthusiastic about it as were law and order conservatives.

2. It assisted in the development of state computerized information systems. In its last annual report in 1979, every state reported using some LEAA money on computerized systems.

According to Gordon, a central problem with crime control under the Panopticon, is that it does not work very well. What it does—surveill, imprison, and extend the range of punishments for intermediate sanctions—is largely divorced from the actual causes of crime. While it is effective at gathering evidence and at imprisoning offenders, those factors associated with the causes of crime are unaddressed. In fact, at the federal level, the U.S. largely dismantled programs in the social welfare arena that addressed root causes of crime.

Moreover, "crime control" is as much about political electioneering as it is about crime control practice. It reinforces policy failures, leads to more crime control, and contributes to stratification in American society. Because crime is concentrated among the poor and minorities, its primary consequences are to polarize American society along class and ethnic lines.

Gordon sees little optimism for a lessening of government surveillance. Two forces are likely to continue the drive for expanded surveillance. The first of these is the political utility of law and order issues, particularly the "war on drugs." Catch phrases like "just say no" and "zero tolerance" contributed to the perception that drugs were indeed a dangerous public problem. No politician wanted to be on the wrong side of efforts to criminalize drugs. With the Anti-Drug Abuse acts of 1986 and 1988, block grants began flowing to state and local law enforcement for the "exchange of intelligence information" (Gordon, 1991:236). Secondly, crime control is reinforced by other policies in the wider policy arena. Law and order politics, Gordon notes, were a "stalking horse" for attacks on the welfare state and other indications of social permissiveness associated with liberalism. The war on drugs was a clear attack on the 1960s counterculture society carried out through the remainder of the century. Welfare grants are tied to work requirements on the one hand, and to random drug and alcohol screening on the other. The likely future of crime control and surveillance is, as Gordon titles the last chapter, "broader and deeper."

Gordon could not have foreseen the specific events of 9/11 and its emotional impact on justice system processes. However, her work clearly foresaw the continued expansion of surveillance in the name of crime control. It may be that the events of 9/11 only hastened practices already well underway in the justice system.

Democratic Politics and the Electorate

Historically, the conservative wing of the Republican party has carried the primary advocacy for the "get tough on crime" mandate. Recognizing the partisan advantages accruing to Republicans for a tough crime policy, the Democratic party has increasingly advocated a toughening posture on crime. This toughening was associated with two electorate dynamics. First, victimization research increasingly showed that minorities were among the most victimized American citizens. Democrats argued for crime control in order to provide protections for ethnic and racial minorities, and for women. Victimization became a way to shore up the base of the Democratic party, while providing the great mass of centrist voters with a reason to support tough law and order and still vote Democratic.

Secondly, Democrats discovered that the electorate was sympathetic to "get tough on crime" advocacy. By taking a politically supportive position in the war on crime and drugs, Democrats could make inroads to that part of the centrist electorate traditionally supportive of centrist Republicans. Nixon's landslide presidential victory in 1968 occurred in part because of his support for a "war on crime." Clinton's strong "war on crime" advocacy was important to his electoral popularity, and many contemporary surveillant practices can be traced to his presidency.

Democrats have effectively used "war on crime" politics to maintain political viability with centrist and undecided voters. On the other hand, civil rights supporters and due process advocates have lost a voice in mainstream politics. In the current age, there is no significant political resistance to hard line crime control policy. The intersection of Democratic politics and surveillant practices is most visible in the 1966 Antiterrorism Act.

Antiterrorism and Effective Death Penalty Act of 1996

The Antiterrorism and Effective Death Penalty Act of 1996, known as the Antiterrorism Act, was a loose set of legislative provisions generally designed to improve antiterrorism efforts by relaxing a variety of controls over due process and privacy rights. As Griset and Mahan (2003:282-283) observe, counter-terrorism legislation was framed in terms of restrictions on citizens' rights. In Figure 4.2 they identify the following elements of the 1996 Antiterrorism Act.

Cole and Dempsey (2002:107) summarized the Antiterrorism Act as follows. It:

> Established a special court that would use secret evidence to deport non-citizens accused of association with terrorist groups; it gave the Executive Branch the power to criminalize fund-raising for lawful activities conducted by organizations labeled "terrorist;" it repealed the Edwards Amendment, which prohibited the FBI from opening investigations based on First Amendment activities; and it resurrected the discredited ideological visa denial provisions of the McCarran-Walter Act to bar aliens based on their associations rather than on their acts The bill also included provisions to create a new federal crime of terrorism, carve further exceptions in the time-honored *posse comitatus* law barring the U.S. military from civilian law enforcement, expand use of pre-trial detention, and loosen the rules governing federal wiretaps.

Several aspects of the Antiterrorism Act, Cole and Dempsey noted, were troubling. First, it addressed no specific anti-terrorist need. When the House Judiciary Committee asked Deputy Attorney General Jamie Gorelick specifically what problems the legislation addressed, Gorelick was unable to provide any such reasons, either avoiding the question or stating that she was not at liberty to respond with specific answers.

Figure 4.2
The 1996 Antiterrorism Act

1. Some terrorist acts were punishable by death This avoided the statute of limitations restrictions on non-death penalty crimes.

2. The Secretary of State was provided with the discretionary authority to develop a list of foreign terrorist organizations.

3 Any organization designated by the Secretary of State as a Foreign Terrorist Organization could have their assets frozen.

4. Penalties up to 10 years in prison were provided for anyone supplying "material support or resources" to a foreign terrorist organization

5. Support for humanitarian activities (schools or hospital support) carried out by foreign terrorist organizations was prohibited.

6. Foreigners could be denied visas based on membership in terrorist groups.

7. Anyone associated with a terrorist group at the time of entry to the U.S , even if the entry was otherwise legal, could be deported.

8 The existing prohibition of opening or expanding an investigation if the basis for it was an activity protected by the First Amendment, such as free speech or assembly, was repealed.

9 Private citizens who were victims of terrorism could sue for damages against state sponsors.

10 A one-year statute of limitations was placed on all *habeas corpus* petitions. *Habeas corpus* permits court review of inmate cases based on constitutional rights.

Source: Adapted from Pamala Griset and Sue Mahan (2003). *Terrorism in Perspective.* Sage Publications, Pp 282-283

Second, it politicized the definition of terrorism by giving the Secretary of State complete discretion to decide who was or was not on the list. And membership on the list had three consequences: (1) contributing money or resources to a group, even if for humanitarian or social reasons, became a crime; (2) members of such groups were barred from entering the U.S. or could be deported if they were already in the U.S.; and (3) banks could freeze the funds of the organizations and their agents. Moreover, these decisions could be based on secret evidence, making challenges impossible to mount. And finally, defendants in criminal actions were not permitted to "raise any question regarding the issuance of such designation as a defense of an objection at a trial or a hearing" (Cole & Dempsey, 2002:121). In other words, a person could be designated an associate or contributor to a terrorist group on the basis of secret evidence, was not permitted to appeal the terrorist designation of the group, and could be exported or criminally prosecuted based on that secret information.

Third, the anti-terrorism legislation permitted the deportation of aliens based on their personal associations. Guilt by association is troubling because it rejects the notion, central to the law, that a person's guilt is determined by some criminal act. The 1996 Antiterrorist Act eliminated the requirement that an individual have any connection to terrorist activity, and substituted a guilt by association standard, refusing entry or making excludable anyone who was a member or representative of a terrorist group, even if that membership was specifically for a humanitarian purpose. Evidence of such associations could be kept secret, with the plaintiff receiving only a government-prepared "summary" of the evidence against him or her.

Some of the items in the 1996 Antiterrorism Act—those having to do with excludable aliens, the criminalization of fundraising, guilt by association, and the use of secret evidence—might seem to have little to do with surveillance. What is important to recognize is that the primary way in which information for these activities was acquired by the government was through surveillance. The history of the FBI demonstrates that it has not always been effective in anticipating crime, but it has been quite effective at using surveillance for the identification of a suspect's associates and background. Hence, although several of these provisions seem to have little to do with surveillant practices, it is through surveillance and its liberalization that the FBI and other intelligence groups could acquire the "secret" information and the associational practices and fundraising background needed to prosecute terrorist suspects.

The 1996 Antiterrorism Act was produced in a national climate of concern about what had been seen as ineffectual military responses to terrorism. President Clinton's early efforts to pass legislation for counter-terrorism measures had languished under partisan infighting in Congress in 1995. However, support for legislation strengthened after the Oklahoma City bombing in April of 1995. The final anti-terrorism bill, a product of the conservative leadership of Speaker Newt Gingrich and a Democratic law and order President, contained a variety of restrictions on personal freedoms and death penalty enhancements and constraints on *habeas corpus* generally unrelated to terrorism (Benjamin & Simon, 2002).

The FISA Court: Bridging Pre- and Post-9/11 Surveillance

Many of the operations carried out under the 1996 Antiterrorist Act and the USA PATRIOT Act, discussed in the next section, require court approval. But the approving court is no ordinary court. It was created especially for jurisdiction over terrorist cases. This section is about that court, called the FISA court, and its jurisdiction. The FISA Court bridges the pre- and post-9/11 eras, because it was originally created in 1978, but its authority undergirds the central provisions of both the 1996 Antiterrorist Act and the USA

PATRIOT Act. Indeed, these acts are only meaningful in the context of the FISA court. Accordingly, this section provides a detailed discussion of this highly specialized court, created for the specific purpose of anti-terrorism.

The Foreign Intelligence Security Act of 1978 established regulations for collecting information about the covert plans or activities of foreign powers that might affect U.S. national interests. This act provided a distinct framework for authorizing surveillance that would result in counterintelligence and counter-terrorism rather than criminal prosecution. While American citizens suspected or accused of criminal activity could continue to expect Fourth Amendment protection from unreasonable searches and seizures, probable cause was not a prerequisite for FISA authorization of wiretapping, electronic surveillance, or physical searches provided the target was a foreign power or an agent of a foreign power.

The Act created a special court, the Foreign Intelligence Security Court (FISC), to authorize such surveillance. Seven federal district court judges, appointed for staggered terms by the Chief Justice, were designated to review applications for counterintelligence warrants that had first been approved by the Attorney General. The basis by which the Attorney General could issue authorization was broad. A targeted individual or group only need be identified as a foreign power or an agent of a foreign power; any facility targeted must be one used by that power or agent. No hostile or criminal intent need be part of the scenario.

The warrant process for the FISA court operates as follows. Each step of the process is carried out in secret. A warrant for electronic surveillance is requested from the Attorney General's office and proceedings are based on information provided by the Department of Justice's Office of Intelligence Policy and Review. The U.S. Attorney General must personally sign off on all warrant requests.

Surveillance wiretaps are authorized after a non-adversarial meeting of the court. The files collected by the court cannot be revealed even to persons whose prosecutions stem from FISA investigations. The application for a FISA warrant must contain (1) the reasons why the target is a foreign power or agent thereof, (2) information on the implementation of the surveillance, (3) a certification from an intelligence official indicating that the information sought is foreign intelligence information, and (4) the reasons why the information cannot be obtained through normal investigative techniques (Tien, 2003).

The warrant then issued is based on probable cause that the target is an agent of a foreign power and that the facilities where the surveillance is directed will be used by the target (Tien, 2003:8). There is no overview of the process to make sure that the warrants are in fact carried out as required by the court.

Since the USA PATRIOT Act was passed, the work of the court has sharply increased. In 2002, the FISA court issued 1,228 special terror warrants. This was an increase from 2001, when 934 were issued. This was paralleled by a decrease in the number of traditional wiretaps in criminal cases. In 2002, judges had authorized all but one of 1,359 requested wiretaps, a nine percent decrease from the 1,491 wiretaps issued in 2001. In other words, increases in terrorist surveillance have been paralleled by decreases in traditional criminal surveillances.

The USA PATRIOT Act of 2001 broadened the basis for FISC authorization of surveillance. Section 218 modified the wording in several sections of FISA that had previously declared "the purpose for the surveillance is to obtain foreign intelligence information." The new wording read "a significant purpose of the surveillance . . .," leaving flexibility for interpretation and leeway as to other purpose(s) that might be involved.

In some cases, surveillance can be authorized without a court order. Foreign intelligence information may be collected for up to one year. This intelligence must be certified by the attorney general, and a notice sent to the Senate and House intelligence committees.

Security versus Criminality

The purpose of the FISA court is markedly different from that of traditional U.S. courts (VanBergen, 2002). Courts have traditionally approved surveillance based on the notion that the fruit of the investigation will result in a criminal prosecution. They are subject to the requirements of the constitution, especially the probable cause requirements of the Fourth Amendment to the U.S. Constitution. This is intended to protect citizens from unreasonable search and seizure. The Fourth Amendment states that "no warrants shall issue, but upon probable cause, supported by oath or affirmation, and particularly describing the place to be searched, and the persons or things to be seized."

Foreign intelligence investigations, on the other hand, do not have to work within the Fourth Amendment because they do not seek the prosecution of an individual. The purpose of intelligence is to "find out what our enemies are up to so we can take counter-measures" (VanBergen, 2002:7). It is unique, because it deals with national security matters in a manner congruent with court processes. Yet it acts outside the traditional jurisdiction of American courts. The court "stands in that no-man's land between the two worlds of espionage and criminal law enforcement and acts as the protector of each" (VanBergen, 2002:7).

As originally defined, the collection of foreign intelligence information was required to be the "primary purpose" of any FISA investigation, and the investigation was not to be used as a subterfuge for prosecutorial efforts to collect evidence in a criminal prosecution (Tien, 2003:4). The relation between the prosecutorial and intelligence purposes of the court were revised under the USA PATRIOT Act. That act changed the wording to "a significant purpose," suggesting that evidence could be acquired where foreign intelligence was not the primary purpose of the investigation. Indeed, there is an expectation under the USA PATRIOT Act that information collected under the intelligence division of the FBI would be passed on to the criminal investigative division (Wolf, 2002).

The shift in prosecutorial role was initially rejected by the FISA court. The May 2002 Memorandum Opinion released through the Senate Judiciary Committee was critical of the Department of Justice for attempting to take advantage of FISA authority to conduct surveillance and then use findings from that surveillance to press criminal charges. The Memorandum accompanied an order signed by FISA Judge Royce C. Lamberth that stated in part:

> law enforcement officials shall not make recommendations to intelligence officials concerning the initiation, operation, continuation or expansion of FISA searches or surveillances. Additionally, the FBI and the Criminal Division shall ensure that law enforcement officials do not direct or control the use of the FISA procedures to enhance criminal prosecution, and that advice intended to preserve the option of a criminal prosecution does not inadvertently result in the Criminal Division's directing or controlling the investigation using FISA searches and surveillances toward law enforcement objectives (Foreign Intelligence Surveillance Court, 2002).

This memorandum was a rebuff of the Justice Department's efforts to use intelligence collected through FISA authorization for criminal prosecutions, and was widely seen as a rejection of the USA PATRIOT Act's approval of the expanded use of intelligence for criminal prosecution. The government appealed the court's decision. The three-person Court of Review, also created in 1976 to oversee the FISA court and whose members were selected by Chief Justice William Rehnquist, unanimously overturned the decision. This has been generally seen by prosecutors as an opportunity to increase communications between national security and criminal investigation. FBI Deputy General Counsel "Spike" Bowman described information sharing as follows:

> Previously, said Bowman, the agent running the FISA investigation would have to worry about any crimes committed by the target, and whether and how he could pass them on, because it might jeopardize his FISA. (The case is one in which several defendants were accused of providing material support to Hezbollah, and the Bureau of Alcohol, Tobacco and Firearms was also pursuing the group for fraud and cigarette smuggling). Now, says Bowman, the agent "can report the crime he sees " More important, there's never going to be a realistic chance of prosecuting everybody in a group on terrorism charges, but they "could break up the cell with criminal prosecutions. The goal here is prevention"—pre-

venting the terrorist act, through whatever means. The more
options law enforcement has at its disposal, the better the chances
of preventing something (Lumpkin, 2003a).

According to this view, the government can collect information on a suspect of interest in a criminal investigation, if a national security interest can
also be identified. Indeed, this is what is occurring in an investigation of
Hezbollah activities. Stemming from the decision of the Court of Review,
the criminal prosecution of terrorism suspects is now accessing "tens of
thousands of pages of wiretap transcripts and reports compiled over many
years by fellow FBI agents who pursued intelligence cases" (Arena, 2003).
The focus of the Hezbollah investigation, the FBI acknowledges, is not
terrorism but fundraising. This ruling will permit the government wider information in its efforts to carry through on prosecutions of the approximately 150 members of Hezbollah who are under surveillance in the U.S.

The American Civil Liberties Union has been less sanguine about information sharing. They have expressed concerns that expanding government surveillance powers would jeopardize other constitutional interests,
such as the First Amendment right to engage in lawful public dissent, and
the warrant, notice, and judicial review rights guaranteed in the Fourth and
Fifth Amendments. Recall that efforts to identify what constitutes a national
security interest are quite flexible and discretionary to the Attorney General, not the courts. Hence a broad range of surveillance activities can be
carried out on whom the person under investigation spends time with,
where they go to church and who goes with them, whom they talk to, and
all their conversations. In subsequent criminal prosecutions, the government
is not required to show its evidence collected under FISA, only to show that
the evidence was collected in a way appropriate with the investigation
(American Civil Liberties Union Freedom Network, 2002). The government, some have worried, can break into a citizen's home, put a bug in their
computer, record all information, then use any collected information in a
criminal investigation without having to tell the judge how it acquired that
information. Defendants may not know that information collected against
them was collected under circumstances of restricted rights.

Concerns about the Court

A principle concern of due process advocates is that the FISA court is
highly secretive in its behavior. Indeed, so much is hidden that it is sometimes likened to the infamous "star chambers" that prosecuted and convicted
British subjects in secrecy. From the view of FISA advocates, security interests outweigh due process concerns associated with the First and Fourth
Amendments.

To understand the secrecy, one must consider the nature of the surveillance authority of the court. Surveillance authority under the FISA court is fundamentally different from that of other courts. Traditionally, courts approve a search warrant based on probable cause that a crime has been committed. FISA permits surveillance based on probable cause that the target is a foreign power or an agent thereof. Agents of a foreign power can include anyone who is an officer or employee of a foreign power, who is a member of a terrorist organization, who acts for a foreign power, or who engages in intelligence activity contrary to the U S. interest. Circumstances that suggest anyone may act or conspire to act contrary to U.S. interests, or may knowingly aid and abet another to do so, are sufficient to trigger a warrant.

Criminal courts evaluate evidence to see if there is probable cause based on the likelihood that a crime has been or is about to be committed. The FISA court can initiate proceedings based on a person's status, that is, their affiliation in some way with a foreign power, rather than their behavior. Moreover, there is virtually no oversight on the FISA court. If a criminal defendant challenges the court action, they are unlikely to gain access to the information that led to the charges. They can only obtain those materials that, as Tien (2003) notes, are "necessary to make an accurate determination of the legality of the surveillance"(2003:9). The source of the information, and hence assessment of its validity and its truthfulness, is unavailable to defendants. One must have great faith in the honesty and integrity of the executive branch in the prosecution of cases, to trust their right and authority to bring terrorism charges against defendants without making documentation available to the defendants.

A secondary concern, is that the FISA function has been expanded to criminal investigations as well. Under the innocuous rubric of "information-sharing" prosecutors can share information regarding both intelligence and criminal investigations. Van Bergen (2002) describes it as follows:

> . . the battle over national security does not belong in the courts. This is one reason why the "national security" argument for secret evidence in criminal trials is bad. If the issue is national security, why is the government bringing a criminal case? [Van Bergen contrasts this with diplomacy, espionage, and meetings between heads of state]. If it is a criminal case, the issues should not rest on national security issues. It should rest on clearly defined criminal conduct.
>
> Likewise, in a case brought by a defendant against the government demanding to know the reasons for his incarceration (known as a *habeas corpus* petition) or one brought by others seeking access to hearings or the release of basic information about who is held and why, courts should not be required to decide a case on the basis of national security. This forces the court to become

a mere instrument of the government since the judge must then
take the DOJ's word as to the weight of the evidence. This is a
breach of the independence of the judiciary (Van Bergen, 2002:7).

Bergen's point is that all the actors in these proceedings are acting on
behalf of the government. No one represents the individual being investigated or perhaps prosecuted. The central problem is this: How can we know
that the government is telling the truth? Are we simply to believe that the
government, in the area where it carries the greatest power in the affairs
of the citizenry, will always be honest and truthful? And the answer is
clear—we cannot. We take the truthfulness of the government in all of these
endeavors involving surveillance and evidence gathering as an article of faith.
And in the history of democratic governments, such acts of faith are both
uncommon and rarely rewarded.

Dimensions of Surveillance in the New Security Environment

Security has been dramatically expanded since the terrorist incidents
of 9/11. The expansion of new forms of surveillance has been justified in
terms of security interests, particularly in regards to terrorism, but with an
eye toward crime control generally. In this section we discuss legislation
passed since 9/11 and consider some of its implications.

The 2001 USA PATRIOT Act

More than any other act, the USA PATRIOT Act is associated with the
post 9/11 security environment. The USA Provide Appropriate Tools
Required to Intercept and Obstruct Terrorism (PATRIOT) Act was approved
by Congress and signed into law by President Bush on October 26, 2001.

The USA PATRIOT Act re-interpreted many of the traditional tools of criminal investigation in terms of security interests. While these tools historically
have been used with regard for the citizen-defining rights which protect U.S.
persons, now the relevance of citizens' rights appears secondary to security
interests. Moreover, the practical utility of the elements of the USA PATRIOT
Act, which are certainly expansive, is difficult to assess. It can only be
determined by the way in which prosecutors and the Attorney General
apply them. That is, the actual meaning of any given element is not a question of legal analysis but a product of the way in which it will be used.

This discussion of the USA PATRIOT Act will make extensive use of material provided by the Electronic Frontiers Foundation (EFF) (2001), because
it provides an excellent contrast of surveillance prior to the Act and changes

that stemmed from the Act. To understand the new surveillance environment, the EFF begins with a review of surveillance under U.S. law. U.S. law recognizes four mechanisms for domestic surveillance.

Intercept Orders

Interception orders authorize the interception of communications. This is the traditional police surveillance strategy, according to which police bug rooms, listen in on telephone conversations, or otherwise obtain real-time electronic communications. The standard of proof for intercept orders is probable cause to believe that the target committed one of a list of serious crimes. The police must report within 30 days what is discovered.

Under the USA PATRIOT Act changes, FISA court intercept orders are not made available to the public beyond an annual report of the number granted. The standard of proof is the certification by the Attorney General that the target is a foreign power or an agent of a foreign power.

The Act also approved the "roving wiretap," according to which a wiretap applies to a person rather than to a location. The FISA court can authorize intercepts on any phones or computers used by the person of interest. Anyone can be required to help the court, and is forbidden to talk to others—they are "gagged." This is controversial because it is inconsistent with the traditional requirement of "particularity" in the Fourth Amendment, according to which a constitutionally legal search can only be carried out in specific places for specific items.

Search Warrants

Search warrants permit the search of physical places and seizure of evidence therein. The execution of a warrant required probable cause, and agents were required to notify persons whose premises were searched that it had occurred. This was usually done by leaving a copy of the warrant at the premises.

Under the FISA court, the Attorney General could authorize searches (1) up to one year if used exclusively by a foreign power, and (2) 45 days after a judicial finding that the target was a foreign power or an agent thereof. The investigation could not be based only on First Amendment protected activities, though protected activities might be recorded as a by-product of the search.

The use of "sneak and peak" warrants is also expanded. The concept of sneak and peak is that the government may enter one's domicile, look for the object of the warrant, and then leave without telling the owner about the search. Notification can be delayed for a "reasonable period" and can be extended if good cause is shown. In other words, a person may not know for an indefinite time that their property has been searched.

The warrant provision is no longer limited to a single jurisdiction. The issuance of a warrant can apply to any jurisdiction where the activity might have occurred or where property pertinent to the warrant exists. In significant part, this was included in the act so that agents in one part of the country could acquire information in another part of the country without having to formally apply for a warrant in that jurisdiction. It was intended to respond to the significant geographic disbursement of information created by the Internet and the explosion of portable phone use. For example, "once a judge somewhere approves a warrant for seizing unopened e-mail less than 180 days old, that order can be served on any ISP/OSP or telecommunications company nationwide, without any need that the particular service provided be identified in the warrant" (EFF, 2001:9). However, it also permitted the government to "judge-shop," seeking friendly justices anywhere in America willing to sign warrants.

Pen Register and Pen-and-Trap Devices

These permit the collection of telephone numbers dialed to and from a device. A pen register device records all numbers dialed from a particular phone line. A pen-and-trap, also called trap-and-trace, identifies the originating phone numbers of all incoming calls on a particular phone line. Historically, these were based on the physical wiring of the telephone system, and law enforcement officers were permitted to obtain all numbers of calls from and to a particular device. The standard of proof was a certification to the court that the information was relevant to an ongoing criminal investigation. The target did not have to be a suspect in the investigation and law enforcement did not have to report back to the court. This standard is quite minimal.

The USA PATRIOT Act expanded the use of pen register and pen-and-trap devices to include e-mail and electronic communications. Intercepting the contents of communications is forbidden; however, dialing, routing, signaling, and addressing information may be collected. For example, the keystrokes an individual uses on his or her keyboard can be targeted to identify the way in which information is routed and what sites are accessed.

The act also expanded the courts' reach. Previously a court could only permit the installation of pen and trap devices in its area. Now it can extend the installation to anywhere in the U.S. provided the U.S. government certifies that the information likely to be obtained is "pertinent to an ongoing criminal investigation" (EFF, 2001:10).

Subpoenas for Stored Information

Grand juries routinely use subpoenas to acquire information to conduct an investigation. The FISA court had previously limited subpoenas to business records, and then only via court order. The Act extended the reach of subpoenas to Internet Service Providers (ISPs), that is, whomever one purchases Internet access from so they can use the Internet at work or at home. This includes stored electronic communications, e-mail communications, and subscriber and transactional records. A court order is no longer required to subpoena ISPs, nor is a court order required to obtain records of session times or durations on the Internet, temporarily assigned network addresses, or means and sources of payments including credit card numbers and bank account numbers. In other words, the government may, without court approval, acquire any U.S. person's bank account, credit card numbers, and other information stored through ISPs.

The USA PATRIOT Act has increased surveillance authority in a variety of other ways.

Information Sharing between Law Enforcement and the Intelligence Community Is Increased

Historically, criminal investigations have avoided the use of intelligence, because the surveillance did not require probable cause and hence criminal investigations could violate Fourth Amendment protections of U.S. persons. This line is effectively erased under the USA PATRIOT Act, which states that foreign intelligence gathering only need be "a significant purpose" of the investigation.

Also, Grand Jury information collected on criminal investigations can be turned over to intelligence investigations when the investigative material involves foreign intelligence or counterintelligence. This raises the question: What constitutes foreign intelligence? It is defined as:

> any info, whether or not concerning a U.S. person, that relates to the ability of the U S to protect against an actual or potential attack, sabotage or international terrorism or clandestine intelligence activities; any info, whether or not concerning a U.S. person, that relates to the national defense or security of the conduct of foreign affairs. (EFF, 2001·11)

Criminal wiretap information (content and evidence derived therein) can be disclosed to any other government official, "including intelligence, national defense and national security" as long as the information deals with foreign intelligence or counterintelligence (EFF, 2001:12).

In other words, if an investigation has a component that is "foreign intelligence gathering," which is loosely defined, the government can turn any information regarding illegal activity uncovered by the intelligence investigation over to local or federal authorities for criminal investigation.

Educational Agencies and Information

The Attorney General can require an educational agency to provide information and records relevant to an authorized investigation of a terrorist offense. Those who provide such information are under legal obligation not to disclose to anyone that they have done so.

Culpability of Facilitators

A facilitator is culpable even if an underlying terrorist offense does not occur. A facilitator is someone who furthers suspected terrorist activity. If a facilitator was certain that some terrorist groups would use his or her information or resources to commit terrorist acts, it is immaterial whether or not the facilitator knows that the criminal conduct will actually occur. For example, if an individual develops a Web site that promotes terrorist behavior, whether or not he actually promotes terrorist activity, that he developed the Web site might be enough grounds for a charge of facilitating terrorism. This seems to be a First Amendment violation of free speech, because many Internet sites, and many terrorist groups, make use of information available in the public domain.

In sum, like the 1996 Antiterrorism Act, the USA PATRIOT Act contained many provisions linked to the expansion of surveillance practices:

> *Practices Directly Expanding Surveillance.* Three aspects of the act expanded surveillance. (1) The act approved the use of roving wiretaps, that is, putting a wiretap on any phone that might be used by the suspect. (2) Wiretaps also have an expanded intelligence function. For approval of a wiretap, terrorism must be a significant reason for the investigation. It need not be the only reason for the investigation. (3) Computers can be treated like telephones, which means that they can be monitored and e-mail communications can be subpoenaed.

> *Practices Enhanced by Expanded Surveillance.* (1) Search warrants can be sought in any federal jurisdiction. Expanded surveillance aids in the gathering of information for these warrants. (2) Immigrants can be held for a longer period, from two to seven days, and in some cases up to six months. Surveillance enhances the ability to gather information on immigrants while

they are being held for extended periods. (3) Intelligence sharing
between local and federal authorities is permitted under the act,
and expanded surveillance is likely to increase the overall quantity of information shared.

Dinh: The "Why" of the USA PATRIOT Act

Viet Dinh (2003), the Assistant Attorney General for Legal Policy under
President Bush, is credited with being the architect of the USA PATRIOT Act.
In a 2003 presentation before the American Bar Association titled "Security
and Privacy in the United States," he provided an explanation for why the
Act is written as it is. Below is a summary of his presentation.

He began his presentation with a quote from a spokesman for the Irish
Republican Army, following a failed assassination attempt on Margaret
Thatcher on October 12, 1984:

> Today we were unlucky. But remember: We only have to be lucky
> once. You have to be lucky always.

This concern, he noted, was central to the USA PATRIOT Act. The USA
PATRIOT Act was put together in a security environment in which the consequences of a failure of security were catastrophic. What was needed was
a series of measures which would allow the U.S. to quickly adapt to a rapidly changing and perhaps extremely dangerous internal security situation.
A lapse had occurred, and the consequence was 9/11. At that time, there was
no way to know if the lapse would lead to other catastrophic incidents.

Viet Dinh stated that the onus of being lucky always, as the IRA put it,
is "a momentous responsibility." He outlined three steps the Justice Department had taken to meet the threat of terrorist attack and to protect the rights
and liberty of the American people. The USA PATRIOT Act is the product
of those three steps.

The first was to update the law to conform with modern technology.
"Even as we seek to think outside the box," he said, "we seek to stay fully
within the Constitution and the bounds of legality in meeting the threat."
The USA PATRIOT Act is an essential tool for dealing with that challenge.
Title III of the Omnibus Crime Act of 1968 regulated the tracking and
monitoring of the communications of criminal organizations, and was
written to address primarily issues of telephone privacy. In the current age,
however, the Internet plays an increasing role in communications, and
the technological capacity of surveillance needed to adapt to Internet
communications.

Dinh emphasized that the authority to intercept Internet communications was restricted under the USA PATRIOT Act. In intelligence terms, communications fall into two categories, content and non-content information.
The pen register discussed above is an example of a device that intercepts

non-content information. It records the numbers dialed from a telephone and the numbers from which calls are made to that phone. The Supreme Court has ruled that the interception of such data is not subject to right of privacy, because the information has already been shared with a third party, i.e., the phone company. The pen register simply makes the collection of the data easier.

By contrast, the interception of content information faces different restrictions. Dinh used the example of cable companies, which are restricted in their ability to disclose information about their customers. Currently, telephone and Internet communication are available through cable lines. Would the Cable Act apply to government requests for content intercept? The USA PATRIOT Act clarifies that it does not, and that the same standard that regulates telephone and Internet companies applies to government requests, with the same level of probable cause required to obtain a judicial order for a content intercept.

Second was a revision of the Attorney General Guidelines, a step Dinh described as "leveling the playing field" by allowing counterintelligence investigators the same tools available to individuals and state and local law enforcement officers. He cited the following section of the Act as being of particular significance:

> For the purpose of detecting or preventing terrorist activities, the FBI is authorized to visit any place and attend any event that is open to the public, on the same terms and conditions as members of the public generally. No information obtained from such visits shall be retained unless it relates to potential criminal or terrorist activity.

While the aim of the revisions was to free the hands of FBI agents, Dinh insisted that the department is mindful of abuses that took place in the past and remains vigilant against any recurrence.

This revision, Dinh argued, also had implications for the traditional centralization of information management by the FBI. Traditionally, the FBI placed investigative decision making at headquarters, while information was gathered and stored at field offices. The new style of organization allows decisions to be made by agents in the field, who are then authorized or required to relay information to headquarters. Dinh describes these changes not as attempts to gain more power but rather as means for agencies to function more efficiently.

Third was an information sharing element: The USA PATRIOT Act aided in the facilitation of information sharing and coordination of the actions of the intelligence, defense and law enforcement communities. In the past, interaction between agencies may have been characterized by competition or even antagonism. Dinh called attention to Section 203 of the Act which permits law enforcement to share information with the defense, intelligence and diplomatic communities. Section 905 requires the Justice Department and law enforcement agencies to share terrorist threat information with the intelligence community. Dinh also noted that there was a "FISA fix," a change in FISA (established under President Clinton) which allows the sharing of information and the coordination of activities between intelligence, counterintelligence and criminal investigators.

Dinh also noted that the FBI has been broadly engaged in the procurement of information. In discussing the search for intelligence since the 9/11 attacks, Dinh said that approximately 18,000 subpoenas and search warrants had been executed, as well as more than 1,500 FISA applications. This massive investigation is warranted, he noted, because:

> The threat is that great. Each and every single one of these activities, we are hopeful and confident, is fully consistent with the laws and Constitution of the United States and therefore fully protective of the privacy needs and liberty of individual Americans, while at the same time deploying every single resource at our disposal, using every single authority we are permitted under the law, in order to counteract this threat

The FBI is mindful of the effects of backlash against Muslims and Arabs as well. A second investigation is being conducted into backlash discrimination resulting from the 9/11 attacks. The Civil Rights Division and the FBI have investigated more than 400 incidents and brought 12 federal prosecutions against 17 defendants, and assisted in 80 state and local prosecutions for backlash crimes. Dinh observed that:

> We take this very, very seriously because we want to carry forth the President and the Attorney General's message, and our abiding belief, that it is *not* Arab-Americans or any particular community that we are targeting, but it is all Americans whom we are protecting against this threat of terrorism.

Dinh pointed out that members of the Justice Department have participated in more than 250 town hall meetings across the nation in order to address citizens' questions. Some of the department's actions have been challenged. Dinh notes, however, "The courts have, on the whole, validated our strategy. We remain vigilant that we protect the liberty of the American people even as we prosecute the war against terror."

The USA PATRIOT Act and the American Library Association

The American Library Association (ALA, 2002) has emerged as a source of resistance to some of the provisions in the PATRIOT Act. The ALA focused their concerns on four of the provisions in the Act, Sections 214,

215, 216, and 218. The broadest sections cited by the ALA (American Library Association, 2002) are reviewed below.

Under Section 215 of the USA PATRIOT Act:

(1) Agents could obtain warrants for "any tangible thing" which included computers, records, and books.

(2) The FBI could compel the production of library circulation records.

(3) The agent does not have to provide probable cause concerning a crime; it is only necessary that the records be related to an ongoing terrorist investigation.

(4) Librarians cannot divulge the existence of the warrant or information disclosed. Library patrons cannot be told that their records were turned over to the FBI.

Under Section 216 of the USA PATRIOT Act:

(1) Pen register and trap-and-trace telephone monitoring laws were extended to all Internet communications and URLs of Web pages.

(2) State law enforcement can also obtain such orders.

(3) Orders can be obtained from any court in the country.

(4) Recipients of monitoring orders are required to participate in the installation of any devices, provide information from their own records, and keep the monitoring of the communications a secret.

(5) If the library provides access to e-mail and Internet services for its patrons, it may become the target of a court order requiring monitoring of the users' electronic services.

In other words, the government can use the library to surveille patrons. The concept of free speech is subverted in efforts to acquire information to assess terrorist threats or, more likely, to build criminal cases against suspects.

The emergence of ALA resistance to the USA PATRIOT Act makes sense when one considers the organization's purposes. In 1981, the ALA passed the "Policy on Governmental Intimidation" which states as follows:

> The American Library Association opposes any use of governmental prerogatives which leads to the intimidation of the individual or the citizenry from the exercise of free expression. ALA encourages resistance to such abuse of governmental power and supports those against whom such governmental power has been employed. Adopted February 2, 1973; amended July 1, 1981, by the ALA Council.

This policy is grounded in an organizational philosophy which views the ALA as a gatekeeper of citizen's right of access to reading materials, with that right codified in the First Amendment. The ALA is particularly concerned about the USA PATRIOT Act's "chilling effect" on free speech and free assembly, an effect that it argues does not substantively contribute to counter-terrorism efforts, and about the gag order on anyone who assists the FBI.

The ALA has become a powerful voice of resistance to many of the USA PATRIOT Act provisions. Make no mistake, the ALA takes an assertive position that the Act is a far-reaching threat to civil liberties, particularly in the library setting. Why is the library so important? In the interpretation of the Library Bill of Rights, the ALA states that, "In a library (physical or virtual), the right to privacy is the right to open inquiry without having the subject of one's interest examined or scrutinized by others." The free exploration and exchange of ideas is fundamental to the concept of public libraries. Kranich (2002) summarizes this position as follows:

> Hours after the terrorist attacks on September 11, 2001, people rushed to libraries to read about the Taliban, Islam, Afghanistan and terrorism Americans sought background materials to foster understanding and cope with this horrific event They turned to a place with reliable answers—to a trustworthy public space where they are free to inquire, and where their privacy is respected
>
> Since 9/11, libraries remain more important than ever to ensuring the right of every individual to hold and express opinions and to seek and receive information, the essence of a thriving democracy. But just as the public is exercising its right to receive information and ideas—a necessary aspect of free expression—in order to understand the events of the day, government is threatening these very liberties, claiming it must do so in the name of national security (Kranich, 2002).

Local Police Surveillance for Federal Security Interests. Local police departments have been provided expanded authority to surveille citizens in their communities. The Justice Department has assembled Joint Terrorism Task Forces (JTTF), commanded by the Justice Department, and comprised of joint local, state, and federal agents. Since 9/11, the number of JTTFs has increased from 35 to 66. The purpose of these JTTF's is to extend the reach of surveillance domestically and make it available to federal analysis. As Lee notes:

> The Bush administration wishes to make raw intelligence from the FBI, CIA, and partner agencies available to the new Department of Homeland Security. The NYPD's [New York Police Department] Cohen [Mayor Bloomberg's anti-terrorism expert] told the

> court of his wish to "work in close partnership not only with fed-
> eral government but with every state, thousands of municipalities,
> and other countries as well." He stated [the] entire resources of
> the NYPD must be available to conduct investigations into polit-
> ical activity and intelligence issues (Lee, 2003:2).

That an expanded notion of surveillance is permitted for these organizations is currently being tested in court. The NYPD had previously been
limited by the Handschu restrictions. These restrictions were the product
of a class action suit against the NYPD, who were accused by political
activists of routinely violating their privacy and misusing information so
acquired. Under the Handschu agreement the police were barred "from starting dossiers, planting undercover agents, photographing protestors, and
reviewing membership lists without any indication of a crime" (Lee,
2003:1). Cohen, an advocate of the removal of the Handschu restrictions,
stated that they "hamper our efforts every day."

New York, though the largest of the departments seeking expanded surveillance authority, is one of many cities that today seek to ease domestic
surveillance laws. However, many of the same cities have in the past experienced charges of domestic spying and face concerns that re-expanding surveillance will invite a recurrence of historical abuses. Powell (2002)
identifies concerns in New York, where city officials want to do away with
the Handschu restrictions that limit their ability to carry out surveillance
on suspected terrorists. Civil libertarians are worried that the police will
return to the "unsavory days of old" when the police had a reputation for
spying on dissidents and for black bag break-ins.

> 'The New York Police Department had no conception of the
> challenge it would face in protecting the city and its people from
> international terrorism' when it signed the consent decree, city
> attorneys argue in a federal legal brief. Clearly, the public inter-
> est in law enforcement's ability to protect it from terrorist violence
> is the most vital priority (Powell, 2002:3).

Civil libertarians note that police abuses have a long history. In the 1950s
the NYPD Red Squad compiled massive files on political meetings involving leftist groups, and names of participants were passed on to the FBI and
to Congress. In the 1970s the Black Panthers were accused of conspiring
to blow up five department stores, a precinct house, the New Haven Rail-
road, and the New York Botanical Garden in the Bronx. A Manhattan District
Attorney conspired with the police to infiltrate the Black Panthers. However, the infiltration raised questions about who initiated criminal activity,
the Panthers or the infiltrators. The jury could not separate the "felonious
impulses of the Panthers and the undercover cops." As Powell (2002:2)
noted, "In one case, a police undercover agent handed the Panthers a map
and a rented car, and urged them to carry out an armed robbery."

Similar concerns have been voiced in other cities. A federal court in Chicago agreed to weaken a decree that had limited surveillant authority that constrained the police. Over the previous two decades, the police had been accused of carrying out more than 500 "black bag" or illegal jobs. They had routinely investigated political opponents of the mayor by going to fundraisers and recording license plate numbers, and tracked the membership of the NAACP and the League of Women Voters.

Organizations such as the American Friends of Service Committee were characterized in the data system as "criminal extremist" groups. A detective, justifying this classification, stated in a deposition that they "have been linked to activities that involved extremist activity, criminal activities." This view of American Friends of Service is troubling, because it suggests that those people who carry out surveillance are unable to distinguish politically and ideologically motivated surveillance from surveillance with a clear security purpose. Also, officers used personal discretion in deciding to label a "criminal extremist" group, and sometimes the "criminal extremist" label was used as a default for groups that did not fit other categories (Fessenden & Moss, 2002:2).

The use of intelligence-oriented software has also sparked controversy. Software developed by Orion Scientific Systems stored, searched, and classified surveillance data. Orion began providing the software to police agencies in the early 1990s with the Pentagon's approval. In 2002, the software was being used by 20 law enforcement agencies. Orion was originally used to track gang members, but converted straightforwardly to intelligence gathering for anti-terrorism.

In Denver, the police had been gathering intelligence on activists since the 1950s. Their records were leaked to an activist for social justice when they computerized the intelligence records using software from Orion Scientific Systems. The documents were subsequently made public.

Several individuals expressed support for the intelligence software. Fessenden and Moss (2002:2) note that:

> 'I think it's imperative after 9/11 that the police department and security agencies have an obligation to track suspicious people, in order to keep the citizenry alive,' said Councilman Ed Thomas, who argued against restrictions In a city council debate, Mr. Thomas waved a list of the dead at the World Trade Center to emphasize his point.

Intelligence has been used to track somewhat innocuous individuals. One of the targets of the intelligence was Sister Antonia Anthony, a 74-year-old nun who had taught indigenous people in the U.S. and Mexico and had worked with a nonviolent group supporting indigenous peoples in Chiapas, Mexico. Denver Mayor Wellington Webb noted that, "There is a role for intelligence gathering." He added that, "There isn't a role for intelligence gathering on Catholic nuns." One of the individuals on whom intelligence was gathered was a local glazier who attended a meeting of Amnesty International. He was listed as belonging to a "criminal extremist" organization and his name and record was circulated to other police departments (Fessenden & Moss, 2002:2).

The interplay between intelligence and criminal investigation is likely to expand. For instance, in a Code Orange alert in December, 2003, the Los Angeles Police Department engaged in what was called an "ongoing post-9/11 roundup aimed at disrupting terrorist activity" (Meserve & Koch, 2003:1). An individual was arrested for forgery after information was obtained from a terrorism-related investigation. The LAPD stated that the arrest was unrelated to terrorism and that it had made 85 arrests since September 11 that were triggered by terrorist investigations, but involved crimes not related to terrorism (McGreevey, Krikorian & Blankstein, 2003).

A common theme characterizes efforts to expand anti-terrorism surveillance in all of these cities. In every instance, police departments seeking expanded powers do so where there is a history of distrust at some level. And in all the large cities, the police have previously surveilled the citizenry for political reasons. The question begged is whether these cities can be trusted to use surveillance more wisely than they have done in the past. A second question is whether they should be permitted to expand the use of surveillance, recognizing that surveillance for political and ideological reasons is likely to accompany genuine anti-terrorist activity. This question carries the concern that, at some point, we may not be able to tell the difference between articulable security threats and activities that are wholly political in aim. A third question is whether local agencies will make use of terrorist task forces to acquire evidence under the less legally strict terrorism laws.

The Future of Surveillance: The USA PATRIOT Act II

On February 7, 2003, The Center for Public Integrity obtained a draft copy of the Justice Department's proposed Domestic Security Enhancement Act of 2003. This draft copy, which quickly came to be known as the PATRIOT II act or "son of USA PATRIOT," extended many of the provisions in the USA PATRIOT Act. The proposed act was originally leaked to the Center for Public Integrity and, following the controversy that accompanied its provisions, was portrayed as no more than an "internal memo" by the Justice Department (Lewis, 2003). The memo, however, had been passed to House Speaker Dennis Hastert for his review.

In the summer of 2003, the Attorney General traveled the country arguing for an increase in legislative protections against terrorism. President Bush, in a speech at the FBI Academy in Quantico, Virginia, in September 2003 said that the Department of Justice authority needed to be expanded;

as he noted, " . . untie the hands of our law enforcement officials so they can fight and win the war on terror" (Brownfeld, 2003). Bush, in this speech, stated that he sought three broad new powers, and these powers were embodied in the new legislation:

> The ability of law enforcement to obtain administrative subpoe-nas without prior review by a grand jury, the ability to hold accused terrorists, like those charged with some drug crimes, with-out bail; and the ability to make terrorist crimes that result in death eligible for the death penalty (Brownfeld, 2003 1).

Proponents have argued that the law would simply give the government the same abilities to fight terrorism that it currently has to fight organized crime Opponents, however, argue that it represents a dramatic overreach of government into citizens' affairs, particularly in the ability of the justice department to bypass courts in the conduct of its war on terrorism Ramasastry (2003) describes these powers and their implications as follows.

> *Enhanced Total Information Awareness:* PATRIOT II gives federal agents access to consumer credit reports, restricted only by the requirement that the information will be used in connec-tion with federal law enforcement duties. No subpoena is required, nor is any court order The citizen would not even be notified that the information had been shared

> *Enhanced Authority to Collect DNA:* A "Terrorist Identification Database" would include DNA samples from terrorists, suspected terrorists, and anyone who is or has been on probation, regard-less of the crime State governments would be obligated to pro-vide the data to the federal government. Anyone's refusal to provide a DNA sample would be a Class A misdemeanor.

> *Enhanced Active Surveillance:* Definitions of "domestic ter-rorists" and "foreign powers" are expanded. They become so broad as to bring almost any criminal investigation into the juris-diction of the FISA Court, where showing probable cause is not a prerequisite to obtaining a warrant As Ramasastry notes, " domestic terrorism is defined very broadly as 'any action that endangers human life that is a violation of any Federal or State law'" (2003 3) If a citizen has not broken a law, they can "alter-natively be deemed 'foreign powers' under PATRIOT II—even if they are American citizens or permanent residents. This allows the FBI to get pen registers on American citizens for a foreign intel-ligence investigation—without having to show any criminal or ter-rorist connection" (2003 3).

Enhanced Immunity for Law Enforcement: Citizens would not be allowed to sue federal agents who conducted searches or surveillance authorized by the President or the Attorney General; nor could they sue any business or employee who might allege suspicious activity and notify law enforcement, leading to surveillance.

Enhanced Regulation of Encryption: The use of encryption of e-mail in the commission of a federal felony would become a separate crime, punishable by five to ten years in prison. Bearing in mind the broad definition of "domestic terrorism," Ramasastry suggests, "you may reasonably fear using encryption even if you are not engaged in any criminal activity at all." The penalty for encrypting "incriminating evidence" would not be restricted to terrorism, but would apply to any federal crime.

Enhanced Government Secrecy: Witnesses in grand jury proceedings would be prohibited from discussing their testimony outside the courtroom. Both federal and state grand juries could be subject to the imposition of federal gag orders, and the federal government would be reserve the right to take over proceedings.

Furthermore, the government would have no obligation to identify detainees, who could be held indefinitely without being accused of a crime. In fact, it would be illegal for a citizen to reveal any information about a detainee whose identity the government wished to keep secret.

Enhanced Expatriation: A citizen may be deported and have his or her citizenship revoked for becoming a member of or supporting a group that has been designated as a "terrorist organization" by the U.S. government, if this was judged to have been done "with the intent to relinquish his nationality."

In short, Ramasastry observes, "PATRIOT II puts in jeopardy the First Amendment right to speak freely, statutory and common law rights to privacy, the right to go to court to challenge government illegality, and the Fourth Amendment right against unreasonable searches and seizures" (2003:5).

The act also includes an expansion of the FISA court, so that the court can focus on "lone wolves," single extremists who are deemed to pose a threat. The court had previously been restricted to terrorist organizations. And the act also will expand wiretap surveillance authorization of the FISA court. The new provisions "carve out a terrorist exception in Title III cases, requiring little or no court supervision in such criminal cases." This permits any American citizen, suspected of terrorism under the definitions of terrorism in the USA PATRIOT Act, to fall under court surveillance (Lumpkin, 2003b). In short, it expands many elements of the FISA court activity regarding suspects from immigrant and foreign to those who are fully citizens.

© Chappatte in International Herald Tribune – globecartoon.com. Reprinted with permission.

At the beginning of 2004, the USA PATRIOT II Act is stalled in Congress. There is a lack of political will to push it through. And questions about the USA PATRIOT Act are emerging as abuses of immigrants, carried out under the act, come to light. For the moment, the government seems to have the limits of its reach into the affairs of its citizens and residents. Yet, that reach has become great, and its full extent will be tested by prosecutors for many years to come.

Conclusion

This chapter has presented a history of key elements and perspectives on surveillance in American society. By dividing the chapter into two sections, it can be seen that the post-9/11 surveillance developments, particularly the USA PATRIOT Act, were anticipated by the 1996 Antiterrorism Act, and the 1978 FISA court. These developments were in turn anticipated by trends favorable to the expansion of surveillance throughout the twentieth century.

Congressional support for additional expansion of surveillance seems to have reached its limit. However, this does not provide insight into surveillance in the practice of criminal justice and counter-terrorism. Many of the tools developed for the prosecution of criminal justice have been creatively expanded to reach into unanticipated areas. For example, the RICO statutes, developed to prosecute gang members for crimes by virtue of association, have been used to prosecute anti-abortion protestors. Hence, the full reach of the law under the recent counter-terrorism and crime control legislation will emerge gradually, and is likely to extend far beyond the legislation's original intent.

CHAPTER 5

Daily Life: Preparing for Terror

Everyday Life in a Security Environment

What does it mean to live our lives inside a security environment? What are the changes we will see from 9/11, and how will it affect our daily routines? This chapter looks at the post-9/11 changes in U.S. security that affect citizens of the United States. It describes the new Department of Homeland Security, its structure, and some of the concerns raised in regard to the Department. Its effect on our daily lives is seen principally through the color-coded terror alerts and through changes in airport security, both of which are examined in detail in this chapter. Also discussed is Northcom, or Northern Command, the first military command encompassing the U.S. and its region. Northcom is an expansion of the Department of Defense, designed to adapt to a military threat that might occur inside the United States. Issues regarding *posse comitatus* are raised and discussed in this section.

Background to the Department of Homeland Security

The Department of Homeland Security (DHS) was a product of concerns that the U.S. lacked a coherent strategy for protecting the homeland from terrorist threat. The DHS was preceded by the Office of Homeland Security, which emerged in the immediate aftermath of 9/11. Richard Falkenrath, Special Assistant and Senior Director for Policy and Plans of the Homeland Security Department, noted that the U.S. had never had a comprehensive national strategy for homeland security (Brookings Forum, 2002). This was in part because homeland security was not a distinct policy area. 9/11 fostered a perception that a distinct area of governance was needed to deal with terrorism. A presidential executive order created the "Office of Homeland Security" on October 8, 2001. (The Office of Homeland Security emerged first because only an executive order of the president is required to establish a new office in the U.S. government. The creation of a department requires legislative approval.) The office had as a mission the development and coordination of a comprehensive national strategy to "secure the U.S. from terrorist threats or attacks." The national strategy was to ensure the adequacy of "detecting, preparing for, preventing, protecting against, responding to, and recovering from terrorist threats or attacks within the U.S." This strategy contained 10 elements, paraphrased from the White House executive order (White House, 2001a):

> *Detection.* Coordinate efforts for collection and analysis of information, both in and outside of the U.S., regarding internal terrorist activities and threats of terrorism against the U.S.

> *Preparedness.* Coordinate efforts to prepare for and limit the consequences of terrorist threats or attacks. This might include the coordination of domestic exercises and simulations, efforts to insure public health preparedness, and the coordination of assistance to state and local authorities.

> *Prevention.* Facilitate the exchange of information such as immigration, visa applications, and cargo shipments; coordinate the investigation of domestic terrorist attacks, and oversee the security of national borders, waters, and airspace to prevent attacks.

> *Protection.* Harden the measures aimed at protecting energy production and distribution, utilities, telecommunications, facilities that make use of nuclear material, and other critical infrastructure. This also includes the protection of transportation systems, livestock, agriculture, and water systems; and prevention of unauthorized access, development, or importation of chemical, biological, radioactive, and nuclear (CBRN) materials that might be used in terrorist attacks.

> *Response and Recovery.* Ensure a rapid recovery of transportation; energy production, transmission, and distribution, telecommunications. Assist in the restoration of public and private information systems; coordinate plans for medical, financial, and other assistance to victims; stabilize financial markets, and contain and remove any hazardous materials including CBRN weapon materials.

> *Incident Management.* Domestic responses for all departments and agencies during an imminent attack and/or its aftermath.

> *Continuity of Government.* Ensure the continuity of the federal government "in the event of an attack that threatens the safety and security of the U S government or its leadership." (White House, 2001a:3).

Public Affairs. With the White House Office of Communications, develop a strategy to communicate to the public in the event of threat or attack. This includes the development of public education programs.

Review of Legal Authorities and Development of Legislative Proposals. Periodic review of the legal authorities who can assist in the functions described in this presidential order. This office will also work with state and local governments to assess the effectiveness of their legal authorities.

Budget Review. The Assistant to the President for Homeland Security will work with the Director of the Office of Management and Budget to identify programs and agencies that can contribute to homeland security. Also this function will seek budgetary assistance for helpful programs and provide a proposed budget to the President.

One of the principle products of the Office was the production of a document called the "National Strategy for Homeland Security." It was designed, Falkenrath noted, around an explicit ends/means relationship. The ends, or the goals of the office, were three: (1) to prevent future terrorist attacks, (2) to reduce the vulnerability of the U.S. to terrorism, and (3) to minimize the damage of attacks and recover after attacks occur. The means are critical mission areas: intelligence and warning, border and transportation security, domestic counter-terrorism, critical infrastructure protection, catastrophic threats, and emergency preparedness and response. This comprehensive list, Falkenrath wryly observed, seemed to "have more activities than his daughter's summer camp" (Brookings Forum, 2002:6).

Developing a list of mission areas requires an assessment of threat and vulnerability, itself a significant project. The breadth of threat potential described by the Brookings Institution below suggests the enormous difficulty in developing a comprehensive counter-terrorist strategy in an open society.

Threat. Determining the number of terrorists is not a straightforward process. Assessing known terrorist activity is insufficient because it merely states what has previously happened. It is not an assessment of future threat. Terrorists are seen as increasingly capable of causing more destruction than previously. Capability is a byproduct of progress, and is increasingly likely to come from non-state actors. Finally, terrorists are strategic. They are not "robots who just mimic what they did before" (Brookings Forum, 2002:7).

Vulnerability. In a free society, vulnerability approaches infinity. We congregate, Falkenrath (Brookings Forum, 2002:8) observed, in very dense packs and in a very predictable, well-advertised way. And people can move around the country without being concerned about being watched by the police, so information is easy to gather. Consequently, we can never reduce our vulnerability to zero, though we can "reduce it a fair bit."

The frustrating complexity of these activities was expressed in a report on Rand Beers, a counter-terrorism advisor who later resigned (Blumenfeld, 2003). The report is discussed in Figure 5.1.

Figure 5.1
Threat Assessment: Day-to-Day

He (Rand Beers) was in a job that would grind down anyone. Every day, 500 to 1,000 pieces of threat information crossed his desk. The typical mix included suspicious surveillance at a U.S. embassy; surveillance of a nuclear power plant or a bridge; a person caught by airport security with a weapon, or an airline flying too close to the CIA; a tanker truck, which might contain a bomb, crossing the border and heading for a city; an intercepted phone call between suspected terrorists. Most of the top-secret reports—pumped into his office from the White House situation room—didn't pan out. Often they came from a disgruntled employee or a spouse . . .

Every time the government raises an alarm, it costs time and money. "There's less filtering now because people don't want to make the mistake of not warning," he said. Before September 11, 2001, the office met three times a week to discuss intelligence. Now twice a day, at 7 a.m. and 3 p.m., it holds 'threat matrix' meetings," tracking the threats on CIA spreadsheets.

It was Beers' task to evaluate them and to act on them. "It's a monstrous responsibility," said William Wechsler, director for transnational threats on Clinton's NSC staff. "You sit around every day, thinking about how people want to kill thousands of Americans.

Source: Laura Blumenfeld, "Former Aid Takes Aim at War on Terror." *Washington Post,* June 16, 2003.

The Department of Homeland Security: Foundation and Structures

Tom Ridge was appointed the first Director of the Office of Homeland Security. An attorney from Pennsylvania, Ridge had twice served as Governor of that state, and was a close friend of the President. His authority was enhanced in January 2003 when, with Congressional approval, the Office was renamed the Department of Homeland Security (DHS) and Ridge was named Secretary of the department. On March 1, 2003, the major agencies were "brought under one roof" (The White House, 2001b).

As the National Threat Initiative (NTI) (2003) noted, the DHS was:

> designed to improve coordination and reduce redundancies
> among the agencies involved with protecting the U.S. homeland.
> In theory, the establishment of one all-encompassing agency
> should result in improved information-sharing and accountability
> among the various players. (National Threat Initiative, 2003).

The NTI cites as an example that "more than 40 agencies" were responsible for border security. The fragmentation of border responsibility increased communication problems, created redundancies, and decreased the likelihood of detecting terrorist activity before an attack. The DHS was created to "defragment" security information and thus increase the likelihood of identifying and effectively responding to a terrorist threat.

Light (2002) identified five reasons for a reorganization of existing agencies into a new Department of Homeland Security:

1. It gives the issue of homeland security a higher priority inside the federal government.

2. It integrates and coordinates policy by bringing lower-level organizations under a single head.

3. It provides a platform for a new governmental activity, or the rapid expansion of government involvement in an activity.

4. It can "help forge a strategic vision for governing." (2002:3) It increases the odds that counter-terrorism will be better served.

5. It increases accountability to congress, the president, and to the public, because its budget and personnel will be more transparent. "Cabinet-status conveys a megaphone that little else in Washington does" (2002:3).

A White House news release defined the mission of the new office as the implementation of a national strategy to secure the United States from terrorist threats or attacks. This strategy would be six-fold, focusing on (1) intelligence and warning, (2) border and transportation security, (3) domestic counter-terrorism, (4) protecting critical infrastructure and key assets, (5) defending against catastrophic threats, and (6) emergency preparedness (The White House, 2001b).

To achieve the goals of the national strategy, the department organized agencies under five major directorates: (1) The Border and Transportation directorate included the U.S. Customs Service and the INS, as well as the Federal Law Enforcement Training Center, and others were added. Such agencies as the Federal Emergency Management Agency and the Nuclear Incident Response Team were overseen by (2) the Emergency Preparedness and Response directorate. Under (3) the Science and Technology directorate came four agencies dealing with environmental issues, disease, and biological weapons. (4) The Information Analysis and Infrastructure Protection directorate would receive information from the CIA, FBI, DEA and NSA. The Secret Service and the Coast Guard would also report directly to the Secretary of the DHS. Budget, management, and personnel would be handled by Janet Hale as Under Secretary of (5) the Directorate of Management. (See Figure 5:1). Eventually, 22 agencies with some 170,000 employees comprised the department. Not since 1947, when President Truman combined the War and Navy departments to form the Department of Defense, had the federal government experienced such a major restructuring (U.S. Department of Homeland Security, 2002).

The beginnings of the DHS were characterized by reorganization and the additions of new agencies. During the first 100 days of its operation, new agencies debuted and several took particularly visible and active roles. Below is a summary of the formative structure of the DHS, not including the Directorate of Management but focusing on the functional areas of security encompassed by the DHS.

Directorate of Border and Transportation Security (BTS)

Former Congressman Asa Hutchinson was selected as the first Undersecretary of the BTS. The BTS encompasses several organizations, discussed below.

Customs and Border Protection (CBP) was charged with the mission of securing borders and ports of entry into the United States. The creation of CBP involved the reorganization of employees from the Department of Agriculture, The Border Patrol, some offices of the INS, and the U.S. Customs Service. Richard C. Bonner had been Commissioner of U.S. Customs, and became Commissioner of the new BCP (True, Walsh & Miller, 2003).

Besides keeping an eye out for terrorists and terrorist weapons, CBP sought to prevent the entry of illegal drugs, contraband, and agricultural pests and diseases. The regulation of international trade was also part of CBP's responsibility. CBP stated its goal as "To facilitate legitimate trade and travel while utilizing all of the resources at our disposal to protect and defend the United States from those who would do us harm" (U.S. Bureau of Customs and Border Protection, 2003). One of this new agency's first actions was to increase the number of "A-STAR" and "HUEY" helicopters used to secure the U.S.-Mexico border (The White House, 2003).

Another important agency under this directorate is the *Transportation Security Administration (TSA)*. It had been established by the Aviation and Transportation Security Act of November 19, 2001, and was originally located within the Department of Transportation. This agency oversees matters concerning the safety of U.S. maritime, air, and land travel, such as airport security and the transportation of hazardous materials. On April 19th, 2003, TSA certified 44 airline pilots who had completed the new Federal Flight Deck Officer Training Program. The training prepared the pilots to carry firearms in the cockpit (The White House, 2003).

The *Bureau of Immigration and Customs Enforcement (ICE)* includes the enforcement and investigation components of Customs, the former INS, and the Federal Protective Services. Michael Garcia, who had formerly been a federal prosecutor and served briefly as acting INS Commissioner, headed the bureau as Assistant Secretary (U.S. Bureau of Customs and Border Protection, 2003). Its primary program areas are immigration investigations, immigration intelligence, customs investigations, customs intelligence, customs air and marine interdiction, and federal protective service (Bureau of Immigration and Customs Enforcement, 2003). The bureau includes the Office of Air and Marine Interdiction (OAMI).

ICE was especially busy during the first 100 days of DHS. Operation Joint Venture investigated the identities of personnel who had access to restricted areas of military installations. As a result, there were 37 arrests and 28 deportations. OAMI provided 'round-the-clock coverage of airspace over Washington, D.C. A multi-agency task force, Operation "Green Quest," investigated the financial infrastructure of terrorist organizations, while Project Shield America partnered ICE agents with U.S. manufacturers and exporters to deter illegal arms exports (The White House, 2003).

While the enforcement of immigration policy fell to ICE, the service functions of immigration were handled by the *Bureau of Citizenship and Immigration Services (BCIS)*. The immediate priorities of the bureau are to improve immigration customer services and eliminate the adjudications backlog, while promoting national security. Eduardo Aguirre, Jr., a former banking executive and a longtime friend of the President, was confirmed as Acting Director June 19, 2003.

BCIS's pilot projects included attempts to standardize the tests required of individuals applying for citizenship, beginning with the English test, and developing a system for online applications for "green card" replacements and Employment Authorizations (The White House, 2003).

Directorate of Emergency Preparedness and Response (EP&R)

The foremost agency in the EP&R directorate is the *Federal Emergency Management Agency (FEMA)*. Created by President Carter's 1979 executive order, FEMA merged many of the separate disaster-related agencies, and absorbed civil defense responsibilities from the Defense Department's Defense Civil Preparedness Agency. It officially became part of the DHS in March, 2003. The similarities between civil defense activities and preparation for natural hazards were emphasized by FEMA's first director John Macy, who led the agency in setting up an Integrated Emergency Management System with an all-hazards approach. The founding director of FEMA under EP&R was Michael D. Brown, a former attorney from Oklahoma.

With national security priority, the agency bears the responsibility for training and equipping the nation's first responders to deal with weapons of mass destruction. Even so, natural disasters—snowstorms, wildfires, floods, tropical storms, hurricanes, ice storms—continue to demand attention and resources. FEMA's mission remains "to lead America to prepare for, prevent, respond to, and recover from disasters with a vision of 'A Nation Prepared'" (FEMA, 2003).

Agency activity in the initial months of the DHS included an Arson Training Course for FBI agents and investigators, the processing of applications for Assistance to Firefighters Grants, and training leaders from volunteer fire departments. In the wake of the Space Shuttle *Columbia* disaster, for instance, FEMA was charged with recovering the debris while maintaining public health and safety, and reimbursing the states of Texas and Louisiana for costs associated with that process (The White House, 2003).

The *Federal Insurance Administration*, which provides flood insurance to property owners nationwide, and the *U.S. Fire Administration* are part of the FEMA organization, as is the *Emergency Training Institute*. FEMA also coordinates *Citizen Corps*, an organization of community volunteers dedicated to public safety, crime prevention, and emergency response. The Corps partners with such groups as the *National Volunteer Fire Council* and the *U.S. Junior Chamber (Jaycees)* to raise awareness in those areas. There are Citizen Corps Councils in 41 states and territories, and in 449 local governments.

Directorate of Science and Technology (S&T)

The S&T Directorate is charged with promoting research and the development of technology. It works with agencies dealing with various aspects of chemical, biological, radiological, and nuclear weapons. For example:

The *Defense Threat Reduction Agency* (DTRA) is a Department of Defense agency. Its purpose is to provide the armed forces of the United States with defense and survival capabilities against chemical and biological weapons. The agency emphasizes a threefold strategy of "shaping, responding, and preparing" in order to control and reduce the threat to America's interests of WMDs.

> **Shaping** refers to attempting to influence the proliferation of WMDs in the international environment. This is undertaken by the Cooperative Threat Reduction program in the Soviet Union,

where the DTRA participates directly in the elimination of weapons and support systems for weaponry. DTRA is also charged with implementing on-site weapons inspections and related activities, both as relating to U.S. treaty rights and in non-treaty matters.

Responding is itself broken down into three commands. *Combat Support* involves working with the Department of Energy, the U.S. Strategic Command, and the Department of Defense in the stewardship of nuclear stockpiles and in missile defense programs. *Technology Development* is geared towards supporting military operations to "neutralize" WDM threats and to sustain U.S. strategic systems in a nuclear environment. Finally, the agency directs and manages *Chemical-Biological Defense*.

Preparing involves working with U.S. and foreign intelligence communities, border security, and customs officials to try to anticipate and deter the proliferation of WMDs (Defense Threat Reduction Agency, 2003).

The *Chemical and Biological Defense Information and Analysis Center (CBIAC)* is a civilian agency under contract to the Department of Defense allied to S&T. It serves as a center for acquiring, compiling, analyzing and disseminating information related to chemical and biological defense technology. For example, it conducts studies, provides training courses, and produces handbooks, databases, reports, training kits, interactive software, and the like.

While the U.S. Department of Energy will provide support from its National and Federal Laboratory System, the *U.S. Coast Guard Research and Development Center* and two laboratories are specifically part of the S&T. These laboratories are the Environmental Measurements Laboratory and the Plum Island Animal Disease Center. The *Environment Measurements Laboratory* is owned and operated by the U.S. government. It focuses squarely on "preventing, protecting against, and responding to radiological and nuclear events in the service of Homeland and National Security" (Environmental Measurements Laboratory, 2003). This includes measuring radiation and radioactivity, developing and evaluating technology, training personnel, and data management.

Scientists at the *Plum Island Animal Disease Center* have worked since 1951 to protect American livestock from foreign diseases. The facility was part of the USDA, which will continue to conduct research and development and diagnostics programs there. (In fact, research staff will remain employees of the USDA.) Foot-and-mouth disease and African swine fever head the current research agenda. The DHS expects the lab to develop countermeasures to protect against high-consequence biological threats to the civilian population and the agricultural system, such as contamination of food supplies (U.S. Department of Homeland Security, 2003).

The DHS still plans to create a new agency, the *Advanced Research Projects Agency*, as well as a 20-member Science and Advisory Committee, which was mandated by the Homeland Security Act (U.S. Department of Homeland Security, 2003).

Directorate of Information Analysis and Infrastructure Protection(IAIP)

The mission of the IAIP is to create a system for identifying threats to the nation by gathering "actionable intelligence," information that can lead to preventing terrorist attacks or to apprehending terrorists. The Directorate is also responsible for issuing timely warnings in the event of an imminent attack, through the Homeland Security Advisory System (National Infrastructure Protection Center, 2003). Retired Marine officer Frank Libutti was serving as the NYPD's Deputy Commissioner of Counter Terrorism when President Bush nominated him to be Under Secretary for IAIP (U.S. Department of Homeland Security, 2003).

IAIP began by assimilating five existing agencies. Principal among these were the National Infrastructure Protection Center (NIPC) and the Critical Infrastructure Assurance Office (CIAO). Second, the Office of Planning and Partnerships (PPO), a new office, took over many of CIAO's responsibilities. The focus of that office was declared to be "to raise issues that cut across industry sectors and ensure a cohesive approach to achieving continuity in delivering critical infrastructure services" (CIAO, 2003).

Third, the National Communications System (NCS) was itself a group of 23 Federal departments and agencies. The NCS was established by President John F. Kennedy in 1963 in response to the need for better communications between the President and defense, diplomatic, intelligence, and civilian leaders during emergencies. National security and emergency preparedness were the goals; interconnectivity and survivability were the essential characteristics of the system (National Communications System, 2003).

Fourth, the Federal Computer Incident Response Center (FedCIRC) was charged with supporting the federal civilian government by receiving reports of computer security incidents, and providing assistance with both prevention and response.

Fifth, the DHS created the National Cyber Security Division (NCSD) on June 6, 2002. The Department has 60 employees providing "24/7 functions" which fall into three categories: risk assessment, incident response, and awareness and education programs. Robert Liscouski, the Assistant Secretary of Homeland Security for Infrastructure Protection, was appointed to oversee the department.

While the routine oversight of the nation's energy supply and its supporting infrastructure remains with the Secretary of Energy, the Energy Security and Assurance Program transfers security functions to the DHS. The mission of this office is to protect the energy infrastructure (including fuel supplies, electric power supplies, nuclear weapons, materials, facilities and information assets) against "disruptions from natural or deliberate causes (which) could compromise our Nation's economic prosperity and compromise our national security"(U.S. Department of Energy, 2003). The goals of the office are to advise the Secretary of Energy on protection activities and on how to coordinate with the DHS, industry, state and local governments to develop training exercises and technical assistance for recovery from an attack.

Organization of the Department of Homeland Security

As broad as the above directorates are, they represent only four of 27 units that report to the Secretary or Deputy Secretary. Figure 5.2 (Organizational Chart, Department of Homeland Security), is a diagram of the entire department. Each of the five directorates is headed by an undersecretary.

At the time of this writing, the Department of Homeland Security continues to be an organization in transition, changing almost daily as agencies adapt to their new locations under the Homeland Security umbrella.

Figure 5.3, adapted from the DHS Press Release "Fact Sheet: A Day in the Life of Homeland Security," shows an estimate of the daily activities carried on by the Department. As the reader will see, the DHS is widely present in both military and civilian pursuits. The DHS is establishing itself as a presence in the daily routines of ordinary Americans.

Figure 5.3 does not display a complete list of DHS daily activities. For example, in addition to the above, the United States Secret Service estimates that it will initiate 23 new financial investigations and suppress two counterfeit operations while continuing its routine protection of the President and other VIPs. The figure is intended to show the extent to which DHS activities permeate everyday life.

Figure 5.2
Organizational Chart, Department of Homeland Security

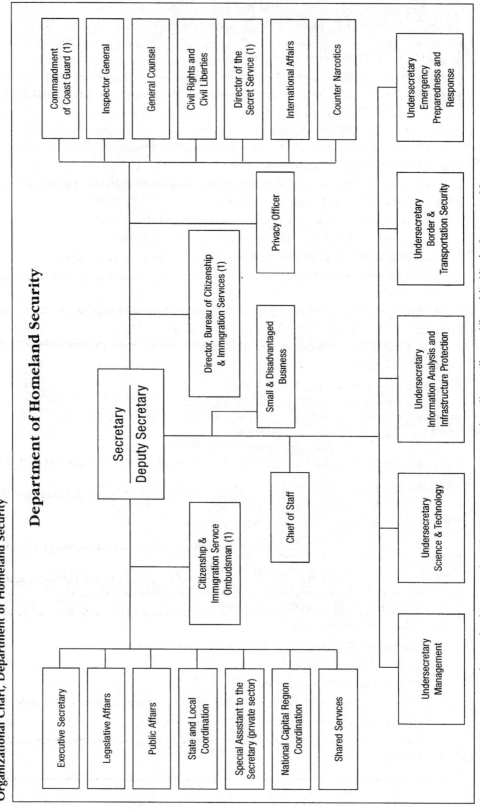

Department of Homeland Security

Source: U.S. Department of Homeland Security (2002). "DHS Organization." http://www.dhs.gov/dhspublic/display?content=20

Figure 5.3
A Day in the Life of Homeland Security

Customs and Border Protection:

- Process more than 1 1 million passengers arriving into our nation's airports and seaports
- Inspect more than 57,006 trucks and containers, 580 vessels, 2,459 aircraft, and 323,622 vehicles coming into this country
- Execute more than 64 arrests
- Seize 4,639 pounds of narcotics in 118 narcotics seizures
- Seize an average of $715,652 in currency in 11 seizures
- Seize an average of $23,083 in arms and ammunition and $467,118 in merchandise
- Deploy 1,200 dog teams to aid inspections
- Make 5,479 pre-departure seizures of prohibited agricultural items
- Apprehend 2,617 people crossing illegally into the United States
- Rescue three people illegally crossing the border in dangerous conditions
- Deploy 350,000 vehicles, 108 aircraft, 118 horses on equestrian patrol, and 480 all-terrain vehicles
- Utilize 238 Remote Video Surveillance Systems, each system using 1-4 cameras to transmit images to a central location
- Maintain the integrity of 5,525 miles of border with Canada and 1,989 miles of border with Mexico

Immigration and Customs Enforcement:

- Make 217 arrests on immigration-related violations
- Make 41 arrests on customs violations
- Remove 407 criminal aliens and other illegal aliens
- Investigate 12 cases involving unauthorized employment threatening critical infrastructure
- Participate in 24 drug seizures resulting in the seizure of 5,511 pounds of marijuana, 774 pounds of cocaine, and 16 pounds of heroin
- Make seven currency seizures, totaling $478,927
- Make grand jury appearances resulting in the indictment of a combination of 32 people and companies
- Launch 20 vessels in support of marine operations protecting the territorial seas of Puerto Rico, South Florida, the Gulf of Mexico, and Southern California
- Fly 25 surveillance flights supporting criminal investigations in Puerto Rico and the Continental United States
- Disseminate 80 criminal investigative leads to field offices
- Review 1,200 classified intelligence cables
- Protect more than 8,000 federal facilities
- Screen more than 1 million federal employees and visitors entering federal facilities
- Make six arrests for criminal offenses on federal property
- Intercept 18 weapons from entering federal facilities to include firearms, knives, and box cutters

Figure 5.3, *continued*

TSA:

- Screen approximately 1 5 million passengers before they board commercial aircraft
- Intercept two firearms. In the month of May, TSA intercepted nearly 516,000 prohibited items, including 50 firearms
- Deploy thousands of federal air marshals to protect the skies

Federal Law Enforcement Training Center:

- Provide law enforcement training for more than 3,500 federal officers and agents from 75 different federal agencies

U.S. Coast Guard:

- Save 10 lives
- Assist 192 people in distress
- Protect $2 8 million in property
- Interdict 14 illegal migrants at sea
- Conduct 109 search and rescue cases
- Seize $9.6 million of illegal drugs
- Respond to 20 oil and hazardous chemical spills
- Conduct 50 Port Security Patrols
- Conduct 20 Homeland Security Air Patrols
- Board two high interest vessels
- Escort eight vessels, such as cruise ships or high interest ships, in and out of port
- Embark Sea Marshals on two vessels
- Maintain more than 90 security zones around key infrastructure in major ports or coastal areas
- Educate 502 people in Boating Safety Courses

Bureau of Citizenship and Immigration Services:

- Provide information and services to approximately 225,000 customers in one of its 250 field locations every day
- Respond to 75,000 daily calls to its toll-free customer service number
- Naturalize approximately 1,900 new citizens every day
- Process approximately 19,000 applications for a variety of immigration related benefits

Source: U.S. Department of Homeland Security, http://www.dhs.gov/display?content=1018.

Issues Related to the DHS

A variety of issues have been raised concerning the DHS. The National Threat Initiative (NTI) identified five general classes of problems: defining roles, making the transition, department funding, privacy concerns, and workers' rights.

Roles. There is uncertainty about the actual role many agencies play in the department. Some departments lack a mission statement that defines their role in the DHS. Some lack any acknowledgment that they are subordinate to DHS. Also needed is some clarification of the roles and responsibilities of state and local governments.

Transition. The NTI raised concerns about the current effectiveness of some of the agencies subordinated to the DHS. FEMA, for example, might be less able to assist local managers in national emergencies because, under DHS, it is now also required to "manage grants and assist local authorities with training," and may not have sufficient personnel to carry out both mandates. Similarly, the customs service will combat terrorism, which might limit its traditional responsibility to monitor commerce.

Funding. Funding for the DHS for 2004 was proposed to be 36.2 billion. The concern is that this seemingly large amount is generally absorbed from previous initiatives, with little new money going to these programs. For example, money and time previously spent by doctors on routine visits now is allocated to preventing and responding to chemical, biological, radiological, and nuclear attacks (CBRN). This has created a vacuum in health care. And many state and local officials are concerned that they have not yet received even the first round of funding for CBRN preparedness, though they have diverted funds from their budgets to implement such plans.

Concerns over funding have been echoed by many local governmental actors (*New York Times*, 2003). The mayor of New Haven, Connecticut, for example, stated that the city was no better off than before 9/11. Only 10 percent of the city's 380 firefighters had received the specialized training and protective equipment for a chemical or biological attack. Chief Gil Kerlikowski, representing the Seattle Police Department, noted that he had to postpone purchasing protective suits for chemical or biological weapons because of delays in funding from Washington. The same article also cited a study by the National Fire Protection Association that found that only 11 percent of the nation's fire departments were ready to respond to building collapses involving more than 50 occupants (Shenon, 2003).

Privacy Concerns. The DHS has great potential to invade citizens' privacy. Under one of the proposed bills for the DHS, the Privacy Act of 1974 would be amended by H.R. 5710 to allow the government access to information such as credit card and bank transactions and travel documents. Hence, the DHS could combine personal information with information from federal and local criminal justice agencies in a search for terrorist activity.

Workers' Rights. A controversial issue is the extent to which workers in the DHS will have any protective rights. The issue is this: Will the President be granted the authority to bypass civil service protections in hiring, promoting, and firing DHS workers? Currently, a compromise has marked negotiations over this issue. Government unions will be permitted to play a role in settling disputes over work rules, and limited collective bargaining rights will be provided, but the President will be given the authority to terminate individuals should national security require it.

Homeland Security in Action: Airline Security and Terror Alerts

In the following two sections, we look at two areas where the DHS has a highly visible influence in the lives of citizens, current airline security practices and the color-coded terrorism alerts.

Airlines and Counter-Terrorism

For those who witnessed the terrifying events on September 11, 2001, the images of hijacked commercial jet aircrafts flying into the towers of the World Trade Center and exploding into fireballs were horrific. It was, one observer noted, like something from science fiction. Even when the images are displayed in retrospect, it is difficult to believe that the camera footage is real. By the end of that fateful day, four commercial airlines had been commandeered by terrorist operatives suspected of being associated with Osama bin Laden. Two aircraft had taken off from Logan International Airport in Boston, one from Newark, New Jersey, and one from Dulles, Virginia. The terrorist strategy was to use the craft as missiles and their fuel as bombs, attacking symbols of American military and economic power.

Three of the aircraft were successfully deployed by the terrorists, two by flying into the upper stories of each of the twin towers, and one by flying into the Pentagon. The fourth aircraft—suspected of being directed at the White House crashed after passengers rebelled against the hijackers. All passengers on all four aircraft were killed. The twin towers collapsed, killing thousands, and outer sections of the Pentagon were breached, killing hundreds. Those events propelled a sea of change in American perceptions of security, and redirected a presidency into a portentous course that has resulted in military occupations of Afghanistan and Iraq and a declared war against terrorism.

The American sense of vulnerability was keenest in the airport industry. One of the immediate results of the 9/11 attacks was that the airline industry shut down temporarily. The industry has slowly and haphazardly recovered since, but only after substantial changes in security and great long-term cost. Today, the airline industry is intensely security focused, and its security measures are the primary way most Americans have experienced counter-terrorism activity in the U.S. since 9/11. In this section, we will review some of those changes, the problems associated with them, and issues associated with airline security today.

Airlines have historically been the focus of terrorism. They are a relatively easy target, and the spectacle of an airline crash or hijacking is big news. Security changes have tended to follow major aircraft incidents. In 1970, Palestinians threatened to blow up four hijacked airplanes, two of which were American. In response, President Nixon put sky marshals on airplanes. One year later, after D.B. Cooper skyjacked an airplane, the industry introduced the "Cooper Vane," preventing the rear stairs from being dropped during flight. In December 1972, the FAA announced a requirement that all passengers and their bags would be searched. Early metal detectors, called magnetometers, were rigged from a device used by loggers (Wu, 2003).

In 1988, Pan Am flight 103 was blown up over Lockerbie, Scotland, killing 270 people. This initiated the next wave of security. The FAA began to screen portable computers and radios, and only bags accompanying a person would be permitted on a plane. It was after the 1996 crash of TWA flight 800 that the most frequently heard airline terminal phrase became: "Has anyone unknown to you asked you to carry an item on this flight?" Critics noted that this ubiquitously heard phrase was based on an erroneous theory of the bombing of the flight—that a flight attendant had carried onboard a package from a person she had met. In any case, existing security measures were either inadequate or wrongly directed, and failed utterly in the face of the 9/11 attacks.

The shortcomings of airport security had been established before 9/11. Yet scant attention was given to those concerns. From 1998 to 2001, the General Accounting Office published five reports, all critical of security at major airports in the U.S. They cited low wages paid to screeners, inadequate training of security workers, and rapid turnover of security personnel. In their most recent report prior to the attacks, the GAO stated that airport security had not improved and in many cases had worsened. They stated that "the security of the air transport system remains at risk" (Fish, 2001:1). As Fish noted, "the watchdogs didn't just bark, they howled over and over again."

Two weeks after the terrorist attacks of 9/11, the White House announced a series of endeavors to enhance airline security (Office of Press Secretary, 2001b). These endeavors fell into four categories:

1. *Expand the federal air marshal program.* The president sought the expansion of the program and support from Congress to make the expansion permanent.

2. ***Establish a fund of $500 million to finance airline modifications to delay/deny access to cockpits.*** These were aimed at restricting entry into the cockpit during flight, fortifying the cockpit doors, alerting the crew to activity in the cabin, and insuring continuous operation of the transponder in an emergency.

3. ***Take over management of airport security.*** The federal government was to take charge of all airport security services. This included establishing new operational standards, supervising passenger and baggage security, overseeing the patrolling of security areas, and carrying out the background checks and training of screeners and security personnel.

4. ***Put in place immediate security measures.*** The president asked the governors of all states to call up the National Guard to augment existing security staff.

These endeavors had a number of visible effects on the flying public. The costs of security were shifted to the public, and a security fee was added to ticket costs. Within 60 days, all luggage had to be inspected, by any means available. Passengers faced pre-screening as well as screening searches, and many passengers were searched multiple times prior to a flight.

Long-term security measures were also ordered. By the end of 2002, all checked baggage was to be inspected with explosives detection machines. Prior to 9/11, less than 10 percent of checked luggage was inspected for such devices. And within a year of the attacks, all 28,000 airport baggage screeners were to be federal workers (Abrams, 2001).

On November 19, 2001, the U.S. Congress enacted the Aviation and Transportation Security Act (ATSA). The Act came into effect in 2002, and it directed the FAA to take action to provide airline security, thereby placing airport security under federal jurisdiction. The ATSA initiated the following changes in security (FAA News, 2002):

1. It established new standards for cockpit doors, to protect them from intrusion and small fragmentation devices. All airplanes were also required to have internal locking devices.

2. The FAA took the initiative to establish an international standard for cockpit doors and monitoring of the passenger cabin from the cockpit, with international monitoring to be carried out to insure compliance.

3. Design improvements for cockpit doors were mandated. The FAA also expedited the approval process for the redesigned cockpit doors, to achieve compliance with the Presidential time line.

4. A federal grants program was approved for the fortification of cockpit doors and monitoring activity in the cabin.

5. The FAA issued guidelines for training crew members in hijack resistance techniques. This was a shift in training from passive to active resistance. Any passenger disturbance was to be considered suspicious, a potential diversion for more serious acts. And the flight crew was instructed to land the plane as soon as possible, to minimize the amount of time available for hijackers to carry out their work.

The ATSA also created the U.S. Transportation Security Administration (TSA), which has since become a component of the Department of Homeland Security. In 2002, the TSA had a budget of $1.3 billion, and in 2003 its budget was increased to $4.8 billion. As of the beginning of 2003, explosive detection machines that could detect 15 categories of chemicals had been installed in many airports, and CAT scanners, at $750,000 each, were installed at 429 airports and screened all 1.5 million bags checked annually at American airports (CDI Terrorism Project, 2003).

A new screening program was proposed by the TSA in 2002. The second generation program called "Computer Assisted Passenger Prescreening System" (CAPPS II), proposed to "analyze passengers' travel reservations, housing information, family ties, identifying details in credit reports and other personal information to determine if they're 'rooted in the [terrorist] community' or have an unusual history that indicates a potential threat" (CDI Terrorism Project, 2003:2). The program was to replace CAPPS I, which airlines began using in 1998. However, the controversial plan was dismantled in 2004 because of concerns over privacy and effectiveness, according to Homeland Security Secretary Tom Ridge. Although the program was never officially begun, the government spent more than $100 million on its planning (*USA Today*, 2004:1A).

Critiques of Airport Security

A variety of criticisms have emerged concerning airport security. Below, we observe three areas of security concerns: (1) they are unduly invasive of personal privacy, (2) they are poorly conceived, and (3) they do not take into account sound security practices.

Invasion of Personal Privacy

This concern is related to programs such as the failed CAPPS II program. Secretary Ridge said in July 2004 that "a new program with a different name might be developed to replace CAPPS II. But if enough people volunteer to provide personal information through a new 'registered travel' program, that alone could replace CAPPS II" (*USA Today*, 2004:1A). Critics have expressed concern that the databases the government uses to formulate the CAPPS II lists, such as credit reports, are "error-riddled." And someone who is subsequently labeled a security risk will not be told why. Hence, someone could be mislabeled and not know how to redeem their reputation. The Federal Registration notice of the program stated that background information will be stored for 50 years. Others have stated that it is no more than complex profiling, and will have as poor a success record as other profiling strategies. A lawyer for the ACLU, Ms. Katie Corrigan, observed, "This system threatens to create a permanent blacklisted underclass of Americans who cannot travel freely" (Associated Press, 2002).

Poorly Conceived

Not everyone believes that airport security is developing in the right direction. One industry critic is aviation consultant Michael Boyd. He has argued that the added security measures are costly and wrongheaded. For example, when asked about random checks at gates, he noted:

> The fact is these aren't enhanced security measures in many cases; they're crackpot. Last-minute random checks of people at the gate where they pick out the first-class passenger who boards regardless or somebody carrying a diaper bag or something . . . We need focused security, not this random scattershot approach (CNN.com, 2002a).

The randomness of airport checks led critics to suggest that this reduced the likelihood of catching a terrorist to no more than random luck. And problems in airport leadership remain unaddressed. Boyd expressed a concern that there was a lack of accountability among security leadership. The person in charge of security at Boston's Logan International Airport, where two airplanes were hijacked on 9/11, was promoted.

Figure 5.4 contains excerpts from an interview with Michael Boyd presented on C-SPAN's the "Washington Journal" (*Washington Journal*, 2003).

Unsound Security Practice

Another criticism of airport security is that it "fails badly." This observation, made by Bruce Schneider, a cryptography expert, was used to describe an event he experienced at Sea-Tac Airport at Seattle, in which someone ran through a metal detector (Mann, 2002). The person was quickly identified, but authorities still had to empty all terminals and re-screen everyone, including passengers who had already boarded planes. According to Schneider, all security systems ultimately fail. But the good ones "stretch and sag" before they fail, the idea being that a single component can fail but leave the overall system unaffected. When the bad ones fail, the entire system becomes vulnerable. The Sea-Tac failure could have been compartmentalized by placing X-ray machines at departure gates. That way, if the most local security were breached, the entire system would not shut down, and the inconvenience would be limited to passengers at that particular location.

Figure 5.4
Airlines and Counter-Terrorism: An Interview with Michael Boyd

Michael Boyd, an aviation consultant, has a company called the Boyd Group Aviation Research Systems Corporation, in business since 1984. Prior to establishing the Colorado-based business, he worked for American International Airlines, Bar Harbor Airlines, Braniff Airlines, and American Airlines. In an interview on CNN, Boyd had this to say:

On Overall Airport Security

No one is still accountable for security failures at our airports. All we've really done is put in a giant bureaucracy to look for pointy objects. Nothing wrong with that. But the real security threat comes from a number of different asymmetrical sources, and we're not even addressing that. What we've basically done is put an unaccountable bureaucracy in place of what we had before . . . We are still very vulnerable. We have not taken the right steps.

We do not have anticipative security. We have legislated security, and we have bureaucratic security, or screening. You know, a real security program would know about these things. They come out two weeks ago and say, "There's a threat that al Qaeda might hijack more airplanes." Well, that's kind of a known issue here. Did they need to, you know, beat up some guy in an orange jump suit in Guantanamo to find that? The real issue here is, real security is anticipating where the next threat will come, and focusing on that. We've just run willy-nilly to put people at screening points at an airport, leave the back door to the airport almost totally unguarded, and then say, "Look at this. We have some threats."

On The Two Questions Asked of Airline Passengers: *Did You Pack Your Own Bag? Did Anyone Unknown to You Give You Anything to Carry?*

As if a terrorist wouldn't lie, you know? It was stupid . . . No benefit at all. That came into place after TWA 800, where they thought that was a bomb that might have gotten on. And again it's some kind of crackpot, half thought through, scarecrow security where you think, "If I ask somebody this, it will look like I have good security." And all it did was gum up the airports. Airlines had spent billions of dollars to maintain systems where you could walk right through an airport, go through security, and get on the airplane without dealing with one of their employees. Then we had huge lines where they had to stop, ask for your ID, which could be easily dummied, and ask those questions. It didn't do any good at all. All it did was again try to make people think we're doing something. And there were some people who said, "You need to change the question to say 'Did *anyone* give you a bag' rather than 'Did anyone *unknown* to you.'" The whole thing was stupid. Rather than really look at security and tighten up security behind the ramp, we just asked Grandma whether she'd packed her own bag.

On Screening

A lot of it is random screening. A lot of this, it's not identifying threats. I put it this way: Random security is like going into the woods, shooting into the forest, and saying that's deer hunting. They do a lot of that stuff, and what they do it for, in my mind, is just for show. Airline crews are picked out very frequently for additional screening. I think that's to show the public that "no one's above

Figure 5.4, *continued*

this." The real issue here is we're looking for pointy objects. They say they got 4.8 million weapons since they started this program. No, they didn't! They got 4.8 million cosmetic items. And the whole idea here is to give the public the impression we have better security.

On Israeli Airline El-Al's Passenger Interviews

Well, sure, it's one thing when you have El Al, which has, like, 30 airplanes. They can do that. But at the morning rush at Chicago, to ask every business traveler why he's going to Omaha; I mean, some people might not even want to admit that. The point is why would you want to ask people this in an environment like that? It makes sense, but if we did that, we would not have an air transportation system. And let's remember: The goal of the terrorists on 9/11 was not to knock down a building; it was to hamstring our economy by making our air transportation system less effective than it can be, less efficient than it can be. What we need to work at is to have good security that does identify threats, and one that is consistent with throughput and efficiency in the system. We can do both. Unfortunately, we don't have the people in place to do that.

On Racial Profiling

Profiling racially or in terms of whether someone has a heavy suntan or not, or looks like that, is wrong. That's not real security. Remember there's people out there today who say, "Let's do a background check on all passengers, and if they have a good background check what we'll do is let them go through less security." I would point out that a background check in 1991 would have identified someone you would want to marry your daughter—a good background in the military, a patriot, and a good work ethic—that would've been Timothy McVeigh.

On Working with the TSA

It's hurting (the airlines). They have very little leeway to complain about it. They have very little leeway to come out and say, "We need to fix this." At the highest levels there are some organizations that are trying to work with the TSA, but again you're working with a giant glue-ridden organization. The thing is airlines don't have a whole lot of control over that, except trying to jawbone on Capitol Hill. And as you saw where Senator (Asa) Hutchinson said, "Everything's fine," and Senator Kay Bailey Hutchison said, "Everything's fine." On both sides of the aisle they say everything's fine. I think that's negligent, because everyone in the industry knows that it's not fine. Everybody in the industry knows that really it's a bureaucracy, not a screening organization. And one of the terrifying things to me is the recent Zogby poll (which is arguably one of the best companies that does polling) came out and said the American public really thinks this is better security and are happy with it. We're right back to where we were before 9/11 and we need to do something about that. But it's the folks on Capitol Hill that are going to have to start to get more responsible.

Source: Excerpts from *Washington Journal* (2003). "Interview with Michael Boyd." August 8. National Satellite Cable Corporation (C-SPAN).

This problem characterized all airport security strategies: They depend on secrecy, and so do not tend to work very well. Airport procedures involving secrecy include screening passengers, examining luggage, and running the autopilot software. The problem with these procedures is that once someone knows the code, they become transparent. It has been widely suggested, for example, that Al Qaeda was aware of the kinds of people profiled at airports, and sent the 9/11 hijackers through because they did not fit the profile. The preferred kind of system, according to Schneider, was one that did not depend on secrecy. Small-scale, compartmentalized systems rather than grand, all-encompassing systems are best. For example, the best defense against hijacking may be cockpit door restructuring and the resistance of passengers en masse. Even if hijackers know about both ahead of time, it does not particularly help them hijack a plane.

Schneider also noted that some of the airport security seemed to address problems that did not exist. Stopping cars from parking within 300 feet of terminals, while passengers were dropped off directly in front of the terminals, for example, did not make sense (Mann, 2002).

Anatomy of a Terror Alert

On February 7, 2003, President Bush raised the terror threat alert to orange status. This was only the second time an orange status alert had been called since the Homeland Security Directive was adopted. An orange status alert is a high state of alert. Figure 5.5 below describes the different alert statuses under the homeland security advisory system.

In the day following, U.S. Fire Marshall David Paulison acted as a spokesperson, providing citizen information on emergency preparedness. He cautioned that citizens might find aid hard to come by after an attack. They should have a variety of items available at home for short term emergencies. He noted that people should have three days' worth of water and food, emergency supply kits for both home and automobile, radios with extra batteries, and plastic sheeting and duct tape to seal windows and doors (Meserve, 2003).

According to the alert, citizens were recommended to designate a safe room protected with plastic sheeting sealed with duct tape, and to have on hand scissors, a manual can opener, blankets, a flashlight, a radio, and spare batteries (Mintz, 2003b). Citizens in New York and Washington were particularly described as vulnerable to a terrorist attack.

The alert affected Americans in a variety of ways. One of these was in the sales and construction of safe rooms. A safe room is a location in the house that provides temporary safety from attack, particularly bioterror attack. The notion of a safe room predates the orange alert. The concept of safe rooms has been used with regard to home invasion and tornadoes. However, the war on terror, and the orange alert particularly, heightened awareness of the concept of safety within the home.

Figure 5.5
Homeland Security Advisory System

Green condition. Indicates a low risk of terror attack. The following is advised.

1   Citizens should develop a household disaster plan and assemble a disaster supply kit.

Blue condition. Indicates a guarded condition There is a general risk of terrorist attacks. The public should

1.   Update the disaster supply kit.

2.   Review household disaster plan.

3.   Have a household meeting; discuss what each member would do and how they would communicate with each other in the event of a terrorist threat.

4   Develop a detailed communication plan

5.   Apartment residents should meet with building plans to develop emergency plans

6   People with special needs should discuss their plans with friends, family and employers.

Yellow condition. Indicates a significant risk of attack. The public should:

1.   Be observant of any suspicious activity.

2.   Contact neighbors, discuss their plans and needs.

3.   Contact school officials. Acquire their plans for emergencies. Obtain their plans to reunite children with parents and care givers in case of an attack

4.   Update the household communication plan.

Orange condition. Indicates a heightened threat alert with a high risk of attack. It carries the following specific recommendations and is described in greater detail here.

1.   Observe all actions for lower levels of alert.

2   If a need is announced, donate blood at designated blood collection centers.

3   Citizens should review disaster plans and recheck supply kits.

4.   Individuals should be ready to shelter in place. Sheltering in place means the following:

    a.   Close and lock windows and exterior doors

    b.   Turn off all fans, heating and air conditioning systems.

Figure 5.5, *continued*

---

    c.   Close fireplace damper.

    d.   Go to an interior room above ground level without windows.

    e.   Bring pets, additional food and water supplies.

    f.   Have a hard-wired phone in the room you select.

    g.   Use duct tape and plastic sheeting (heavier than food wrap) to seal all cracks around the door and any vents into the room.

    h.   Keep listening to the radio or television until told you are safe or you are told to evacuate.

Red condition. Indicates the most severe risk of terrorist attack. Protective measures are not intended to be sustained for substantial periods. The public should:

1.   Avoid public gathering places.

2.   Follow official instructions about restrictions of normal activities.

3.   Contact employers about work status.

4.   Listen to radio and TV about possible advisories.

5.   Prepare for protective actions such as sheltering in place or evacuation.

Adapted from Mason Booth, "Individual Preparedness Steps for Orange Alert." In the News. American Red Cross; Federal Emergency Management Agency, "National Security Emergencies."

In the marketplace, a variety of safe rooms had been available. During the cold war, fallout shelters were widely disseminated, but their perceived utility declined in the latter part of the twentieth century, and many scoffed at them as representing unreasoned fear. However, the social acceptance of them and their marketability has been spurred in the current age by fears of terrorist attack. Donn (2003:1) describes this transition as follows:

> By the late 1960s, a new mindset began taking hold . . . how could a personal shelter protect against an apocalyptic nuclear war between superpowers? Shelter builders began to seem like eccentrics and shelters seemed even more superfluous with the breakup of the Soviet Union.

> 'When you had civil defense in the 1960s, that was ridiculous,' says physicist Ed Lyman, who is scientific director at the Nuclear Control Institute, a research group in Washington, D.C. 'Now, in the context of the risks associated with a terrorist who might have a small number of . . . Radiological weapons, it's not necessarily bad to think if there are procedures that might avert casualties.'

Sales of emergency products were brisk. Many retail stores experienced a run on plastic sheeting. One of the leading suppliers of plastic, 3M, reported a run on plastic sheeting. Fears of imminent attack were cited. An official with 3M stated that two ladies were buying duct tape and plastic. When asked why, the official stated, "They both said the terrorists are coming and they needed help when they attack with gas" (de Bono, 2003). Yet, while some leading security experts were advocating preparedness, others were cautioning that even a period of time in a sealed room as short as three hours could lead to asphyxiation. Sales of duct tape were reported to be robust. Outside of Washington, an Alexandria, Virginia, Home Depot store announced that sales of duct tape increased three-fold overnight. Another store in Alexandria, Lowe's, sold out of duct tape (Meserve, 2003).

In a *Time* magazine article, a sidebar titled "How to Talk to Your Kids" noted that many youths were anxious about terrorism, and advised parents to take three actions. First, parents should avoid conveying their own worst fears. Consider duct tape. "If a 5-year old asks 'Why are you buying that duct tape?' it may be enough to answer "It's a handy thing to have around" (Ratnesar, 2003).

What was the evidence of an impending attack? According to *Time* magazine, a senior U.S. official stated that Al Qaeda operatives "are in the execution phase of some of their operations" (Ratnesar, 2003:24). Others stated that there was "credible evidence" that Al Qaeda had attacks prepared to begin at the end of hajj, the five-day Muslim pilgrimage to Mecca. Some of the concerns were quite specific. Members of Congress were warned that specific information indicated that they might be the objects of assassination attempts. Telephone calls and e-mails between suspected terrorists led the FBI to suspect a plot involving nerve gas, poisons, or radiological devices. Tom Ridge, Secretary of the Department of Homeland Security, placed the probability of attack at greater than 50 percent.

On February 14, 2003, seven days after the alert went into effect, federal law enforcement officials stated that some of the information that led to the alert had been fabricated. An informant who had stated that terrorist attacks were timed to coincide with the hajj failed a lie detector test. Official noted that other evidence was involved in the decision for the heightened state of alert, particularly an increase in communications and money transfers by Al Qaeda members. However, the only information specific to a terrorist threat had been provided by the informant, and it was the informant who suggested that attacks might coincide with the hajj (McCaffrey, 2003).

The terror alert was lowered from orange status to yellow status on February 27, 2003. A yellow alert indicates that a significant threat of terrorist attack continues to exist. The reason for lowering the level was the lack of attacks following the end of the hajj. Both Attorney General Ashcroft and Secretary of Homeland Security Ridge stated that the hajj had ended without incident, and concerns that an attack might coincide with the hajj had passed (Stout, 2003). This observation suggests that counter-terrorism activity is mobilized by religious considerations, whether or not an actual terrorist threat appears to be imminent.

Several observers criticized the use and timing of the orange level threat alert. The President's advisors suggested that the heightened alert level may have led terrorists to postpone any attacks. This prompted a retort from the *Washington Post* that the comment suggested that there was an inverse relationship between the level of the alert and threat of terrorism, in which the higher the level of alert, the greater the deterrence and the less likely the threat. The *Post* asked how Americans were to prepare for attack if there were an inverted relationship between the alert level and likelihood of attack. Many cartoons appeared in daily newspapers mocking the use of duct tape as a counter-terrorist protection strategy (see Figure 5.6 below).

Figure 5.6
Duck and Cover or Duct Tape and Cover?

Source: © Copyright 2003 Jeff Parker, *Florida Today.* All rights reserved February 13, 2003 caglecartoons com. Reprinted with permission.

Fears of "crying wolf" were raised by some who observed that an over-use of the code alerts might inure the civic population to a real threat should one materialize. The problem with the "cry wolf" concern is two-fold. First, the decision to raise the alert level is made through the analysis of intelligence and is not open to public scrutiny. Hence, concerns that the alert might be raised for partisan political reasons rather than for security purposes cannot be assessed. Some accused the President of raising the threat level in order to bolster his efforts to build political support for a war against Iraq. Without publicly available evidence of an actual increase in terrorist threat, the argument is impossible to refute. Second, the ability to "connect the dots," that is, assess the actual threat of terrorism from disparate communications among suspected terrorists is, at best, an inexact art. Security analysts fear that if they do not give the public adequate warning, they risk attack on an unprepared population. However, by lowering the threshold for public warning to vague or unsupported threats, they risk undermining the public's faith in their capacity to identify and act against real threats. As Ridge himself acknowledged on February 14, "I would like to remind everyone that the information we have to work with, more often than not, is very vague. It does not tell us when, where or how the terrorists might try to harm us" (U.S. Department of Homeland Security, 2003b).

Perhaps the sharpest criticisms of the orange alert were directed at the home shelter. Many observers noted that a shelter constructed as recommended might lead to loss of life, because it is designed to keep out life-sustaining oxygen. The Mayor of New York, Michael Bloomberg, had called the duct tape advice "preposterous" (Gibbs, 2003). By the end of the alert, even Ridge had noted that the protective utility of a home shelter might be overrated. Several political pundits provided their commentaries on the alert in Figure 5.7.

Figure 5.7
Quotable Pundits and the Heightened State of Alert

James Carville, Democratic Campaigner: Suggests the development of a company that prepares a person's house for terrorist attack. This service would be called the "Fristiciser" for Senate Majority Leader Bill Frist who wrote a book about bioterrorism. "This is my idea," he stated, "I want 10 percent."

Grover Norquist, President of the Conservative Americans for Tax Reform: A room should contain surgical masks, a week's worth of water and canned tuna, "and probably several months worth of liquor. In case I have to wash out a cut."

Ken Duberstein, President Reagan's Chief of Staff: "Yes, I have tuna fish; yes, I have an ample supply of batteries; and yes, I have the black and white battery operated television. (But) I haven't sealed anything since Hechingers went out of business . . . They're telling us to get all this plastic. My son says 'when we seal this room, what are we going to breathe?' And he's right. Count on an 11-year-old to be smarter than Homeland Security.

Robert Reich, Clinton's Secretary of Labor: "I'm doing nothing. I'm getting on with my life." The idea that individuals can prepare for terrorist attacks, he noted, was "as bizarre as survivalists in the 1950s who tried to turn their basements into nuclear bomb shelters."

Source: Adapted from Mark Leibovich and Roxanne Roberts (2003). "Ready or Not: A Capital Question." *Washington Post.*

By the end of the alert, something truly fascinating had happened in the United States. Duct tape had become politicized. The concept of a safe room for chemical attack in one's house had undergone a moral metamorphosis, from a safety recommendation put forth by the American Red Cross, to an object of biting political punditry, representing a moral commitment to the war on terror to conservatives and an example of paranoia to liberals. Lost in the debate was the history of safe room practice, a history in which safe rooms have provided protection from a variety of external threats.

In Israel, changes in civil defense regulations were instituted after the Gulf War. All buildings were required to have a "built-in protected space constructed of reinforced concrete, with sealed and blast-resistant windows" (Israel Defense Front, 2003). The purpose of these spaces was to protect those inside from conventional, chemical, and biological attack. These spaces were designated as Apartment Protected Spaces (APS) and Floor Protected Spaces (FPS). Both contained blast-resistant doors opening outwards, an internal sealed security window, and preparations for internal ventilation. In the event of chemical or biological attack, a ventilation and air filter system was recommended. Central to air system ventilation is the concept of over-pressure—more pressure has to be generated inside than outside, so that a filtration system is not accidentally constructed that draws air into the room from the outside, poisoning the inhabitants inside.

The construction of the rooms is carefully regulated. The installation of the system should only be carried out by the Home Front Command, and constructed in terms of regulatory policy Israeli Standard 4570. The insulation of the room should be done by an authorized laboratory, in accordance with Israeli Standard 4577. The construction of the safe rooms carries the weight of legal code: Failure to provide a safe room can result in fines and/or imprisonment.

Yet, even in Israel, safe rooms pose hazards. On March 16, 2002, shortly after the end of the orange alert, a mother and two teenage sons suffocated in a sealed room created to protect them from the threat of Iraqi missile attack. The room was designed to permit air to escape but not enter. A coal fueled heater in the adjoining room sucked out the oxygen. The family was well prepared: The room contained nylon sheeting, duct tape and rags along the bottom of the door, and gas masks with filters. The family had decided to sleep in the room because they feared Iraq would fire chemical-loaded scud missiles at them if the U.S. launched a war against Iraq (Associated Press, 2003a).

The preparations for safe rooms in Israel are motivated by a clear and present security threat. Israel is in a state of war and its civilian populations are routinely attacked. How reasonable are such preparations for citizens of the United States? Clearly, when a safe room in Israel is contrasted to some of the creations during the orange alert, the differences are palpable. When one contrasts the heavily regulated and robustly designed safe rooms in Israel with the work of one U.S. resident who covered his house in plastic sheeting and duct tape, one can only be dismayed. Yet, the daily security threat in the United States from Islamic radicals will never be as great as it is in Israel.

Consider the nature of the threat: A young Muslim, with no reasonable future and living in a torn landscape, meets with a bomb-maker who offers to take care of her family when the young person carries out a suicide mission. Such young people seem to be common, and many are available who carry grievances against the Israeli Defense Front. Dying in the name of Allah, the young Muslim will rejoice in heaven forever. She straps on a vest loaded with dynamite, is driven across a narrow stretch of ruptured landscape, walks up to a bus, and detonates the explosive, killing herself and 20 passengers.

There is no reasonable way that the pathways of this bomb-maker, this hapless young bomber, bomb-making equipment, and easy access to a bus will routinely come together in the United States. This does not mean that there is no threat to American citizens from terrorism, but for terrorism to become a routine security issue it would have to develop internally and be fostered by groups indigenous to the U.S. With this in mind, maybe the highly deregulated and mostly defective safe rooms currently constructed by citizens carry an important purpose. They enable citizens to move forward with their lives, feeling like they've done something constructive to protect themselves. And given the overall infrequency of death and injury by terrorism in the United States, perhaps this is the most that can be asked from safe rooms.

USNORTHCOM: The Military Component of Internal U.S. Security

One of the less widely recognized aspects of the war on terrorism is the establishment of the U.S. Northern Command, also called USNORTHCOM, as a military component in the Department of Defense aimed at assisting the war on terrorism. USNORTHCOM became a new division in the U.S. military's Unified Command Plan, operational as of October 2, 2002. It combines under its defense the United States, Mexico, Canada, Puerto Rico, and waters up to 500 miles off shore. Its headquarters are located at Peterson Air Force Base in Colorado Springs, Colorado. It also absorbs NORAD (North American Air Defense), which was located under Cheyenne Mountain in that city.

USNORTHCOM is a direct result of the 9/11 attacks. Its emblem displays three stars, "honoring the victims and heroes of the attacks in New York, Washington, and Pennsylvania" (usgovinfo, 2002). The purpose of USNORTHCOM is to locate the military defense of North America under a single, unified command. In that sense, it is a military version of the Office of

Homeland Security, which seeks to accomplish a similar defensive objective under a unified civilian authority. It has a two-part mission statement:

1. It will conduct operations to deter, prevent, and defeat threats and aggression aimed at the United States, its territories, and its interests.

2. It will provide military assistance to civil authorities. It has few assigned forces (about 500 civilian and military forces) but will be assigned forces as ordered by the President. Assistance includes "consequence management operations," which means the provision of military assistance to civilian authorities for "terrorist attacks, natural disasters, and drug intervention operations" (usgovinfo, 2002).

USNORTHCOM joins the other four military commands, the European Command, the Central Command, the Southern Command, and the Pacific Command. Because of the creation of this command, for the first time the U.S. military command is global in breadth.

The command does not create a new military service but realigns existing services, and acts under the following limitations. It does not liaison directly with Homeland Security, conduct law enforcement operations, secure airports or borders, train or maintain operational forces, or conduct homeland security in Hawaii (U.S. Northern Command, 2003). Nor does it provide a first responder role, noting that there are already 11 million first responders to terrorism incidents in the U.S.

One of the controversies associated with USNORTHCOM is whether it employs military activity inside the U.S. Even in a law enforcement role, such actvity would be a violation of Posse Comitatus. The Posse Comitatus Act, originally passed as a rider to an appropriations bill in 1878, states:

> From and after the passage of this act, it shall not be lawful to employ any part of the Army of the United States, as a *posse comitatus*, or otherwise, for the purpose of executing the laws, except in such cases and under such circumstances as such employment of said force may be expressly authorized by the Constitution or by act of Congress . . . (Chapter 215, Section 15, Army as Posse Comitatus: See Baker, 1989:1).

The Posse Comitatus Act was the result of two political concerns. The first and most important was to end the use of Federal troops to police state elections in former Confederate states. The second was to curtail the use of military Fort Commanders in the West, who in many cases exercised civilian law enforcement responsibilities. The results of their actions were sometimes seen as unacceptable to elected civil officials (Baker, 1989).

Several exemptions to the Posse Comitatus Act have been enacted. These exemptions are (1) National Guard operating under state authority;

(2) active duty military and federalized National Guard under presidential authority to quell domestic disturbances; (3) areal surveillance by military personnel, and a "drug exemption," permitting the Secretary of Defense to make available equipment, training, and military advice in the "war on drugs;" (4) use of the Judge Advocate Corps as a special assistant prosecutor; (5) the use of the Coast Guard during peacetime; and (6) the use of the Navy to assist the Coast Guard in anti-drug trafficking activities (though the Navy is prohibited in all other cases).

Moreover, the Posse Comitatus Act prohibits only the Army from involvement in citizen affairs in the U.S. It does not expressly prohibit the Navy, Marine Corps, or National Guard. However, the Department of Defense has extended the prohibition to the Navy and Marine Corps, except for the exceptions noted above.

In spite of USNORTHCOM's prohibitions, a variety of concerns have been raised about the command. The President has demonstrated a willingness to use the military inside U.S. territory since the 9/11 terrorist incidents. Air Force pilots, for example, were put on patrol and authorized to shoot down commercial airliners, and the Pentagon has taken actions to participate in homeland defense training. This willingness is troubling to civil libertarians, for several reasons cited by the Center for Defense Information (2002).

1. Soldiers are not trained, as are the police, to protect Americans' rights to privacy and due process. This concern has been reinforced by the extended detention of legal immigrants and proposals to try them by military tribunal.

2. From a military perspective, assignment to homeland duties further dilutes an already small military. The current military is one-third smaller than it was in 1990 and is already stretched thin.

3. The military is not well organized or trained to deal with home security missions. Police are trained to operate in small groups, while the military acts with large units. Nor are the roles wholly compatible: the military mission is search and destroy, while the police mission is search and capture.

On the other hand, the actual mission of USNORTHCOM has been questioned. Several issues were also raised in a symposium held by the U.S. War College (Tussing & Kievet, 2003). The discussion was framed around the general issue of the contribution of the military to a homeland defense threat. The following is a brief summary of some of the observations.

1. The current perception of the Department of Defense is that it is the *Department of Foreign Wars* (Italics in original). USNORTHCOM's position has left state and local governments concerned about military support. USNORTHCOM,

rather than being restricted, needs to be encouraged—indeed required—to develop a Theater Engagement Plan with state and local governments (2003:1-2).

2. Elements of the guard should specialize in homeland defense. The National Guard is the unit that will provide the "Federal solution" to state, local, and regional shortcomings in a national emergency.

3. Because the military role in homeland security will be a support function "in 99 percent of the time," USNORTHCOM should develop regional coordination centers for intelligence, resources and standards for response and responders.

4. The military should train first responders to avoid "tactical myopia." This means that first responders need to learn how to recognize second and third order threat indications. And the executive leadership of first responders needs to be taught about the importance of continuity of command, understanding threats, planning for regional responses, and developing conceptual training for first responders.

An additional function for USNORTHCOM was noted by Naef (Infocon, 2002). In the event of a catastrophic event it will be critical that the Northern Command communicate with lead agencies such as FEMA and the FBI. In such a circumstance, USNORTHCOM provides a unity of command that enables a high level of communications capability. It may provide the most efficient way to "connect the dots" as information comes in, or as one person put it, "the best way to transform a voice report from an emergency responder who is first on the scene of a terrorist attack or natural disaster into a digital format that provides reports to all coordinating agencies" (Infocon, 2002:2).

Substantive differences in perceptions of issues involving USNORTHCOM are noted when the Center for Defense Information is compared to the symposium held at the U.S. War College. The Center for Defense Information reveals a concern about the appropriateness of the U.S. military in civilian affairs. This concern stems from the role differences between military and the police, and related concerns over due process. Moreover, the Center expresses a concern about the over-extension of military forces, already spread thin. However, the symposium perspective seems to display an opposing view, one that seeks greater capacity for involvement in internal U.S. affairs. Their view stems from the position that we are in a "new reality" where a threat can be both domestic and foreign.

Both perspectives give the National Guard a central role in the event of domestic attack. The Center for Defense Information, though, advises that caution and proper training are central to their use. They remind the reader of the four students who were killed, and the nine students who were injured, at Kent State University in Ohio in 1970 by National Guard members that resulted from poor training and lack of threat understanding.

Conclusion

In summary, this chapter has looked at the reorganization of defense in the United States, aimed at the elevation of terrorism as a principal defense concern. In the civilian arena, this reorganization involved the establishment of a new cabinet, the Department of Homeland Security, and in the military arena a new command, USNORTHCOM. The DHS is a large and unwieldy bureaucracy, bringing together many previously separate federal entities under a common umbrella and counter-terrorism mission. It is in a period of continual development. Its final form, like all cabinet posts, will be determined both by political influences and by practical concerns of the needs of counter-terrorism. To an extent, its form and function will change in the event of another significant terrorist action, and if counter-terrorism activity is increasingly normalized in the everyday lives of citizens or if counter-terrorism laws are normalized into crime-fighting activities. USNORTHCOM is a bold change in military command, uniting various pre-existing military elements in a common defense function. It has yet to deal with a significant internal threat. When it does so the fundamental notions of posse comitatus in the United States may well be rewritten.

CHAPTER 6

Middle-Eastern Immigrants in the U.S. Since 9/11: Detainment and Seizure

Many of the most compelling issues associated with 9/11 bear on immigrants. In order to understand the world in which immigrants today find themselves, we must separate these issues into specific categories, each of which have differing implications for immigrant life. In this chapter we will consider issues related to detainment and seizure. In Chapter 7, we will consider the registration and surveillance of immigrants.

Overview: Immigration, Immigrants, and Constitutional Rights

Since 9/11, a great deal of attention has focused on the presence of Middle-Easterners who have immigrated to the U.S., are visiting, or are in the United States illegally. When the subject of terrorism enters the picture, the discussion is often characterized by a belief that the Constitution only applies to citizens of the United States; others are not constitutionally protected, and the executive branch of the government has the authority to deal with these populations in any way it wants. This belief about the rights of immigrants and visitors is untrue on both counts and reveals a profound misunderstanding of the Constitution.

Foreign Travel and Immigration in the U.S.

Figure 6.1 shows 2000 levels of migration of all kinds to the United States and is included to show the scope of travel to and from the U.S. Contemporary changes in the law affect all migrants, not only Middle-Easterners (although they have been singled out in various policy directives); consequently any consideration of the reach of legal changes applies to the entire group. Overall migration also provides a backdrop against which we can focus on current efforts to institute counter-terrorism programs.

Figure 6.1
Foreigners Entering the United States, by Category, 2000

The appropriate perspective for understanding Middle-Eastern migration to the United States is viewing it in the context of all migration to the U.S.

Category, 2000

Category	Number
Immigrants	849,807
Immediate relatives of U.S. citizens	347,870
Other family-sponsored	235,280
Employee-based	107,024
Refugees and asylees	65,941
Diversity immigrants	50,945
Other immigrants	42,747
Estimated emigration	220,000
Nonimmigrants entering U.S.	33,651,072
Visitors for pleasure/business	30,511,125
Temporary workers/trainees	634,788
Foreign students and dependents	676,283
Illegal immigration	
Alien apprehensions	1,814,729
Aliens deported	184,775
Alien smugglers located	14,403
Unauthorized foreigners (estim.)	8,500,000
Annual increase (1995-2000)	700,000

Source: Immigration and Naturalization Service, Legal Immigration Fiscal Year 2000 (2002) and J. Passell, "Estimates of Undocumented Immigrants" (Urban Institute, 2001) In Martin and Widgren (2002). "International Migration: Facing the Challenge." *Population Bulletin*, March: p. 12.

Figure 6.1 describes three categories of foreigners in the U.S. First are immigrants, who are those who enter the U.S. for the purposes of residency. In 2000, immigrants numbered nearly 850,000. Most of these, 69 percent, came to the U.S. to be with their families. Employment reasons accounted for the second largest percentage of immigrants, 13 percent. Individuals forced to relocate, including refugees and individuals seeking asylum, make up the third group at 7.8 percent. The emigration number represents those who left the United States. We can see that one person leaves for every four who enter for residency purposes.

The second category is non-immigrants. More than 33 million non-immigrants entered the U.S. in 2000. Most of these, more than 30 million, were visitors for pleasure or business. These foreign visitors are encouraged by the U.S. because they contribute to tourism and local economies.

This category also includes temporary workers or trainees, who account for more than 600,000 individuals. This group represents almost 30 percent of the net growth of U.S. employment, and for that reason has been quite controversial. Many employers want to maintain minimal restrictions for this group, arguing that this is a readily available pool of skilled workers important to the well-being of the U.S. economy. But many American employees would like to restrict the numbers of these individuals, arguing that U.S. companies should shoulder the burden of training and educating an American workforce. Finally, foreign students and their dependents number about 676,000 and account for 2 percent of all non-immigrants entering the U.S.

The third category of foreigners in the U.S. is illegal immigrants. Unauthorized foreigners, also called illegal aliens, either enter the U.S. illegally or enter legally and then violate the terms of their entry, for example, by not leaving on the scheduled departure time, by working when on a tourist or student visa, or by committing a crime. The actual number is unknown but is estimated to be 8.5 million. This number is increasing annually by about 700,000. About one in five (21%) are apprehended annually, and of these 184,775 (or 2.2% of all illegal aliens), are deported.

This table is illuminating. When we think about immigration and the United States, we see that the numbers of people we are talking about are substantial. And these numbers, it should be emphasized, represent only a single year of foreigners entering the U.S. Kaplan reminds us that the U.S. is becoming the first truly international society. Pulled for reasons of the heart or of the purse, foreigners enter the U.S. in very large numbers. Many decide to stay.

Middle-Eastern immigration, the target of much of the current anti-terrorism effort, has increased sharply in recent decades (Gross, 2003). Numbering 200,000 in 1970, the number of Middle-Eastern immigrants in the year 2000 increased to nearly 1.5 million. By 2010, this number is expected to grow to 2.6 million. The religious identity of Middle-Easterners has changed over this period as well. In 1970 only about 15 percent were Muslim, compared with 73 percent in 2000. They are also highly educated, with nearly half entering the U.S. with a college degree (compared with 28% of Americans of the same age). Rates of self-employment for Middle-Easterners are also higher than for those who are native-born. However, rates of poverty have recently begun to rise.

It is against the backdrop of foreign entry into the U.S. generally and Middle-Eastern foreigners specifically that current counter-terror efforts should be considered. This is the socio-demographic context within which most of the counter-terror policies and laws are being carried out, and where we can most vividly witness the impact of these laws.

Immigrants and the Constitution

Be it for political interest, curiosity, or simple attraction to the bizarre, many of us watch political talk shows on the television. A number of these shows have offered debates over aspects on the war on terrorism, during which one often hears dialogue (read "loud argumentation") over how to treat foreigners. It is commonly heard on these shows that foreigners in the U.S. have no constitutional rights. Yet, this view is simply wrong. Foreigners in fact have many rights, although those rights have important qualifications.

If there is a general principle that guides the rights of foreigners in the U.S., it is the Fourteenth Amendment. Section 1 of the Fourteenth Amendment states:

> All persons born or naturalized in the United States, and subject to the jurisdiction thereof, are citizens of the United States and of the State wherein they reside. No State shall make or enforce any law which shall abridge the privileges or immunities of citizens of the United States; nor shall any State deprive any person of life, liberty, or property, without due process of law; nor deny to any person within its jurisdiction the equal protection of the laws.

The final sentence is generally taken to refer to anyone legally inside the United States or its territories. The due process protections that apply to citizens, in other words, also apply to non-citizens in the U.S. legally. A narrow body of administrative rights are provided to individuals who illegally enter the U.S., who overstay or violate the terms of their visa, or who have committed crimes or misdemeanors. Lucas Guttentag, an immigration advocate of the ACLU, describes these rights as follows:

> Under the Constitution, non-citizens are entitled to basic procedural fairness. They are entitled to due process. They are entitled not to be discriminated against based on race or ethnicity, and other fundamental rights guaranteed to everyone. If someone is here in violation of the immigrant laws, they are subject to deportation based on the legal procedures that are in the law. Those procedures have to be followed (CNN.com, 2001).

With regard to illegal immigrants, the ACLU notes that those here illegally are subject to deportation. And the Bureau of Immigration and Customs Enforcement (ICE, formerly part of the INS and now an agency in the

Department of Homeland Security) has the authority to question anyone they believe might be illegally in the U.S. However, according to *Yamataya v. Fischer* (1903), deportation proceedings must meet constitutional due process standards. This means that the suspects are provided with (1) a hearing before an immigration judge and review by federal court, (2) representation by a lawyer, (3) reasonable notice of the hearing time, (4) a reasonable opportunity to examine evidence against them, (5) interpretation for non-English speakers, and (6) clear and convincing proof that the grounds for deportation are valid (American Civil Liberties Union, 2003). Yet, in recent years all, of these elements are being contested. The remainder of this chapter discusses areas of contestation.

Legislative Precursors to 9/11: The 1996 Immigration Act

Contemporary concerns about security and immigration policy can be traced to the Illegal Immigration Reform and Immigrant Responsibility Act (IIRAIRA) passed by Congress in 1996 and signed into law by President Clinton.

This act, a partner to the more heralded 1996 Antiterrorism and Effective Death Penalty Act, was aimed at controlling illegal immigration in the U.S. Supporters of the act argued for the need to control borders and expedite cumbersome bureaucratic procedures. The numbers of border patrol agents were doubled. Penalties were increased in an effort to deter illegal immigration. It sought to limit illegal immigrant access to government benefits. And it mandated the construction of fences at the most heavily trafficked border crossings. The Illinois Coalition for Immigration and Refugee Rights described the act as follows:

> IIRAIRA broadened many of the grounds for which an immigrant can be removed, and in particular expanded the definition of "aggravated felony" to include many minor offenses, including crimes of theft or violence carrying a sentence of one year (even if that sentence was suspended or involved probation).

> IIRAIRA added several new grounds for which immigrants can be refused admission or deported. These new grounds include unlawful voting and false claims to U.S. citizenship, including instances in which an immigrant may truly believe she is a citizen (as happens with many adopted immigrant children) or may inadvertently claim citizenship (as may happen when an immigrant renews his or her drivers license and is asked to register to vote).

> IIRAIRA also created the 3- and 10-year bars for unlawful entrants. Anyone who is in the U.S. unlawfully for 180 days or longer and

who leaves the U.S. can be barred from reentering for three years; anyone in the U.S. unlawfully for one year or more can be barred for ten years.

In addition, IIRAIRA effectively closed off many avenues for challenging and gaining relief from deportation. IIRAIRA cut off court review for many types of immigration decisions made by the INS, including waivers of inadmissibility, cancellation, voluntary departure, and ineligibility for asylum.

Finally, IIRAIRA required that INS detain any immigrant who is being deported based on criminal and certain other grounds, regardless of whether the immigrant actually posed any threat to the community. This "mandatory detention" policy in effect subjected immigrants who had already served their criminal sentences to another term of incarceration, and separated them from their families and communities, and thus from key sources of support, while their cases were in process. Furthermore, detainees were often confined to facilities such as county jails that do not have the resources needed to handle longer-term detention, and are commingled with the criminal population (Illinois Coalition for Immigration and Refugee Rights, 2003).

These changes carry profound implications. For example, the IIRAIRA created an expedited removal process, according to which anyone seeking illegal entry can be summarily removed by an immigration officer, and can be barred by that office from reentering the U.S. for an extended period, perhaps permanently. This is a non-reviewable decision, and in practice has been extended not simply to those with fraudulent documents but to those "whom an inspector believes may have intent to violate the terms of an otherwise valid visa" (Thal, 2003). These applications have effectively stripped the courts of their traditional role to review ICE decisions. Under "expedited removal" circumstances, there is no judicial review of individual decisions of ICE officers or procedures. An inspector, acting on his prejudgments of a person's future behavior, may remove a person from this country without fear of judicial review.

The Act also changed the law permitting removal for aggravated felonies in two important ways. Immigrants who commit aggravated felonies are removable. However, the definition of aggravated felony was dramatically expanded to include minor felonies such as shoplifting, and crimes for which no time may have been served. More importantly, the law applied retroactively. "As a result, many immigrants who had been convicted of such offenses as shoplifting or petty theft many years ago—and who were not deportable until IIRAIRA—are now being deported, even though they have long since served their sentences and rehabilitated themselves" (Illinois Coalition for Immigration and Refugee Rights, 2003).

Concerns have been raised that the mandatory detention statute is disruptive of the lives of many immigrants, and has been associated with what many observers consider to be abuses of governmental power. If an individual is detained for having violated their visa or other immigration violation, they can be held at the discretion of the ICE, and if that person is a seizure under the expedited review process, they can be held without court review, and hence without any of the legal safeguards normally associated with court procedures. In this way, IIRAIRA effectively blocked individuals seized by the ICE from constitutional protections available through the courts, including the right to see if they were entitled to constitutional protections.

The 1996 Immigration Act was not the only legislation passed in 1996 dealing with immigration rights. President Clinton also signed into law a sweeping welfare reform package called the Welfare Reform Law. This law had a broad impact on aliens as well:

1. It prohibited legal immigrants who entered the U.S. after 1996 from food stamps, Medicare, and other federal need-based programs.

2. It raised the income and legal criteria for U.S. residents who sponsored aliens.

3. It denied eligibility for illegal immigrants from most federal, state, and local public assistance.

The 1996 Immigration Act and Welfare Reform Law, passed in conjunction with the 1996 anti-terrorism act and the 1978 FISA court noted in Chapter 5, provided the immediate pre-9/11 environment for aliens and immigrants. The laws and policies passed after 9/11 were possible because these acts provided critical legal groundwork. In this historical progression of acts, we can see how the 2000 Bush administrations policies did not represent a dramatic break from the past, but represented an extension of already existing legal trends in the treatment of immigrants and visitors to the U.S.

Post-9/11: Legal Changes in the Lives of Immigrants

The IIRAIRA anticipated many of the changes in law and policy that were enacted after 9/11. In this section, we look at specific areas of change in the relationship between the government and immigrants, particularly those of Middle-Eastern descent, since 9/11. This and subsequent sections makes extensive use of the chronology of decisions bearing on immigrants assembled by the Migration Policy Institute (2003).

Increased Legal Flexibility in Detaining and Jailing Aliens

The government has sharply broadened legal authority to detain, seize and jail immigrants. The capacity for seizure, particularly when coupled with the secrecy surrounding many seizures, is among the most controversial of the government's newly asserted authorities. Excerpts from a list provided by the Migration Policy Institute are first presented, followed by a discussion of selected elements. It should be noted that the abbreviations INS and ICE are both used below. This may seem confusing, but it is done because the INS was restructured and relocated to the Department of Homeland Security during this time period (see Chapter 5). We see in the list below that authority to seize and detain has several administrative dimensions.

September 17, 2001: Immigration and Naturalization Services (INS) amends regulation to provide itself with more flexibility to detain aliens prior to determining whether they will be kept in custody or released on bond or recognizance, and whether a notice to appear and warrant for arrest will be issued. Unless voluntary departure has been granted, the INS must make such determination within 48 hours of arrest, except in the event of "emergency or other extraordinary circumstance."

September 20, 2001: Department of Justice issues interim regulation allowing detention without charge for 48 hours (or an additional "reasonable period of time") in the event of an emergency.

September 21, 2001: Chief Immigration Judge Michael Creppy sends an e-mail containing a memorandum to all immigration judges (IJs) and immigration court administrators discussing the procedures to be followed in cases requiring additional security measures. Procedures require IJs to hold the hearings separately from all other cases on the docket, to close the hearings to the public, and to avoid discussing the case or otherwise disclosing any information about the case to anyone outside the Immigration Court.

October 31, 2001: INS and the Executive Office for Immigration Review (EOIR) publish an interim rule expanding the existing EOIR regulatory provision for a temporary stay of an immigration judge's decision to order an alien's release in any case in which a district director has ordered that the alien be held without bond, or has set a bond of $10,000 or more.

April 22, 2002: The INS publishes an interim rule, which became effective April 17, 2002, stating that officials at non-federal detention facilities will not release information relating to detainees, reserving for the INS the decision to release such information.

May 29, 2002:   Judge John W. Bissell of the U.S. District Court for the District of New Jersey rules unconstitutional Chief Immigration Judge Creppy's directive closing immigration hearings deemed of "special interest" to the investigation into the September 11 attacks.

June 28, 2002:   The Supreme Court blocks Judge Bissell's May 29, 2002, order which had prohibited the government from holding closed immigration hearings, until the U.S. Court of Appeals for the Third Circuit issues a formal ruling on the government's challenge.

June 28, 2002:   The Supreme Court agrees to consider whether the government can jail immigrant criminals without bail to keep them from fleeing before deportation hearings.

October 4, 2002:   The FBI begins to use a boilerplate memo to oppose bond in all post-September 11 cases. The memo states that "the FBI is gathering and culling information that may corroborate or diminish our current suspicions of the individuals who have been detained."

November 18, 2002:   In its efforts to appeal Judge Kessler's August 2, 2002, ruling, the Department of Justice argues before the U.S. Court of Appeals for the D.C. circuit that disclosing the names of those arrested on immigration charges after Sept. 11, 2001, would help terrorists figure out how the government is conducting its antiterrorist campaign.

March 17, 2003:   The Bush administration launches Operation Liberty Shield to "increase security and readiness in the United States." As part of this security effort, the Department of Homeland Security implements a temporary policy of detaining asylum seekers from 33 countries where Al Qaeda is known to have operated (Migration Policy Institute, 2003).

A review of these decisions shows the following patterns. The decisions provide the ICE greater time flexibility in deciding what to do with immigrants it is holding. Recall that the 1996 Antiterrorism Act shifted legal authority over suspected terrorists from the jurisdiction of courts to the INS administrative process. In the decisions above, immigration judges are required to hold hearings separately and under secret circumstances. Generally, these decisions involve a shift of authority from the courts to the ICE, and place court decisions under the review of the ICE. The overall pattern is to increase the authority of the executive branch of the government to deal with anyone deemed of interest by the Attorney General. The object of this expanded flexibility is to (1) increase the authority of the ICE to keep aliens in custody while deciding what to do with them, (2) increase the length of detention permitted while deciding what to do with aliens, (3) give the ICE authority to override immigration court's decisions, (4) keep court proceedings in secrecy, (5) allow use of federal agents to track down and prosecute whomever they think might have terrorist connections, (6) prohibiting officials at non-federal detention facilities to release information relating to detainees, (7) closing immigration hearings on cases involving individuals with any connection to the investigations into 9/11, and (8) permit state and local law enforcement officers to also carry ICE arrest responsibilities with regard to aliens.

An important part of the increased ICE flexibility is the interim rule passed on September 20, 2001. This interim rule is summarized below:

> The interim rule amends Sec. 287.3(d), "*Custody procedures.*" The current language of that section provides that unless voluntary departure has been granted pursuant to subpart C of 8 CFR part 240, the Service has a period of 24 hours following the arrest of an alien in which it must determine whether the alien will be continued in custody or released on bond or recognizance and whether to issue a notice to appear and warrant of arrest . . . the Service is amending the rule to provide that unless voluntary departure has been granted pursuant to subpart C of 8 CFR part 240, the Service generally must make the determinations as to custody or release of the alien and as to the issuance of the notice to appear and warrant of arrest within 48 hours of arrest. The Service may often require this additional time in order to establish an alien's true identity; to check domestic, foreign, or international databases and records systems for relevant information regarding the alien; and to liaise with appropriate law enforcement agencies in the United States and abroad.
>
> In situations involving an emergency or other extraordinary circumstance, the Service may require additional time beyond 48 hours to process cases, to arrange for additional personnel or resources, and to coordinate with other law enforcement agencies. Therefore, the interim rule provides an exception to the 48-hour general rule for any case arising during or in connection with an emergency or other extraordinary circumstance, in which case the Service must make the determinations as to custody or release and as to the issuance of the notice to appear and warrant of arrest within an additional reasonable period of time. (Immigrationlinks.com, 2001, exerpted from Federal Register: September 20, 2001, Volume 66, Number 183).

This interim rule provided broad authority to the INS to hold immigrants beyond the traditional 24 hours. Importantly, it provided authority for indefinite detention for any case "arising during or in connection within emergency or other extraordinary circumstance," in this case, the war on terrorism. The issue raised by many is that the war on terrorism, carried out against an enemy without identifiable allegiances or boundaries, creates a quasi-permanent status out of "emergency or other extraordinary circumstance." How long can one be held under emergency procedures? The answer is unknowable, given the ubiquitous nature of the war on terrorism.

By shifting immigration decisions away from the courts and to the INS, the government effectively circumvented any recognition of normal court processes associated with due process. The decisions above continue to expand this authority, removing the various constitutional protections afforded those prosecuted in courts. Where courts are used, their behavior is shrouded in secrecy.

On March 17, 2003, President Bush launched Operation Liberty Shield (OLS). This program was designed to provide increased protections of the physical infrastructure of the U.S. Among its elements was a program permitting indefinite detention of asylum seekers. OLS described this program as follows:

> Asylum Detainees—Asylum applicants from nations where Al Qaeda, Al Qaeda sympathizers, and other terrorist groups are known to have operated will be detained for the duration of the processing period. This reasonable and prudent temporary action allows authorities to maintain contact with asylum seekers while we determine the validity of their claim. DHS (Department of Homeland Security) and the Department of State will coordinate exceptions to this policy (White House, 2003a).

According to DHS Secretary Tom Ridge, the program was put into place because of a heightened threat from Al Qaeda senior leadership. According to Ridge, Al Qaeda was "on the defensive" in anticipation of a U.S. military attack against Saddam Hussein, and intelligence reports had indicated that various groups might use the current time to launch attacks against the U.S. OLS was a response to this heightened threat of alert (NBTA, 2003). With regard to those seeking asylum, Ridge stated "We want to make sure, during this period of time, that you are who you say you are" (KOMO, 2003).

Amnesty International (AI) responded with a statement asserting that OLS was an assault on the rights of asylum-seekers. OLS, they noted, "could leave thousands of traumatized men, women, and children languishing in U.S. detention centers and jails for many months, not for having committed a crime, but simply because they looked to the U.S. for protection (Amnesty International, 2003a). The policy, AI noted, was "blatantly discriminatory." They called on Secretary Ridge to (1) remove the discriminatory basis for selecting asylum seekers for detention, (2) make decisions on an individual (rather than national origin) basis, (3) provide prompt review for those selected for detention, and (4) house detainees in reasonable settings, not with criminals in local prisons (Amnesty International, 2003a).

Status of Detainees

This section focuses on the individuals detained and characteristics of their detention. These "detention" characteristics generally flow from the legal changes described above. As in the previous section, we open below with the chronology provided by the Migration Policy Institute (2003).

September 28, 2001:   Attorney General Ashcroft announces that 480 individuals have been detained in a post-September 11 sweep.

October 25, 2001:   Attorney General Ashcroft announces that "to date, our anti-terrorism offensive has arrested or detained nearly 1,000 individuals as part of the September 11 terrorism investigation."

November 8, 2001:   Department of Justice announces that it will no longer provide a running total of all individuals detained in connection with the investigation, but only of those charged with federal crimes or immigration violations, and that it will only release information on the number of detainees currently in custody, not the total number detained in the course of the investigation.

November 27, 2001:   Attorney General Ashcroft holds a press conference and releases a list of 93 individuals who have been charged under federal criminal laws and a document entitled "INS Custody List" which contains 548 cases with no names provided.

November 28, 2001:   Attorney General Ashcroft identifies 93 people charged with crimes arising from the related investigation, many of whose identities have already been released. Most of the charges are for violations such as credit card fraud or making false statements on passport applications. Ashcroft also releases an accounting of 548 people, including their nationalities, dates of birth, and the charges against them (but not their names) who remain in custody on immigration law charges resulting from the investigation. He asserts that the law allows him to withhold their names and that he is doing so in order not to aid Osama bin Laden by revealing which of his associates are in custody.

December 4, 2001:   Senator Russ Feingold holds hearings on the status of post-September 11 detainees. The Attorney General states that those who question his policies are "aiding and abetting terrorism."

December 19, 2001:   Department of Justice announces that there are 460 individuals still in custody on immigration charges.

January, 2002:	National Association of Immigration Judges (NAIJ) proposes the creation of a separate executive branch agency to house the trial-level Immigration Courts and the Board of Immigration Appeals. The NAIJ says this step is needed because of "disturbing encroachments on judicial independence." The NAIJ expresses concern about actions taken by the President, the Attorney General, and the Department of Justice in the aftermath of September 11.
February 15, 2002:	Department of Justice states that 327 individuals are still in custody on immigration charges.
April 30, 2002:	INS turns over list of post-September 11 detainees held in secret to the General Accounting Office (GAO).
September 26, 2002:	The Inter-American Commission on Human Rights invokes an emergency procedure that orders the U.S. to take immediate steps to protect the rights of individuals taken into immigration detention as part of the post-September 11 sweep of immigrant communities (Migration Policy Institute, 2003).

The seizure and imprisonment of foreign nationals, largely carried out in secret has generated a great deal of controversy. The items above show a pattern of seizure, followed by subsequent efforts to find out who was seized and learn their status. This action has been carried out by the families of immigrants so seized, sometimes with the support of legal aid such as the American Civil Liberties Union and various Immigration Advocacy Centers.

The interim rule described in the previous section, particularly the section providing indefinite detention in emergency situations, has provided the legal basis for the extended period of these detentions. Importantly, the decision for the indefinite detention of someone was wholly in the hands of the INS, who carried out the recommendations of the Attorney General. Because the detentions were treated as administrative matters, no provision allowed for review of the detention. Hence, immigrants could be held indefinitely, without review and without opportunity for appeal, and regardless of hardship to themselves or to their families (Human Rights Watch, 2001). Immigrants so seized sometimes simply disappeared without their families knowing what happened to them (Worldlink, 2003).

We see in the seizure of immigrants one of the central dilemmas involved in assessing the merits of government actions in the war on terror. The immigrant group's position is publicly available, and their efforts to free immigrants are advocated by rights groups in a variety of public forums. The government's position is much more difficult to assess because much of it is carried out secretively. The answers to questions such as who is being held, how many are held, why are they being held, what administrative review will be made available to them, will their visas be revoked, and how long will they be held are available to the public only at the discretion of the Attorney General.

One location where immigrants have been held is the Metropolitan Correctional Center in New York, New York. Romano and Fallis (2001) describe immigrants being held in the facility as follows:

> In a high-security wing of Manhattan's Metropolitan Correctional Center, an unknown number of men with Middle-Eastern names are being held in solitary confinement on the ninth floor, locked in 8- by 10-foot cells with little more than cots, thin blankets, and if they request it, copies of the Koran. Every two hours, guards roust them to conduct a head count.
>
> They have no contact with each other or their families, and limited access to their lawyers. Their names appear on no federal jail log available to the public. No record can be found in any court docket in New York showing why they were detained, who represents them or the status of their cases.
>
> Authorities will say virtually nothing about the detainees in the Metropolitan Correctional Center or hundreds of others who have been held during the investigation. The Justice Department has also refused to reveal the names of the lawyers representing them.
>
> It is unknown whether the detainees are considered conspirators in the worst act of terrorism in U.S. history, valuable witnesses or merely people who might have information because they crossed paths with the terrorists responsible for the deaths of nearly 5,000 people Sept. 11.
>
> The government is relying mainly on two legal methods to detain people in the terrorism investigation: immigration violations and the material witness statute. At least 165 of the 698 people detained have been held for violations of immigration law. Their detentions can be virtually indefinite if deportation proceedings have begun. The material witness statue allows prosecutors to hold people who may have information pertinent to the case. They must demonstrate a witness's value to a case and show that he or she may be otherwise unavailable to the court if released.
>
> Some legal experts are concerned that secrecy can affect a client's representation. Some of the lawyers on the case have been cautioned not to talk about their clients and are routinely prohibited from keeping copies of confidential court records. At least one attorney said he would not talk publicly for fear of angering public officials (Romano & Fallis, 2001).

The government, as these authors note, justifies secrecy for several reasons. In the New York case, secrecy rules were imposed by the grand jury, and federal judges ordered certain matters to be filed under seal. Ashcroft justified using the Material Witness statute to insure that they go before a grand jury. Because many of the individuals seized were undocumented, a flight risk was a concern. David Cole, a professor of constitutional law at Georgetown University, countered that they were being held indefinitely so the government could search for clues (Romano & Fallis, 2001). Indefinite holds increase pressure on individuals to provide government with information. Such pressure can backfire: There may be an increased likelihood much of the information will be false, submitted by individuals motivated by ending an indefinite detention by whatever means possible.

In more colorful governmental justifications for secrecy, it was suggested that immigrants were being secretly held so that, if they are members of Al Qaeda, the government can acquire information about ongoing operations and respond accordingly before the terrorist organization has an opportunity to find out who is arrested. Were this argument to be correct, it would suggest an astonishingly fragmented and decentralized Al Qaeda organizational structure, certainly not the top-down organization directed by Osama bin Laden celebrated by the government in its prosecution of the war on terrorism.

The seizure and detention of immigrants typically occurs within a broader investigation. Wilgoren (2001) describes one such investigation, and how it affected its target. Ali al-Maqtari was among those arrested and placed in detention, in his case in Mason, Tennessee. He was initially picked up by immigration on his way to Ft. Campbell, where his wife was reporting for army duty, because two box-cutter knives were found in his car and he had post cards of New York City. At a hearing, an immigration judge requested more solid evidence, a request the government declined, stating that "he was part of a larger terrorist mosaic"(2001:3). The affidavit to the court also stated that the government couldn't reject the idea that al-Maqtari was linked to the 9/11 attacks.

On October 1, the judge ordered him released on $50,000 bail, but the INS appealed, expressing concerns that he was a danger to the community. The board, in response, asked for further proof of his danger. The INS was unable to come up with additional proof, and al-Maqtari was released.

Al-Maqtari's wife was also the subject of scrutiny. While he was in Memphis being questioned, she was tailed by guards on the base for weeks. Base officers "encouraged her to take an honorable discharge," which she ultimately did. We see in this example that the seizure is part of a broader investigation into events and individuals, carried out in this case evidently with minimal evidence that it is likely to be fruitful. Again, we must caution that we don't know what the real evidence is because of the secret way in which the government's case is carried out.

So how many individuals were ultimately arrested? The last complete tally by the Justice Department, in November 2001, indicated that 1,182 people had been picked up in the post-9/11 sweeps (Lawyers Committee for Human Rights, 2003), after which the Department announced it would no longer maintain tallies. Of these, 752 were held on immigration charges and

129 on criminal charges. By June 2002 the number had dropped to 147, with 74 for immigration problems and 73 for criminal charges. Similar but different numbers were provided by the Assistant Attorney General—81 on immigration charges and 76 on criminal charges, a discrepancy raising concerns about overall accuracy. To the public knowledge, no one involved in terrorism activity has been identified among the detainees.

On December 18, 2003, Justice Department Inspector General Glenn Fine released a report on the treatment of detainees at the Metropolitan Detention Center in Brooklyn, New York. That report stated that foreign nationals held after 9/11 were subjected to physical and verbal abuse by guards. The report noted that officers had "slammed and bounced detainees against the wall, twisted their arms and hands in painful ways, stepped on their leg restraint chains, and punished them by keeping restrained for long periods of time." Meetings between detainees and lawyers were improperly tape-recorded because they were audio- as well as videotaped—audiotaping is against the law—and strip searches were used as punishment. Some detainees were kept for months in cells that were illuminated for 24 hours a day. Most troubling was an American t-shirt, hung on a wall in the prisoner receiving area, with the slogan "These colors don't run." Four officers reported that it was covered with blood stains, including "some that appeared to have come from detainees being slammed into the wall" (Eggen, 2003:A01).

Fine's investigators had interviewed facility officials who denied wrongdoing, and claimed that tapes of the incidents no longer existed because they were routinely destroyed. However, 300 videotapes were found that substantiated the accusations recorded in the report (Eggen, 2003). It should be noted that none of these detainees were ultimately charged any counterterrorism activities or with involvement in 9/11.

Alien Absconder Apprehension Initiative

One of the prongs of the counter-terrorism effort is called the Alien Absconder Apprehension Initiative. The initiative can be traced to January 8, 2002, when, according to the Migration Policy Institute:

> In an effort to identify and remove them from the U.S., the Department of Justice adds to the National Crime Information Center database the names of approximately 6,000 men who have ignored deportation or removal orders, all of them originally from countries believed to be harboring al-Qaeda members. The Department uses country, age, and gender criteria to track down the "absconders."

On January 25, 2002, a memo was circulated from Deputy Attorney General Larry Thompson of the Justice Department to anti-terrorism officials with instructions to apprehend and interrogate illegal Middle-Eastern immigrants residing in the U.S. in violation of deportation orders. This memo was in reference to the "Alien Absconder Initiative," focused specifically on 6,000 immigrants believed to be from Al Qaeda strongholds (National Immigration Law Center, 2002).

To search for the absconders, apprehension teams were assembled of agents from the FBI, from the U.S. Marshals Service, and from the INS. According to Eggen (2002), agents were instructed to find methods of detaining some suspects for criminal charges rather than simply expelling them as historically practiced.

By July 12, 2002, the INS had stated that 758 persons had been arrested as part of the Absconder Apprehension Initiative (Migration Policy Institute, 2003). The initiative differed from the voluntary interview program (discussed in Chapter 7) in that it was directed at persons who violated the law, either by failing to comply with a deportation order or by committing an illegal act. Those apprehended were to be "afforded all standard procedural rights and constitutional protections." Investigators were encouraged to "feel free to use all appropriate means of encouraging absconders to cooperate, including reference to any reward money that is being offered and reference to the availability of an S-visa." Investigators were cautioned not to promise that inducements would be forthcoming in particular cases (National Immigration Law Center, 2002).

One complaint aimed at the Alien Absconder Initiative was in the selective targeting of Middle-Easterners. There were about 314, 000 total absconders in the U.S. in 2002, most of them from Latin America. The DOJ described the selective focus on the 6,000 as a prioritization appropriate for current concerns over terrorism. They were deemed "priority absconders" who might "have information that could assist our campaign against terrorism" (National Immigration Law Center, 2002). Critics charged that the initiative was a further example of racial profiling. The initiative was seen as a justification for a broad police sweep against people, the vast majority of whom had committed minor visa infractions that had been historically viewed as not serious, particularly the charge of overstaying one's visa (Porter & Randall, 2002). Whether the prioritization for the war on terrorism was justified or not, there was no debate that particular ethnic and national groups were being targeted for arrest under the Initiative. Indeed, precisely that was the purpose of the initiative.

The sweeps were not simply for the purpose of arresting and removing illegal aliens. Under the war on terrorism, the sweeps were intended to create an intelligence opportunity through interrogation of Middle-Easterners arrested. In turn, investigators could hold out the "carrot" of the S-visa to acquire information, and the "stick" of deportation or prison for those who do not comply. The process capitalizes on coercive interrogation, conducted wholly beyond relief in American courts. In the exchange between Angela Davis and Rodney Smolla reported in Chapter 2, Davis argued that the program is used against people who are what she called "hard-working people" who carry out the menial jobs in American society, and who have not been traditionally targeted by the immigration authorities because the infractions they are charged with are trivial. Others have countered that "sleeper-cells"—secret and inactive terrorist cells that could become active upon the receipt of an order—had led to 9/11 and this sort of tool was necessary to root them out. The S-visa is discussed further in the next section.

The S-Visa

The S-visa was signed into law by President Bush on October 1, 2002. The purpose of the bill was to provide aliens who had information to contribute to anti-terrorist efforts the opportunity to remain in the United States. According to the Migration Policy Institute (2003), the legislation "amends INA § 214(k) to provide permanent authority for the admission of "S" non-immigrants (S. 1424). Such visas are issued to aliens who possess and will supply information regarding terrorist organizations to U.S. law enforcement officials."

On November 29, 2001, Attorney General Ashcroft formally announced the use of S-visas for people who provide the government with information regarding terrorist activity. Even illegal immigrants could avoid deportation if they provided tips to federal investigators about terrorists (*St. Petersburg Times*, 2001). He stated that "People who have the courage to make the right choice deserve to be welcomed as guests into our country and perhaps one day to become citizens." The initiative had been around since 1994, and was a product of the Clinton presidency. It was created under the Violent Crime Reduction Act of 1994, and was set to expire on September 12, 2001. The Attorney General renamed the initiative the "Responsible Cooperators Program."

Immigrants have 12 different kinds of visas they can apply for, one of which is an S-visa. There are two kinds of S-visas. To obtain the S-5 visa, a person must have reliable information about a crime or pending crime and be willing to share that information with law enforcement officials or testify in court. The S-6 visa places the same requirements, but the information must be for an "important aspect of a terrorist organization or plot." The petitioner for an S-visa of either kind is a law enforcement agency, and the application is titled the Inter-agency Alien Witness and Informant Record.

The S-visa holders must report every three months to the Attorney General regarding their whereabouts and activities. They cannot have committed a felony (any crime punishable by more than one year in prison), agree not to contest a deportation order, and agree to any other provisions stated by the Attorney General. If they "substantially contribute" to a successful investigation or prosecution of a crime, or if they substantially contribute to the prevention of an act of terrorism, they are eligible to have their status adjusted to full citizenship (Immigration.com, 2003).

The S-visa plays an important role in the war on terror. When immigrants or other aliens are contacted or seized through the voluntary interview program or the Alien Absconder Initiative, investigators are instructed to discuss the availability of S-visas with potential informants (National Immigration Law Center, 2001:2002). In the voluntary interview program, U.S. attorneys were instructed in the proper form of interrogations, including the offer of an S-visa if information was substantially useful to the prevention of a terrorist attack. The S-visa offer was more enticing when linked to the Alien Absconder Initiative: Individuals with pertinent information could avoid arrest and imprisonment as well as deportation, and receive the prize jewel the U.S. has to offer to immigrants if their information was good enough—U.S. citizenship.

Critics have not been kind to the S-visa. They refer to it as the "snitch visa." The criticism is that it will induce people who have nothing to lose to fabricate stories for prosecutors in order to stay in the U.S. That informants have fabricated terrorist stories in order to avoid prosecution has been established. For example, the Code Orange alert issued on December 29, 2002, for five suspected terrorists was in response to fabricated information. Michael Hamdani, an accused immigrant in custody in Canada, had provided the information in order to avoid deportation to the U.S. (Mintz, 2003). The newspaper *Iran Today* stated, "This offer reminds us somewhat of the communist era under Stalin where citizens spied on their neighbors . . . In the end, everyone was a suspect of a totalitarian government . . ." (Akbarpour, 2001). The editorial expressed concern that individuals who had no training or knowledge about how to recognize terrorism were encouraged to spy on their neighbors.

Also of concern was the impact of the tips program on Arab-American communities. One Arab-American described the Arab-American community in Dearborn, Michigan, as "like being in a dark lake. You don't see the 'gators, but they're down there" (Akbarpour, 2001).

Individuals have used the government's willingness to take tips as an opportunity to settle old scores as well. In a case reported by the *Detroit Free Press* (2002), one informant agreed to help a divorced friend get even with his estranged wife by telling the FBI that she and her brother were smuggling weapons and making death threats. In 2003, the *New York Times* reported several cases of false terrorism tips (Moss, 2003). Three of these are briefly summarized below:

1. Shortly after the 9/11 attacks, nine men were arrested, on a tip, shackled, "paraded in front of a newspaper reporter and jailed for a week." The tip was false. However, four of the men were placed on the national crime registry, preventing them from flying, finding work, and renting apartments. After 19 months, a federal judge ordered that the men's names be removed from all federal crime records.

2. A student from Morocco was detained after being accused of plotting terrorism by his former wife. She was sentenced to

a year in prison for making a false statement, but he was charged with immigration violations. He contested that he violated the terms of his visa because he was under arrest for the false charges.

3.   A tipster accused a Michigan trucker, Mr. Alajji, of plotting a bomb attack. His rig was searched and friends and associates were interviewed. He was finally charged with Social Security fraud and, based on the tip and other information, agents sought to prevent bail. However, a "skeptical judge" asked investigators to talk to the tipster, which they had not done. When they did so, the tipster recanted. However, prosecutors decided to keep the case open anyway. Fearing for his safety in the U.S., Mr., Alajji returned to his home in Yemen.

At least in the early days of its inception, the "Responsible Cooperators Program" was not used extensively. In its first two months, no immigrant took advantage of it. Some observed that the program was founded on the notion that there were "large numbers of people with useful information, particularly people from the Middle East, and that they are withholding that information," commented a spokesman for the Arab Anti-Discrimination Committee. He suggested that anyone who actually knew about terrorist activity would not be swayed by the offer of possible citizenship (Cantlupe, 2002).

Prison Communications of Detainees Associated with Terrorism

On October 31, 2001, the Bureau of Prisons published an interim rule titled "Prevention of Acts of Violence and Terrorism" (Department of Justice, 2001). The interim rule authorized "the agency to monitor the attorney-client mail or communications of inmates or detainees in federal custody, in cases where the attorney general has certified that reasonable suspicion exists that an inmate may use such communications to further or facilitate acts of violence or terrorism" (Migration Policy Institute, 2003). Controversial in the popular press for a brief period after publication, it quickly fell out of public review. However, it effected fundamental and far-reaching changes in a variety of First Amendment issues related to prison communications.

The interim rule amended existing special administrative measures (interim rule, 61 FR 25120) with respect to inmates:

> where, based on information provided by senior intelligence or law enforcement officials, the Bureau of Prisons determines it to be necessary to prevent the dissemination either of classified information that could endanger the national security or other information that could lead to acts of violence and terrorism (The Federalist Society, 2001).

The interim rule is controversial because it provides for the monitoring of communications between an inmate and his or her attorney if ordered by the Attorney General. The monitoring is permitted if there is "reasonable suspicion" that the communication with an attorney will facilitate acts of terrorism, and that the monitoring will reasonably deter those acts.

Proponents of the rule note that it provides for oversight of the communications. First, a special "privilege team" monitors the inmate's communications with regard to "established firewall procedures." The rule is seen as minimally intrusive, affecting only 16 out of 158,000 inmates, and these inmates are themselves informed in writing of the monitoring procedure. Moreover, the context for the rule is the "war on terrorism," in which the individuals so subjected are viewed as unlawful belligerents and so, for this small group of individuals, national security trumps civil liberty concerns (The Federalist Society, 2001).

Finally, the executive branch, through the authority of the Attorney General, takes the position that particular procedures are needed to counter the threat created by potential terrorist acts; that we must first act to protect the country. As Attorney General Ashcroft noted, "We cannot wait for terrorists to strike to begin investigations and to take action. The death tolls are too high, the consequences too great. We must prevent first—we must prosecute second" (The Federalist Society, 2001).

Critics of this act focus on attorney-client privilege. They challenge that, "If a lawyer is to work effectively on behalf of his or her client, it is essential that the lawyer and the client be able to communicate candidly, without fear that agents of the government are listening" (Boston Bar Association, 2001). The basis for candid communication stems from the Sixth Amendment, which guarantees right to counsel.

Moreover, decisions about attorney-client privilege are shifted from the courts to those carrying out any monitoring and who are members of the executive branch of government. Like many of the changes in procedure in the war on terrorism, decisions about the treatment of prisoners are relocated out of the judicial arena and into the executive arena, thus bypassing the body of due process and civil rights law that the judicial branch of government affords. Hirshon, the President of the American Bar Association, summarizes this concern as follows:

> If the government has probable cause to believe criminal activity is occurring or is about to occur, it can ask a judge to approve the type of monitoring proposed by these regulations. But prior judicial approval and the establishment of probable cause—the standard embodied in the Fourth Amendment—and not "reasonable suspicion," are required if the government's surveillance is to be consistent with the Constitution and is to avoid abrogating the rights of innocent people (American Bar Association, 2001).

The concern here is twofold. First, the concern focuses on the constitutional division of authority. The rule relocates important decisions about information out of the judicial branch and into the executive. What if, during the course of a terrorist investigation, information about criminal activity is uncovered? The rule seems to suggest that such criminal activity could be turned over to investigators. This is clearly inconsistent with the Sixth Amendment right to counsel, unless one accepts the position that right to counsel is trumped not only by concerns over terrorism, but by criminal activity, a position that wholly circumvents the Sixth Amendment. It should be noted that the interim rule is not only directed at terrorism but at "acts of violence" as well.

Secondly, there is a suspicion that the executive is scornful of due process and is using the war against terrorism as a pretext to diminish the reach of due process in all forms of investigation. The Boston Bar Association, in their position paper, for example, observed that "This (government monitoring) is as true as ever in today's environment—particularly when the highest ranking law enforcement officer in the nation expresses the view that the spirited defense of civil liberties is a 'tactic that aids terrorists . . . erodes our national unity . . . diminishes our resolve (and) gives ammunition to America's enemies . . .'."

Conclusion

The impact of 9/11 on aliens, particularly those from Muslim countries, has been far-reaching. Many individuals were caught up in the various sweeps discussed in this chapter. Given the changes to immigration law, they were unable to extricate themselves through appeals to American courts. Some were treated violently and later released without charges. Some were deported. Some still languish in jails. Of those caught, none were ultimately linked to 9/11 or to terrorist acts directed against the United States. In view of this, one should ask whether any of the post-9/11 programs reviewed in this chapter have contributed to safety from terrorism. One might argue that the pervasive pressures from these programs has had a deterrent effect, keeping potential terrorists from acting because of unrelenting justice system activity. On the other hand, of all those caught up in the various programs, none has been linked to terrorism even after exhaustive background checks. These individuals are all examples of false positives, individuals who by some criteria look like potential terrorists but are not. Hence, with regard to these individuals, counter-terrorism has been at best misplaced, a case of mis-spent resources, and at worst has created a hostility toward America that previously was not present. Put bluntly, the primary outcome of the sweeps may have been to create enemies within where we previously had friends.

The sweeps picked up many individuals who, though not terrorists, were in the country illegally and/or had committed violations of the law. In this sense, post-9/11 sweeps have carried out the principle goals of the 1996 Immigration Act, whose purpose was to more effectively prohibit the entry of illegal aliens and to locate and to remove them when found. However, this is a different goal than counter-terrorism, and one cannot conclude from it that counter-terrorism purposes were served.

CHAPTER 7

Middle-Eastern Immigrants in the U.S. Since 9/11: Registration and Surveillance

This chapter continues the themes initiated in the previous chapter. Chapter 6 covered the aspects of the impact of 9/11 on Middle-Eastern immigrants bearing directly on interrogation and seizure. This chapter looks at other changes in the law that have dramatically affected the lives of Middle-Eastern immigrants, those changes that have to do with registration and surveillance.

The war on terrorism encompasses many different programs. Those covered in this chapter include the National Security Entry-Exit Registration System (NSEERS), the Enhanced Border Security and Visa Entry Program, the crackdown on student visas, and the voluntary interview program. A variety of decisions regarding surveillance were also made by the government. These programs, their reach into the lives of immigrants, and the response of local municipal governments and police departments are discussed.

NSEERS and the Registration of Aliens

The registration of aliens has been a controversial part of the war on terror. The discussion below lists the dateline of decisions regarding registration, as compiled by the Migration Policy Institute (2003), and discusses controversies associated with the act.

June 5, 2002:   Attorney General Ashcroft announces a new entry-exit system that will require certain non-immigrants who are deemed to be a national security risk to register and submit fingerprints and photographs upon their arrival in the U.S.; to report to INS field offices within 30 days, then annually;

after arrival to re-register; and to notify an INS agent of their departure, with possible criminal prosecution for those who fail to comply.

August 12, 2002:   Attorney General Ashcroft issues a final rule requiring certain non-citizens to register (fingerprints and photographs and other information) upon entering the U.S., at 30 days after entry, at one-year intervals thereafter, and at exit, which must be at designated exit points.

September 11, 2002:   The Department of Justice implements the National Security Entry-Exit Registration System (NSEERS), which authorizes the INS to keep track of the arrival and departure of non-immigrants to the U.S. who were born in Iran, Iraq, Libya, Sudan, or Syria and who may be citizens of those countries. NSEERS requires that these individuals be photographed and fingerprinted and have their entry into and exit from the U.S. verified.

October 30, 2002:   The Canadian Department of Foreign Affairs and International Trade issues a travel advisory warning Canadian citizens born in Syria, Sudan, Libya, Iraq, or Iran to reconsider any travel to the United States because of the implementation of the NSEERS program.

November 6, 2002:   INS expands NSEERS by issuing a notice requiring male nationals and citizens of Iran, Iraq, Libya, Sudan, and Syria ages 16 and older who were admitted to the U.S. on or before September 10, 2002, (and who will remain in the U.S. until at least December 16, 2002) to appear before, register with, and provide requested information to the INS by December 16, 2002. Failure to report to an INS office for fingerprinting, a photo, and an interview will result in deportation. Among those excluded from the requirement are permanent residents and asylum applicants who applied for asylum by November 6, 2002, or who have been granted asylum.

November 7, 2002:   Attorney General Ashcroft announces that since the implementation of NSEERS on September 11, 2002, the INS has fingerprinted and registered more than 14,000 visitors to the U.S. and arrested 179. According to INS records, the INS has been averaging more than 70 fingerprint "hits" a week nationwide.

December 16, 2002:   The INS adds certain non-immigrant males 16 years or older from Saudi Arabia and Pakistan to its list of those subject to NSEERS special registration requirements.

December 19, 2002:   Thousands of Iranian Americans demonstrate against the arrest of hundreds of Middle-Eastern immigrants in the southern California area who voluntarily registered with the federal government under the NSEERS special registration program.

December 24, 2002:   The American-Arab Anti-Discrimination Committee, the Alliance of Iranian Americans, the Council on American-Islamic Relations, and the National Council of Pakistani Americans launch a class action lawsuit against Attorney General Ashcroft and federal immigration officers over the detention of hundreds of Muslim men.

January 16, 2003:   U.S. officials announce that they have detained nearly 1,200 men during the NSEERS special registration program for foreign visitors from 20 mostly Middle Eastern nations. The statistics were released as the government added five countries—Bangladesh, Egypt, Indonesia, Jordan, and Kuwait—to the list of 20 whose male citizens, 16 and older, must register with the INS and be fingerprinted. INS also states that those who have missed earlier deadlines to register will get another chance to do so without fear of penalty.

February 13, 2003.   The House and Senate approve a $397.4 billion appropriations bill, restoring the $362 million for the INS' special registration program NSEERS, on the condition that the INS provide a detailed explanation by March 1, 2003, of the program's origins, its efficacy, and the reasons for a large number of resulting detentions. The bill also blocks funding for research on the Pentagon project called Total Information Awareness, citing worries that the project would invade Americans' privacy (Migration Policy Institute, 2003).

January 5, 2004:   NSEERS ended and was replaced by US-VISIT, an extensive tracking program for all foreigners (see surveillance, next section).

On September 11, 2002, the National Security Entry-Exit Registration System (NSEERS) was implemented by the Department of Justice. According to the Justice Department, NSEERS was designed as the first step toward a "comprehensive entry-exit system" applicable to all foreigners (www.usembassy.si, 2003). The system was developed in response to the USA PATRIOT Act, which required that the Justice Department develop an entry-exit system to track aliens in a way that afforded increased protection to the United States. NSEERS has three characteristics:

1.   Fingerprinting at the borders is upgraded to make use of state-of-the-art imaging systems. Fingerprints are run against a known terrorist data-file, from a felons file, and from unknown fingerprints collected from training camps and elsewhere.

2. Periodic registration and confirmation of visitors activities will be an ongoing process. NSEERS combines a European registration model with an ultranet model to provide "real-time" updating of files.

3. A system of exit controls will be instituted. Visitors who are enrolled in NSEERS must complete a departure check when they leave the country. This allows the INS to immediately know if a high-risk alien overstays his or her visa.

NSEERS, though designed to be comprehensively used, focused primarily on individuals from states that the government considered as sponsors of terrorism. In its first round of registrations, NSEERS required registration of individuals from Iran, Iraq, Lybia, Sudan, and Syria, as well as "aliens from other countries who warrant extra scrutiny" (Department of Justice, 2002). Aliens could be identified by either the State Department or by INS agents at the port of entry (www.usembassy.si, 2002). Individuals so identified were required to (1) register upon arrival to and departure from the U.S., (2) be interviewed by the INS if remaining in the U.S. for more than 30 days and/or over one year, and (3) notify the INS within 10 days of any changes regarding place of residence, employment, or educational institution.

The first "special registration" was carried out on December 16, 2002, focusing on the terror countries and requiring registration by all males 16 and older. The bureaucratic formality of additional registration, for many Muslims, went badly in some areas. For several hundred, the formality turned into a narrative of mass arrest. In Southern California, an estimated 500-700 individuals were arrested when they showed up. In Los Angeles, nearly 1/4 of those who sought to register were arrested (Pugliese, 2002).

Most of those arrested were Iranian, many of whom lived there in exile from the 1979 Islamic Revolution. The INS claimed that those arrested were guilty of criminal acts or visa violations. Advocates of NSEERS have noted that a detainee is not necessarily arrested, and that of those arrested, a number were felons who were fugitives from justice. Critics countered that active terrorists and criminals were unlikely to take part in a registration program (BBC News, 2002a). Many of those who were arrested had already become aware of green card violations and had made appointments to address their problems.

The arrests sparked mass demonstrations on behalf of those arrested. The following story describes the narrative of one arrest:

> One attorney, who said he saw a 16-year old boy pulled from the arms of his crying mother, called it madness to believe the registration requirements would catch terrorists. 'His mother is 6½ months pregnant. They told the mother he is never going to come home—she is losing her mind,' said attorney Soheila Jonoubi, who spent Wednesday amid the chaos of the downtown INS office attempting to determine the status of her clients. Jonoubi

said the mother has permanent residence status and that her husband, the boy's stepfather, is a U.S. citizen. The teenager came to the country in July on a student visa and was on track to gain permanent residence, the lawyer said (Pugliese, 2002).

In other areas, NSEERS registrations went smoothly. The *Salt Lake Tribune*, in an investigation of registration at the INS office in Murray, found that no one had been detained (Sullivan, 2003). This was attributed to the population of Muslims in the state, most of whom are legal citizens. Only students were likely to face problems at that office, and most of these stemmed from a lack of awareness about the NSEERS program.

As of March, 2003, 110,534 individuals from 149 countries had registered in all components of NSEERS. Of these, 49,712 were port of entry registrants. According to the Attorney General, eight suspects were detained, including one individual suspected of Al Qaeda membership. The special registration program that focused specifically on in-country individuals from "terrorist" states had registered an estimated 60,822 men (Jachimowicz & McKay, 2003).

The Migration Information Source identified 6 public criticisms of the NSEERS program.

1. The special registration program uses nationality as a basis for registration, implicitly assuming that all citizens of particular states are suspects of terrorism. (It should be noted that several of these states have raised objections).

2. The INS conducted virtually no outreach to Muslim communities about the registration initiative.

3. Immigration officials were inadequately prepared and staffed for the registration procedures.

4. The foreign visitor database was flawed. Many individuals were detained on violations even though their visa applications were pending.

5. The program diverted resources from other more effective INS programs.

6. The program is no more than a public relations effort to placate American citizens, instituted without evidence of overall effectiveness. Critics have stated that the few individuals picked up for felony violations would have been picked up in any case, and thus there is no evidence that any potential terrorist has been detained (Jachimowicz & McKay, 2003).

The controversies surrounding NSEERS prompted a congressional investigation into the program. The omnibus bill passed by the Senate suspended funding for the program (Carroll, 2003). A subsequent House-Senate Conference meeting reinstated the funding, but also initiated an inquiry into the program. The Department of Justice was instructed to submit all materials pertaining to the creation, assessment of scope and effectiveness, and future plans of the NSEERS program. The DOJ also was asked to explain why individuals with pending status-adjustment visas were detained. The role of the FBI and the use of information gathered are also subjects of the inquiry (National Iranian American Council, 2003).

That the ICE (former INS) uses the special registration of in-country individuals as an opportunity to detain and sometimes arrest suspects reveals contradictions in policy regarding ICE enforcement and tracking. As an enforcement tool, the ICE was able to take advantage of the registration process to assess the legality of their status and arrest those who had visa problems or were otherwise in violation of the law. However, this tended to backfire, lowering likelihood of registration.

The danger in using NSEERS for seizure and detention was that it undercut trust in the purposes of the government, added a dimension of fear in the group being registered, and ultimately was likely to decrease registration effectiveness because of no-shows. If individuals fear that the government is using the special registration as a pretext to find reasons for exporting Muslims, it is likely to scare off those who are not particularly dangerous—anyone who may worry their "illegal" summer job with McDonald's was discovered by the government, for example. The result of this might be an increasingly large number of immigrants who elect to remain illegally because they fear that their efforts to renew their legal status will result in seizure and deportation.

The policy of enforcement of the ICE in some of these incidents carries backfiring dangers similar to urban police sweeps through dangerous areas in the early 1970s. These sweeps had the short term effect of lowering serious crime but backfired over the long term because they alienated local communities and led to the breakdown of communications between local communities and the police. This breakdown complicated the ability of the police to obtain victim and witness testimony, core elements of evidence essential for the functioning of the criminal justice system. Similarly, the long term effects of ICE seizures during the NSEERS registrations could be a loss in connections to the Muslim Community and a loss in ICE effectiveness in immigration registration.

On December 1, 2003, the Bush administration announced that it was ending the NSEERS special registration program. According to Asa Hutchinson, its director, the NSEERS program cast too wide a net. Of the 83,519 individuals who came forward voluntarily, about 17 percent, or 13,799, were placed into deportation proceedings. Most were for overstaying a visa (Alonso-Salvidar, 2003). According to the government, only 23 remained in custody in December, 2003.

Future programs, Hutchinson observed, needed to focus on individuals, not categories of people. The NSEERS program was replaced by a new system aimed at tracking visitors from overseas. Called US-VISIT, it required foreigners who enter the U.S. on tourist, student, or business visas to be digitally photographed and fingerprinted, and some foreigners may undergo extensive interviews.

Surveillance

In Chapter 4, contemporary trends in surveillance were discussed extensively. In the section below, surveillance decisions and practices specifically related to 9/11 are presented. These decisions generally show two trends: (1) the expansion of existing federal databases to include information on aliens, and (2) expanded tracking of U.S. persons to include noncriminal activity.

December 6, 2001:   INS Commissioner James Ziglar announces that his agency is providing the FBI with the names of more than 300,000 aliens still in the U.S. despite prior deportation or removal orders, for inclusion in the FBI's National Crime Information Center database.

April 11, 2002:   Attorney General Ashcroft orders that the names of thousands of "known or suspected" terrorists be listed in the government's three major law enforcement databases, including one used by police officers nationwide when making routine arrests or traffic stops.

May 17, 2002:   The Foreign Intelligence Surveillance Court issues an order refusing to give the Department of Justice broad new powers, saying the government has misused the law and misled the court dozens of times.

July 15, 2002:   Department of Justice Web site announces a surveillance pilot program, to be launched August, 2002, whereby U.S. citizens can act as informants to report "suspicious activity."

November 18, 2002:   The Foreign Intelligence Surveillance Court of Review rules that the USA PATRIOT Act gives the Department of Justice broad authority to conduct wiretaps and other surveillance on terrorism suspects in the U.S., thereby overturning the May 17, 2002, Foreign Intelligence Surveillance Court order.

January 3, 2003:   INS announces a proposal that will require all airline and ship travelers, including U.S. citizens, to provide personal information such as name, date of birth, citizenship, and passport number when arriving in or departing from the United States. The information will be conveyed to the INS before the traveler arrives in the United States or departs from it, to be matched against security databases. The measure is intended to help detect potential terrorists or criminals and to enhance the government's ability to track whether visitors to the United States leave as planned (Migration Policy Institute, 2003).

January 5, 2004:	US-VISIT, an extensive tracking program, is established.
May 28, 2004:	US-VISIT contract awarded to ACCENTURE. Controversy erupts over the awarding of an $18 million contract to the company because of its offshore, tax-sheltered location.

The above decisions reveal a variety of surveillance strategies aimed at tracking aliens. Surveillance practices have expanded to include the listing of deportable aliens in the FBI's data-base, the use of U.S. citizens to act as eyes for the government in efforts to identify "suspicious activity," the expansion of the authority of the FISA court, and the tracking of and acquiring of detailed information about U.S. individuals departing or entering the United States. Importantly, many of these elements of surveillance are not limited to aliens, but apply equally to U.S. citizens.

These elements of surveillance reveal a general across-the-board expansion of surveillant strategies applied to all U.S. people, citizens, immigrants, and visitors alike. Many of these elements are being contested in the courts. It is likely that the shape and practice of surveillance will be contested for many years to come.

Border Security

One of the significant areas of concern following the 9/11 attacks was the security of the U.S. borders. Border concerns over security took two forms: the tightening of the screening and tracking of visa applicants to the U.S., and the expansion of the ability of the ICE to carry out border control activity. This concern led to the enactment of the Enhanced Border Security and Visa Entry Program of 2002. Important dates leading to the establishment of this program, and characteristics of it, are presented below.

February 25, 2002:	Department of Justice and Department of Defense (DOD) enter into a cooperative arrangement that allows the DOD to assist the INS on the northern and southern borders for up to six months.
April 12, 2002:	INS issues a proposed regulation establishing a presumptive limitation on visitors to the U.S. of 30 days, or a "fair and reasonable period" to accomplish the purpose of the visit. The regulation also prohibits a change of status from visitor to student, unless the student intent is declared at the time of initial entry.
May 8, 2002:	House of Representatives passes the "Enhanced Border Security and Visa Entry Reform Act of 2001," clearing the way for President Bush's signature. As approved by Congress, the bill would increase funding for INS staffing and infrastruc-

ture, and for State Department consular functions. It would also require information sharing between intelligence agencies and the INS/State Department.

May 14, 2002: President Bush signs into law the "Enhanced Border Security and Visa Entry Reform Act" (H.R. 3525).

February 20, 2003: Charles Andrew, the outgoing director of the Alabama Department of Public Safety, and U.S. Senator Jeff Sessions announce that Alabama is working on an agreement with the INS and the Department of Justice to provide training for state troopers that will allow them to arrest illegal aliens (Migration Policy Institute, 2003).

June 25, 2004: The DHS announced the first civilian use of unmanned aerial vehicles (UAVs). Two UAVs will be used to curb illegal activities in the Tucson, Arizona sector. Flights will be monitored by the border patrol.

On May 14, 2002, President Bush signed into law the Enhanced Border Security and Visa Entry Program. This program had many different components, including expanding the technology, real-time database information on visas at ports of entry into the U.S., INS training, tightening control of foreign students, and barring nationals from the seven countries that are listed as state sponsors of terrorism. Characteristics of the program are:

1. It authorized the hiring of additional Immigration and Naturalization Service inspectors and associated personnel. The allocation of funds for Department of State consular functions related to the review of visa applications was also authorized.

2. Security improvements at borders were approved. This included technology to facilitate the flow of commerce and persons at the point of entry.

3. INS was funded to fully integrate all databases and data systems. The fully integrated data system was to become a component of an electronic data system that accessed federal law enforcement agencies and the intelligence community to determine the admissibility and deportability of an alien and whether to grant a visa.

4. The development of machine readable, tamper resistant visas and other travel documents that used biometric identifiers. Also, installation at all U.S. ports of entry of equipment that allowed biometric comparison and authentication of all U.S. visas and entry documents of aliens.

5. For all commercial aircraft and vessels transporting people to U.S. seaports from any place outside the U.S., an official must provide the INS with manifest information about each passenger, crew member, or other occupant. This is to be provided prior to arrival at the port (U.S. Maritime Administration, 2002).

Given the disputes surrounding the implementation of other elements of the counter-terror program, this act generated little controversy. The American Immigration Lawyers Association (AILA), for example, supported the passage of the act even while arguing that the NSEERS special registration program was deeply flawed and should be suspended (AILA.org, 2002). The program had broad bipartisan support. For instance, Senator Edward Kennedy, a frequent critic of the administration, was a Democratic co-sponsor of the program.

A few groups were concerned about the aspect of the bill which prohibited the entry of foreign nationals from states identified as sponsors of terrorism. These states were Cuba, Iran, Iraq, Lybia, Syria, Sudan, and the Democratic People's Republic of Korea. The Iranian Foreign Ministry spokesman described the visa restrictions as "backward." It was, he stated, "contrary to the spirit and interests of nations for expanding mutual scientific and cultural ties" (People's Daily Online, 2002).

The act has had an impact on cultural programs, though the extent of the impact is difficult to determine. For example, the Cuban artist Salvador Gonzalez was denied entry into the U.S. for an October 11, 2002, premiere of a documentary film about his life. Similarly, the Iranian director Abbas Kiarostami was denied entry to attend the screening of the film "10" at the 40th New York Film Festival. Twenty-two Cuban artists were denied visas to attend the Latin Grammy Awards in Los Angeles in 2002 (Hernandez, Brooks & Mitchell, 2002). And in 2004, Cuban musicians invited to the Grammy Awards were again denied U.S. visas. Among those denied was singer Ibrahim Ferrer, a multiple grammy award winner of the Buena Vista Social Club. Since 2001, when the laws over visas were toughened, no Cubans have been permitted to attend the Grammys (Martin, 2004). We see in the denial of visas to Cuban Grammy winners how the war on terrorism is subverted for other political aims, in this instance the long-standing foreign policy restrictions aimed at Cuba because of President Fidel Castro's leadership.

SEVIS: Tracking Foreign Students on Visas

One of the areas of greatest concern in domestic counter-terrorism has been the granting of student visas. Visas are commonly provided for aspiring students: In 1999, the INS granted approximately 560,000 F-student visas, and an additional 10,000 were given for short-term vocational training.

However, three of the 9/11 terrorists had entered the U.S. on student visas, prompting calls to reconsider the student visa system. Below is a review of legislation and discussion of issues related to foreign student visas.

April 8, 2002.   INS tightens visa rules for foreign students. Foreign students wishing to study in the U.S. must obtain a student visa before beginning classes and must have received the appropriate security checks before entering the country. Previously, foreign students were able to begin course-work while their visa applications were being processed. In addition INS proposes a 30-day limit to the time millions of tourists and business people may stay in the country.

April 12, 2002: INS issues an interim rule prohibiting a visitor from attending school while an application for a change to student status is pending.

May 16, 2002: Attorney General Ashcroft issues a proposed regulation that implements a new foreign student reporting system, SEVIS. The system will become voluntary on July 1, 2002, and mandatory for all covered schools on January 30, 2003. The new SEVIS system will require reporting of student enrollment, start date of the next term, failure to enroll, dropping below full courseload, disciplinary action by school, early graduation, etc.

September 11, 2002: The State Department's Bureau of Consular Affairs implements the Interim Student and Exchange Authentication System (ISEAS). The system dictates that no F, M, or J visas may be issued without sponsoring institutions providing consular officers overseas electronic notification that the visa applicant has been accepted to the educational institution or exchange visitor program. The interim procedures will remain in operation until the INS' foreign student reporting system (SEVIS) is fully operational, as required by the Enhanced Border Security and Visa Reform Act.

November 24, 2002: In reaction to FBI requests for information on foreign students, the American Association of Collegiate Registrars and Admissions Officers posts an advisory on its Web site to its 2,300 member institution, asserting that under the Family Educational Rights and Privacy Act of 1974, as amended, "a subpoena or court order MUST accompany" a request from the FBI for information involving a student's citizenship or there could be "significant legal consequences" (Migration Policy Institute, 2003).

August 1, 2003: Congress mandates this date as deadline for U.S. educational systems to certify participants and have information about current participants submitted.

June 28, 2004: GAO report claims that DHS is not monitoring or adequately reporting on key performance requirements for SEVIS.

September 1, 2004: Expected implementation of $100 processing fee for SEVIS applicants. Higher education officials resist, saying it is bureaucratic, burdensome on students, and unfairly lengthens visa application process.

Many people associate the student visa program with terrorist acts of 9/11. However, the vulnerability of the program as a terrorist entry point was identified and remedies were sought earlier. On February 26, 1993, a terrorist attack on the World Trade Center resulted in six deaths and more than 1,000 injuries. A Jordanian national, Eyad Ismoil, carried out the attack. He had entered the U.S. in 1989 on a student visa and attended Wichita State University in Kansas. He attended school for three months and dropped out (Pinsker, 2003). In response to the trade center bombing, the Congress in 1996 passed a law requiring electronic tracking of foreign students in the U.S. However, as Pinkster observed, the "system all but fell through the cracks until the events of September 11" (Pinkster, 2003:1).

After 9/11, an electronic tracking system, titled Student and Exchange Visitor Program (SEVIS) was implemented for all educational systems that accepted foreign students. SEVIS is a school-based registration program. Students who participate are fingerprinted. Schools are to report whether students drop out, fall below the required full time workload, graduate early, or face disciplinary problems (Sinha, 2003). Information is also kept on addresses, and the specific courses students are taking.

Traditionally, in order to acquire a visa, foreign students had to apply to a U.S. institution and be admitted. The admission letter enabled the person to go to a U.S. consulate and receive an F-student visa. When students arrived at U.S. ports of entry, the INS notified the school that the person had arrived. If the student failed to enroll, the school was in turn supposed to notify the INS, which could remove the student for violating the terms of the visa (Martin & Martin, 2001). However, there was little "watchdog" activity in schools and foreign students were not tracked. For many people, 9/11 revealed the inadequacies of the tracking system. As Diane Feinstein, congresswoman from California observed, "We've got a deeply flawed system and we've got to have accountability" (Norris, 2001).

Tracking has been complicated by increases in the demand for student visas in recent years. In 1970 there were only about 50,000 foreign students in the U.S. on F-visas; by 2000, 284,000 applied and received F-visas. Schools are required to register by February 15, 2003, in order to enroll foreign students. Some schools, however, expressed reservations about the new system. One assistant director noted that the program only provided cursory statistics; one could be a full time student and still be engaged in terrorist activities. Summary statistics cannot tell immigration authorities "who is good and who is bad" (Sinha, 2003:3). Many students expressed concern that the changed rules are complicated, and an error by them or by the school could result in deportation.

Other students were concerned about being stigmatized. One director of international students stated that the program lent itself to racial profiling. Universities, she observed, were supposed to make students feel welcome; they should not be required to participate in a system that found them guilty of visa related infractions without a presumption of innocence (Norris, 2001). Others noted that the new rules conveyed the image that foreign students were not welcome in the United States.

Their concerns may be justified. A student at the University of Colorado, Denver, was jailed when he was one hour shy of a full-time load, 12 credits. Yet he had been approved by the University to drop the class. Other Middle-Eastern students were jailed up to 48 hours and required to post a $5,000 bond. None of the students were suspected of any other offenses (Associated Press, 2002).

Voluntary Interviews

One of the many programs initiated by the Department of Justice was the voluntary interview program. Beginning November 13, 2001, voluntary interviews of 5,000 men would be undertaken by several groups, including federal prosecutors and local police. Most of the men interviewed were from Middle-Eastern countries (National Immigration Law Center, 2001). The program is coordinated through the anti-terrorism task forces located in each of the U.S. attorney districts. The purpose of the program was to identify and disrupt potential terrorist threats.

November, 2001:   Deputy Attorney Larry Thompson issues guidelines for "voluntary" interviews of up to 5,000 aliens from countries suspected of harboring large numbers of terrorists.

November 23, 2001: INS issues a memo stating that officers conducting the so-called "voluntary" interviews of aliens "may discover information which leads them to suspect that specific aliens on the list are unlawfully present or in violation of their immigration status." The memo directs INS to provide agents to respond to requests from state and local officers involved in the interviews.

November 26, 2001: U.S. attorneys in Detroit issue a letter to potential interviewees stating that the meetings are voluntary, but that "we need to hear from you by December 4."

March 19, 2002:   Department of Justice announces interviews with 3,000 more Arabs and Muslims in the U.S. as visitors or students.

November 21, 2002: The FBI's Washington, D.C., field office begins voluntary interviews of young Arabs, Muslims, and Arab-Americans in the Washington, D.C., metropolitan area.

March 24, 2003:   FBI officials announce that the FBI has interviewed more than 5,000 Iraqis who live in the United States and has detained around 30 on immigration charges since the war with Iraq began. The interviews are part of an FBI wartime effort to prevent possible reprisal acts of terrorism by Iraqi agents of Al Qaeda operatives. According to the FBI, the interviews were voluntary (Migration Policy Institute, 2003).

According to the Department of Justice, interviews carried out are wholly voluntary. They are aimed at acquiring information on such topics as (1) current foreign travel, (2) where they have visited, (3) knowledge of September 11 attacks, (4) what foreign countries they have visited, (5) any involvement in terrorism, and (6) knowledge of weapons.

The interviews were preceded by letters mailed out to individuals. One of the U.S. attorneys who wrote letters stated that he had no reason to believe that individuals interviewed had direct terrorist connections. In a letter, he stated that "... you may know something that may be helpful to our efforts. In fact, it is quite possible that you have some information that may seem irrelevant to you but which may help us piece together this puzzle" (Yancho, 2001).

The program began shortly after 9/11 and sought to acquire information on the terrorist attacks of 9/11. Individuals selected were advised that they came to the attention of federal agents because they came on a visa and "from a country where there are groups that support, advocated, or finance international terrorism." Individuals contacted are given a deadline for complying with the interview. The initial interviews of 5,000 foreign nationals were followed by an additional 3,000 interviews, and during the period of Iraq-U.S. hostilities were supplemented by interviews of Iraqi men.

The voluntary interview program came under scrutiny from a variety of sources. Concerns were raised that the program was little more than profiling, a controversial police practice that singles out individuals of interest based on racial or ethnic characteristics. The Council of American-Islamic Relations (CAIR) (2002) stated that "rounding up the usual suspects based on nothing more than race, religion or national origin is not an effective law enforcement technique and creates the perception of profiling." CAIR recommended that an advocate or member of the Muslim community be present at any questioning (Council on American-Islamic Relations, 2002).

The American Civil Liberties Union (www.aclutx.org, 2001) expressed similar concerns. They observed that many of the questions asked interviewees to report on their political behavior and the behavior of their families, and also to provide telephone numbers of all associates. Also, many of the questions were the sort of questions associated with a criminal investigation, yet because of the "voluntariness" of the program suspects were not informed of their legal rights. This was troublesome to critics of the program, because individuals were not told that they could have a lawyer present or decline to answer questions, and the government has not demonstrated any reasonable evidence or specific information that the people to be interviewed are related to the 9/11 terrorist incidents. Moreover, although the interviews were themselves voluntary in principle, they may be experienced as coercive by those interviewed. And, according to the ACLU, the Justice Department stated that anyone found in violation of immigration laws during the interview could be jailed without bond. The interviews were more realistically described as "coercive interrogations based on racial and ethnic profiling" (www.aclutx.org, 2).

Municipal Resistance to Interviews

One of the controversial issues is the recruitment of local police forces to help identify individuals for interviews. The ACLU noted that many local police stations have demurred from participation. Departments in San Francisco and San Jose in California; Detroit, Portland, Eugene, and Corvallis in Oregon; and Richardson and Austin, Texas, have all declined to participate in the interviews.

Reasons for refusing to participate fell into three categories: concerns over invasion of privacy rights, often associated with a history of unwarranted governmental intrusion; concerns over particularity; and fears of loss of community goodwill.

Invasion of Privacy Rights

Portland was the first city to refuse to participate, and cited reasons of intrusion into privacy coded into state law. Portland city officials noted that three of the guidelines issued by federal authorities would violate state law: (1) that all telephone numbers used by an individual and his family or close ties should be obtained, (2) the identities of others the individuals lived with should be obtained, and (3) whether or not the individual knew anyone who had ever lived in Afghanistan should be asked (Associated Press, 2001a).

Particularity

Most concerns involved the lack of particularity in the decision regarding the selection of interviewees. The police, as agents of the law, have to be able to show particularity before interviewing suspects—they must demonstrate that, at a minimum reasonable suspicion standard, the individual interviewed has committed or is about to commit a crime. The interview process does not satisfy this legal notion of particularity. The individuals interviewed are not associated with specific crimes but instead are identified by country of origin.

Eugene, the second city after Portland to refuse to allow their police to be involved in the interviews, expressed concerns about interrogating individuals not accused of a crime. As a Eugene police spokeswoman noted, "Give us some legitimate reason to talk to the people—other than that they're from the Middle East—and we'll be glad to" (Associated Press, 2001b).

Good Will with the Arab Community

Others indicated that they had built up good will and trust with their Muslim communities and did not want to engage in practices that would undermine that goodwill. Guilford, the Chief of Dearborn, Michigan, noted that "We don't want to lose our trust that we built up through the years with the Arab community . . . This is strictly voluntary. If they don't want to talk, they don't have to talk to anybody. Nobody is going to twist their arms" (Butterfield, 2001).

The Detroit City Council passed a "Local Resolution to Protect Civil Liberties" on December 6, 2002. This document revealed concerns over both particularity and governmental intrusion into privacy. The part of that document relating to police services stated:

Be it resolved that the City of Detroit directs the City of Detroit Police Department to:

1. Refrain from enforcement of federal immigration laws, refrain from engaging in the surveillance of individuals or groups of individuals based on their participation in First Amendment protected (activities);

2. Refrain, whether acting alone or with federal or state law enforcement officers, from collecting or maintaining information about the political, religious, or social views, associations or activities of any individual or group UNLESS such information directly relates to a criminal investigation;

3. Refrain from undertaking or participating in any initiative, such as the Terrorism Information and Prevention System (TIPS) that encourages members of the general public to spy on their neighbors, colleagues or customers;

4. Refrain from the practice of stopping drivers or pedestrians for the purpose of scrutinizing their identification documents without particularized suspicion of criminal activity (Bill of Rights Defense Committee, 2002).

Not every community or police department resisted assisting the DOJ in the interview program. Chief Flynn, of Arlington County, Virginia, stated that Constitutional issues were "overblown." He compared the interviews to a standard police canvass of a neighborhood after a crime. However, many chiefs thought that there was a communications problem between the DOJ and local communities.

A General Accounting Office investigation into the voluntary interview program in 2003 identified numerous problems with it. The interviews had been expected to end in May, 2002, but as of March, 2003, only about 42 percent of the individuals on the government's list at that point had been interviewed. Of those interviewed, the government noted that "fewer than

20" had been arrested, and none had been arrested on terrorism charges. A statement from the committee leadership asserted that the Justice Department "cannot provide a shred of evidence" that the interviews were successful, and encouraged the Justice Department to redirect its resources "to better protect us from future threats." The Justice Department responded that the interviews provided useful leads, but declined to provide examples of those useful leads because of the sensitivity of anti-terrorism efforts. This secrecy was of concern to the GAO, who stated that they could not conduct an analysis of the success of the interviews because of governmental secrecy (Associated Press, 2003b).

Conclusion

The government has expanded the tracking of aliens in the United States in several ways. Through NSEERS a national entry and exit registration system was implemented. At the borders, the Enhanced Border Security and Visa Entry Program was put into place. For students, the SEVIS program was established. And a voluntary interview program was used to interview suspicious individuals from terrorist countries. A variety of other surveillant operations were also put into place, including the inclusion of suspected terrorists on the national crime control databases, encouraging citizens to inform on suspected terrorists and suspicious activities, and tracking U.S. persons, including citizens, for noncriminal but suspicious activities.

What we see in all this is a dramatic expansion of the Panopticon discussed in Chapter 4, to include ordinary citizens both as watchers and as watched, and carried out under the authority of the Executive with the thin review of the FISA court. Though collecting information on activities that are not themselves criminal, it makes its information available through major criminal databases used by local police and the FBI. The Panopticon is sharply focused for foreigners, whether they be visa-holders, legal immigrants, criminal immigrants, or individuals who have overstayed legal visas. These individuals face extensive detailed tracking and interviewing. And as we saw in the previous chapter, they also face deportation and indefinite imprisonment without charges.

Many municipalities are resisting the new Panopticon: The *Christian Science Monitor* reported in November, 2003 that 200 communities in 34 states had passed resolutions opposed to the government's anti-terrorism tools (Miller & Stern, 2003). This is, as Miller and Stern note, a grass-roots movement—organized resistance among citizens has generally not taken root. And as we noted in Chapter 7, many police departments are either expanding their counter-terror tools for wider surveillance or are developing counter-terrorism task forces with the support of federal agencies. One can only conclude that the future of the counter-terror Panopticon, like its crime control and war on drugs progenitors, looks to be a future of growth and expansion.

CHAPTER 8

Guantanamo Bay and the Treatment of Foreign Prisoners

In the popular political lexicon we are fighting two wars, the war on terrorism and the war on drugs. We have fought many such wars; for example, President Lyndon Johnson fought the war on poverty. The war metaphor serves an important purpose: It suggests that national leaders are prepared to mobilize their energies on behalf of a cause in which they believe.

The war on terrorism cannot be understood only in this metaphorical sense. It is in important ways a real war, declared or not. Aspects of it are being fought with U.S. military troops. Terrorism has been used as a basis for invasion and military occupation of Afghanistan and provided part of the legitimating rationale for the military invasion and occupation of Iraq. Military actions have also take place in other countries; we launched predator missile strikes against a military target in the Sudan killing several suspected Al Qaeda members and an American citizen, for example.

As a result of this aspect of the "war on terrorism," we have acquired prisoners. And our treatment of these prisoners has created a firestorm of controversy, both in the U.S. and among international rights organizations. This chapter focuses on how we are dealing with these prisoners, primarily on the military base at Guantanamo Bay, where many of the prisoners are currently located. Also discussed are two issues pertinent to the treatment of prisoners—military tribunals and coercive interrogation of prisoners.

Guantanamo Bay

One of the controversial aspects of the war on terror is the detention at U.S. Naval Base Guantanamo Bay, in Cuba, of fighters captured in the Afghanistan war. The reasons for detention at Guantanamo Bay were straightforward; the base had a U.S. military facility, and the facility was outside of the jurisdiction of U.S. courts. Consequently, prisoners held there could not avail themselves of due process protections and legal relief available to all held inside U.S. jurisdictions. This section reviews issues associated with these detentions. The Migration Policy Institute (2003) identifies the following chronology concerning detention.

July 31, 2002:   Judge Colleen Kollar-Kotelly of the U.S. District Court for the District of Columbia rules that the U.S. legal system has no jurisdiction over the detainees held in Guantanamo Bay and, thus, the detainees have no access to U.S. courts.

October 18, 2002:   Department of Justice asks the U.S. Court of Appeals for the District of Columbia Circuit to uphold Judge Kollar-Kotelly's July 31, 2002, ruling, which states that suspected Taliban and Al Qaeda fighters held at the U.S. Naval Base in Guantanamo Bay have no right to access American courts. Attorneys representing the families of some of the 600 prisoners are appealing the lower court ruling, arguing that Guantanamo Bay is under the *de facto* control of the U.S. and that the detainees have legal rights under international law. The appeals court will hear the arguments in the case on December 2, 2002.

November 18, 2002:   The U.S. Court of Appeals for the Ninth Circuit rules that a coalition of clergy and professors has no legal standing to represent the detainees being held at Guantanamo Bay Naval Base in Cuba.

October 28, 2002:   Four detainees, three Afghanis and one Pakistani, are the first to be released from Guantanamo Bay and are returned to their home countries. Thirty more prisoners arrive, however, increasing the number of detainees to "approximately 625," according to a Pentagon spokeswoman.

March 11, 2003:   The U.S. Court of Appeals for the D.C. circuit rules that the 650 suspected terrorists and Taliban fighters held at a U.S. naval base in Guantanamo Bay, Cuba, have no legal rights in the United States and may not ask courts to review their detentions (Migration Policy Institute, 2003).

The pattern of these decisions is a general reluctance of the courts to challenge the government's contention that Guantanamo Bay is outside the U.S. jurisdiction. In the sections below, we review the history and character of prisoner detainment at Guantanamo Bay, Cuba.

History and Conditions of Confinement

On November 13, 2001, President George W. Bush issued a military order titled the "Detention, Treatment, and Trial of Certain Non-Citizens in the War Against Terrorism" (Office of Press Secretary, 2001a).

Section 3 of that order provided detention authority to the Secretary of Defense, Donald Rumsfeld. Under that authority, the Secretary of Defense could direct that anyone subject to the order:

1. Be detained in an "appropriate location" designated by the Secretary of Defense in or outside the U.S.

2. Be provided humane treatment, without adverse condition based on race, color, religion, gender, birth, wealth, or similar criteria.

3. Be provided adequate food, drinking water, shelter, clothing, and medical treatment.

4. Be allowed free exercise of religion consistent with requirements of the detention.

5. Be detained in accordance with any other conditions determined by the Secretary of Defense.

In response to the order, the Secretary undertook the establishment of a high-security detention facility at the U.S. Naval Base in Guantanamo. The detention facility was staffed by the "Joint Task Force 160" and about 1000 soldiers from various bases under the U.S. Southern Command, based in Miami. It was initially designed to handle 100 prisoners, but was anticipated to expand to receive up to 2,000 (CNN.com. 2002b).

The first group of 20 prisoners arrived on Friday, January 10, on a C-141 transport from Kandahar, Afghanistan. The prisoners, a mix of alleged Al Qaeda and Taliban individuals, debarked from the plane dressed in "turquoise blue face masks, orange ski caps and flourescent jump suits, their hands in manacles" (CNN.com, 2002c). From the plane, they were loaded into a bus and then a ferry. They arrived at Camp X-Ray, where they were photographed and fingerprinted, and underwent initial interrogation. Thus began the uncertain sojourn of Afghanistan prisoners under U.S. custody.

From the outset, they were perceived and treated as dangerous individuals. General Richard Myers, chairman of the Joint Chiefs of Staff, stated in reference to the observation that they were shackled on the flight: "These are people who would gnaw through the hydraulic lines in the back of a C-17 to bring it down" (CNN.com, 2002c). They were housed in cells that measured 1.8 meters (about 6 feet) wide by 2.4 meters (about 7.9 feet) long by 2.4 meters (about 7.9 feet) high. The cells had corrugated metal roofs, wire mesh walls, and a concrete base. Daytime temperatures ranged from 71 at night to 88 during the day (BBC News, 2002b). Secretary of

Defense Donald Rumsfeld, responding to the charge that the prison conditions were unjust, responded "To be in an 8 by 8 cell, in beautiful, sunny Guantanamo Bay, Cuba, is not inhumane treatment" (NewsMax.com, 2002).

The official description of the circumstances of detainment was as follows: Each cell contained two buckets, a foam mattress, and a 1-quart canteen. Prisoners were provided with two orange suits, one pair of flip-flops, two bath towels, a washcloth, toothpaste, soap, shampoo, and a copy of the Koran. Detainee's daily routine was as follows: Breakfast, followed by the opportunity to shower; "personal time," a euphemism for confinement to a cell; lunch; an exercise period in the afternoon; mail call, with letters written under supervision; dinner, again followed by a shower opportunity.

Outsiders reported seeing prisoners handcuffed, blindfolded, and masked. Other images showed them manacled and clamped into leg irons on trolleys that were wheeled into interrogation rooms. The U.S. said that these were used only for transit, and that the prisoners were living better than before they were captured. Secretary Rumsfeld refused to call the detainees "prisoners," arguing that such a designation would confer legal status on them (Serrano & Hendren, 2002). Given a legal status, they might be able to argue for court relief, an outcome steadfastly resisted by the U.S. government.

By the end of 2002, questions were raised about the actual danger posed by many of the detainees. The *Los Angeles Times* (Miller, 2002) reported that at least 59 of the detainees were "deemed of no intelligence value after repeated interrogations in Afghanistan." All had been recommended for repatriation well before being transferred to Guantanamo Bay. Many were caught up in bureaucratic processes that led to their confinement. They had been given a low priority, but with the relocation of individuals to Cuba, their names showed up on flight manifests. It has been suggested that, once a name was on a roster for interrogation, it remained in the system regardless of the outcome of the interrogation, and gradually filtered to the top of the list and ended up in Cuba. Once on the manifest, their names could only be removed only if senior intelligence officers "work(ed) through a thicket of military red tape." One was described as a 22-year-old Afghan who sold firewood at a bus station in Konduz, and was picked up by Northern Alliance Forces when he and six others were traveling to Kabul. There was no evidence that he had ever had any knowledge of the Taliban or Al Qaeda (Miller, 2002).

Some officers expressed concerns about the impact of long-term detention on the detainees, some of whom were previously deemed appropriate for release. Detaining innocents without opportunity for appeal could only breed distrust for the U.S., both among the inmates and in their home countries. Also, even with the security, there was significant indoctrination of the detainees by radical Islamists. As one military official observed, "If they weren't terrorists before, they certainly could be now" (Miller, 2002).

A common complaint was the small cells. Prisoners noted that they slept, ate, prayed, and went to the toilet all in their small cell. Because the sides were wire, the tropical sun entered the cells in the afternoon, making the cells quite hot. The exercise was initially restricted to walking around a cage once a week. Those released complained of an enormous sense of injustice, combined with a lack of knowledge about the length of their detention.

According to one prisoner, they were taken out for showers only once a week for one minute (Gall & Lewis, 2003). After a hunger strike by some of the prisoners, the shower time was extended to five minutes, and exercise was permitted once a week. A spokesman for the military also noted that, by 2003, there had been 28 suicide attempts by the prisoners. One of those who tried to commit suicide stated that he was surrounded by Arabs and could not understand their language. He attempted suicide four times, and was later released without charges.

In April 2002, Camp X-Ray was closed and prisoners were relocated to Camp Delta. By April of 2003, about 664 prisoners continued to be held at Guantanamo Bay (Lewis, 2003). By nationality, the largest number, about 150, were from Saudi Arabia, followed by 83 Yemenis and 53 Pakistanis. These facilities had blocks of 48 cages, with two rows of mesh cages separated by a narrow corridor. Each cell had a "through the floor" toilet, a sink and a bed. The cells had electric ventilators in the ceilings, to help compensate for the scorching temperatures of Cuban summers. Prisoners who cooperated were placed in Camp Four, where they were rewarded with dormitory-style life. A block was set aside for the three juvenile prisoners, and Delta Block was used for prisoners with mental problems. India Block contained punishment isolation cells. These were windowless metal boxes where prisoners were kept in isolation for infractions (Meek, 2003a).

The detainees received two hot meals a day at Camp Delta, and were rewarded with dates and ice cream when they cooperated. A call to prayer was heard five times a day over loudspeakers. A medium security center was also built as a half-way house before release. The 40 prisoners there were allowed to congregate and were given improved rations (Lewis, 2003).

POW Status

> "If you want a definition of this place, you don't have the right to have rights" (Meek, 2003a:2).

This comment, from a prisoner in Guantanamo, was one of the few political statements to slip past the censors (Meek, 2003a). It reveals the extraordinary frustration of prisoners in Guantanamo who are held on indefinite terms and without charges. And, according to many observers, it contributed to the high successful and attempted suicide rate among prisoners.

Prisoners at Guantanamo Bay had no rights because the justice department had refused to grant them either U.S. or international legal status. Indeed, one of the many controversies surrounding the Guantanamo imprisonment of war-on-terrorism detainees was the refusal to accord them Prisoner of War (POW) status under the Geneva Convention. According to a White House Fact Sheet issued in February of 2002, the President determined that the Geneva convention did not apply to the Al Qaeda detainees—"Al-Qaida is not a state party to the Geneva Convention; it is a foreign terrorist group. As such, its members are not entitled to POW status." The Taliban, the fact sheet continued, are covered by the convention, because Afghanistan was a signatory to the Convention. However, under the terms of the convention, the Taliban detainees did not qualify as POWs.

What was the basis for the decision to deny POW status to both Al Qaeda and the Taliban? According to the Geneva Convention, to be considered POWs irregular militias must satisfy four criteria: "(1) that of being commanded by a person responsible for his subordinates, (2) that of having a fixed distinctive sign recognizable from a distance, (3) that of carrying arms openly, and (4) that of conducting their operations in accordance with the laws and customs of war" (Dorf, 2002).

Al Qaeda, the government claimed, did not meet these conditions for several reasons. They try to blend into civilian populations, they do not carry a fixed distinctive sign, and they target civilians, in violation of the laws and customs of war. The Taliban resemble a traditional army, and appear to be commanded by individuals responsible for their subordinates. However, Dorf noted, "Taliban members did not appear to satisfy the second and third criteria, for they did not wear uniforms that bore a 'fixed distinctive sign recognizable at a distance,' nor did they invariably 'carry arms openly'"(Dorf, 2002:2).

The combination of detention at Guantanamo and non-POW status served four purposes for the Bush Administration. The first purpose was prisoner interrogation, and failure to accord Geneva Convention protections is integral here. Under the Convention, prisoners must be treated humanely. An element of this treatment is they not be interrogated. But interrogation has been central to their detainment. Secretary Rumsfeld noted that, "To stop future terrorist attacks, we have detained these people, and have and will be questioning them to gather additional intelligence information" (Newsmax, 2002). That goal could not be achieved under the principles of the Geneva Convention.

Second, detaining individuals at Guantanamo Bay placed them at a location off U.S. soil. Under *Johnson v. Eisentrager* (1950) enemy aliens who have not entered the U.S. are not entitled access to U.S. courts. Consequently, as long as Al Qaeda and the Taliban are held at Guantanamo, their only appeal is within the executive branch. As Dorf (2002) stated, "Put more bluntly, they will have only the procedural recourse the Administration allows them."

Third, under Article 118 of the Geneva Convention, prisoners of war must be "repatriated without delay after the cessation of hostile activities" (Dorf, 2002:3). This was troubling, Dorf pointed out, because it was based on the notion that repatriated soldiers in a conventional war will return home and take up civilian roles. However, members of Al Qaeda acted out of an ideology committed to the killing of American civilians as a means of entering heaven. It was unlikely that a formal conclusion to hostilities in Afghanistan would stop this commitment.

Fourth, if the prisoners were granted POW status, the Administration could not carry out military tribunals, one of its stated goals. According to the President's military order of November 13, 2001, Al Qaeda and those who harbored them could be tried by military tribunals. According to the 1942 case *Ex Parte Quirin*, "only unlawful combatants can be tried by the sort of irregular tribunals at issue in that case and contemplated by the President's order" (Dorf, 2002:3) If they were treated as lawful combatants, they were subject to a variety of procedural protections available under the Geneva Convention.

Concerns over Terms of Confinement

Detainees face an uncertain future. It is likely that many will eventually be released. It is equally plausible that many will be kept in the camp indefinitely, and also that some will face military-style tribunals. Some may be executed. It is the absence of a clear legal identity for detainees that has concerned many observers of U.S. practices in Guantanamo. The absence of a legal standard is a deliberate effort to prevent U.S. court or international legal relief. As long as they are not assigned a legal status, no international tribunal can determine what their rights should be—no status, no rights. One of the consequences of this is that their confinement was, until 2004, potentially indefinite and unreviewable.

The U.S has publicly stated that some of the detainees may be kept indefinitely. It intends to assemble a three-member panel to act as a "quasi-parole board" and prisoners could plead their cases before them. A Defense Department official noted that:

> We feel very much like we are in an active war . . . while some critics worried about the rights of the detainees the Pentagon was more concerned with "the rights of the soldiers having these people not going back to the battlefield" and the rights of the soldiers' families not to have their relatives face the same men in combat.

> The military, according to the *New York Times*, is operating along two lines of action. Less serious threats are gradually being released to return to their countries. At the same time, a 'hard-walled traditional prison' is being built alongside the metal units that have been used to house Guantanamo detainees. The prison is expected to be ready in the summer of 2004 and will house about 100 inmates. There were no plans for an execution chamber in the prison (Lewis & Schmitt, 2004:1, 3).

Observers question the United States' motives regarding open-ended confinement. The U.S., believing that some of the detainees are too dangerous to release, may have already decided to hold them for their natural lives. Only by refusing them any status can the U.S. achieve that goal without actually having to prove that the detainees are in fact dangerous. Hence, by holding prisoners in Guantanamo and resisting efforts to assign them some legal status the U.S. has efficiently trumped all legal standards, national and international, that apply to humans.

The Internationalization of American Prisonization

Criminal justicians have widely noted the dramatic growth of the American prison population. In April, 2003, the Justice Department announced that 2,019,234 prisoners were held in prisons or jails, more than in any other country in the world. Its rate of imprisonment is 702 individuals per 100,000. With this growth, the U.S. has surged ahead of Russia, which, holds 655 individuals per hundred thousand (*Baltimore Sun*, 2003).

A less noted aspect of prison growth is the internationalization of American prisons. The most well known of these prisons is located in Guantanamo, the primary subject of this chapter. But there is a context for Guantanamo—it is one of many prisons where individuals are being held outside the U.S. in order to hold individuals for military matters, avoid the due process requirements available to those inside the U.S. geographic jurisdiction, or to increase the pressures available to interrogators. These facilities are generally run by the CIA.

One of these other locations for prisoners is Bagram Air Force Base in Afghanistan. Many Taliban and Al Qaeda were housed there during the Afghanistan occupation and an unknown number continue to be. Detention facilities have also been used Kandahar and Kabul. Some Al Qaeda figures were also held in a facility in Thailand. In Iraq, a detention facility at Baghdad International Airport has been established for Iraqi prisoners, and the Abu Ghraib prison, infamous as a torture center under Hussein, was refurbished to hold prisoners (Risen & Shanker, 2003). In 2004, Abu Ghraib received notoriety for torture carried out by U.S. troops against detainees. The U.S. has announced that some of the lower-ranking or less important Iraqi prisoners will be sent to its facility at Guantanamo (Risen & Shanker, 2003). Additionally, the CIA coordinates prisoner renditions with friendly countries such as Egypt, Jordan, and Morocco. Through the process of rendition, detainees are turned over to these countries so that interrogations can be conducted outside U.S. jurisdiction, but with a list of questions provided by the CIA (see Figure 8.4).

Who is being held, how many are held, whether American citizens are held, the circumstances of their confinement, and their actual treatment is classified. Occasionally a high profile figure such as Saddam Hussein is known to be at one of these facilities. Information about these prisoners is provided by the U.S. government, which means that no oversight independent of the government is available to verify the government's pronouncements of the terms of their confinement. Except for a rare few, they are beyond hope, facing only a bleak and indefinite future of imprisonment interrupted only by the occasional interrogation.

Military Tribunals for Non-Citizens

Tied to the imprisonment of detainees at Guantanamo Bay is the Bush administration's decision to try some of the detainees via military tribunal. Why are individuals confined indefinitely, without legal representation, in Guantanamo? Meek suggests that three reasons account for this. First, the use of imprisonment as a counter-terrorism tool was made explicit by Attorney General John Ashcroft. According to his view, large-scale incarceration and execution are the way to fight wrongdoing, both nationally and internationally. In a speech given near the second anniversary of 9/11, Ashcroft noted that, "We have proven that the right ideas—tough laws, tough sentences, and constant cooperation—are stronger than the criminal or the terrorist cell" (Meek, 2003b:2).

Secondly, indefinite detention increases the power of interrogations. As Meek noted, each prisoner at the camp has been interrogated 10 to 20 times and, assuming interrogations lasted about an hour, that would have generated about 15,000 hours of transcripts. When prisoners asked how long they would be held, interrogators responded, "We don't know when you will be set free. Only our bosses know. We are here to do our job" (Meek, 2003a:3).

Third, the presence of prisoners with enemy combatant status under indefinite detention in Guantanamo is a potent interrogation threat for prosecutors in other cases in the U.S. For example, Meek noted that the Lackawanna Six, a group of Yemeni-Americans from a Buffalo, N.Y., suburb accused of helping Al Qaeda, only pleaded guilty after prosecutors "dropped heavy hints that they would be declared 'enemy combatants' if they didn't" (Meek, 2003a:3).

On November 13, 2001, President Bush issued an executive order authorizing the creation of military tribunals to try non-citizens an charges of terrorism and provided Secretary of Defense Rumsfeld with authority over detention of Guantanamo prisoners (see Figure 8.1). Secretary of Defense Rumsfeld followed this order with Military Commission Order No.1, titled "Procedures for Trials by Military Commissions of Certain Non-United States Citizens in the War on Terrorism," on March 21, 2002. Defense Secretary Paul Wolfowitz was given authority over military tribunals on June 21, 2003. This authority included approval of charges against detainees, sending detainees to trial, selecting military officers to sit on the commissions, and making final decisions on procedures, motions, and facts (Migration Policy Institute, 2003).

Figure 8.1
Summary of President George Bush's November 2001 Military Order

---

Section 2 defines individuals subject to the order as those who have engaged in, aided or abetted, or conspired to commit, acts of international terrorism, or acts in preparation therefor; that have caused, threaten to cause, or have as their aim to cause, injury to, or adverse effects on the United States, its citizens, national security, foreign policy, or economy; or who have knowingly harbored someone described above.

Section 4 states that such individuals will be tried by military commission and may be punished in accordance with penalties provided under applicable law, including life imprisonment or death. This section also defines the authority of the Secretary of Defense regarding these trials. As a military function, the Secretary of Defense shall issue orders and regulations, including orders for the appointment of one or more military commissions, and rules for the conduct of the proceedings of the military commissions, including pre-trial, trial, and post-trial procedures, modes of proof, issuance of process, and qualifications of attorneys.

Section 4 specifies the minimum provisions for military commissions, including:

- To sit any time and place chosen with the Secretary's "guidance."
- A full and fair trial, with the military commission sitting as the triers of both fact and law.
- Admission of such evidence as would, in the opinion of the presiding officer of the commission, have probative value to a reasonable person.
- Protection of information classified or classifiable under Executive Order 12958 or otherwise protected by statute or rule from unauthorized disclosure.
- Conviction and sentencing by concurrence of 2/3 of the members of the commission present at the time of the vote, a majority being present.

Section 7(b)(2) states that individuals tried "shall not be privileged to seek any remedy or maintain any proceeding . . . [or to have any sought on their behalf] in (1) any court in the United States, or any state thereof, (2) any court in any foreign nation, and (3) any international tribunal.

Source: White House (2001a). Press Release, November 13, 2001.

The document discussed in Figure 8.1 thus lays out a set of criteria for the development of military commissions for the trial of suspected terrorists. It is a matter for historians to determine why the President elected not to use existing military protocols for the trial of combatants. However, the decision to develop the courts in accordance with the criteria stated above has created a hailstorm of controversy in many sectors, a storm that is likely to increase as a trial date approaches for prisoners subject to this order. The criminal guidelines were revised in 2002 to blunt some of the criticism of their lack of due process.

Military tribunals, as currently proposed, are different from civilian courts on several dimensions. Figure 8.2 describes these differences.

Figure 8.2
Differences between Tribunals and Regular Courts

According to the revised guidelines, military tribunals will have the following characteristics:

(1) They will use juries of 3-7 panelists who are military officers. Federal courts use 12 panelists.

(2) Conviction and sentencing will require a 2/3 majority. Death penalty sentences will require a unanimous 7-panelist decision.

(3) Evidence will have "probative value to a reasonable person." This includes secondhand and hearsay evidence excluded from traditional courts.

(4) Prosecutors do not have to show a "chain of custody," that is, where evidence came from and how it arrived to the courtroom.

(5) Defendants will be provided with military attorneys and will be permitted to hire civilian attorneys at their own expense.

(6) Defendants cannot appeal to the federal courts. They may petition a panel of review, which can include civilians and military officers. The President has final review.

The tribunals have some traditional protections. These are:

(1) Defendants can review the evidence against them.

(2) Most sessions will be made public.

(3) Jurors can convict only when the case is proved beyond a reasonable doubt.

Defendants will have the following:

(1) copy of charges in English.

(2) presumption of innocence.

(3) right to remain silent.

(4) access to evidence known to the prosecution that will exculpate the accused.

(5) right to obtain witnesses and documents for defense.

(6) access to sentencing evidence.

(7) right to submit plea agreement.

(8) cannot be tried again my military tribunal once verdict is final.

Sources: Council on Foreign Relations, 2003; Addicot, 2002.

Under continued pressure, the Pentagon in February 2004 announced that it would relax some of its amended rules for tribunals. Lawyers would have more information about whether the government might eavesdrop on their conversations with suspects, and lawyers would not have to sign an affidavit that made it appear they condoned the eavesdropping. Under the new rules, the government will retain its right to eavesdrop. However, the rules add clarity on how suspects for eavesdropping are selected for monitoring, a defense lawyer will be notified in advance, and the lawyer can object to the planned electronic monitoring at trial. Also, lawyers can get help from their home offices or other outside lawyers, even if they are not members of a Pentagon-approved pool (Associated Press, 2004).

Arguments Favorable to Tribunals

The issue of military tribunals has been intensely polarizing. Supporters argue that the use of tribunals for wartime crimes is appropriate. John Dean (2001a), former aid to President Nixon, argues that military tribunals have played an important role in American history. Citing examples from the Mexican-American war, the Civil War, and the Second World War, Dean argues that the history of tribunals is, as he puts it, "(mostly) honorable." During the Civil War alone, as many as 4,000 military tribunals may have been held. Many of these were in response to terrorist acts carried out by the defendants.

The trial of the defendants in the assassination of President Lincoln was carried out by the Hunter Commission, a tribunal of nine officers who also tried those who attempted to assassinate Vice President Andrew Johnson, Secretary of War Seward, and General Ulysses Grant. All defendants had right to counsel and called witnesses on their behalf. More than 350 witnesses testified. Dean observes that, given the mood in the District of Columbia after the assassination of Lincoln, it is unlikely that the defendants could have received as fair a trial in a civilian court as they did before the military tribunal.

Dean cites the testimony of Attorney General John Ashcroft that President Bush relied on the precedent set by Franklin Roosevelt in 1942, dealing with Nazi saboteurs who had landed on U.S. shores. Roosevelt instructed his Attorney General, Francis Biddle, to try all eight of the saboteurs—two of whom had once been American citizens—by military tribunal. Dean wryly noted that the President selected a military tribunal because it would give the outcome to the trial that Roosevelt wanted, fast convictions with no opportunity for protracted appeals. "I want one thing clearly understood, Francis," Roosevelt said. "I won't hand them over to any United States Marshall armed with a writ of *habeas corpus*. Understand!" Roosevelt's decision went before a special commission of the Supreme Court. The court handed down an opinion, titled *Ex Parte* Quirin, that unanimously supported the president (Dean, 2001a).

Dean concluded that the military commission should be authorized by Congress. Both Lincoln and Roosevelt had the support of Congress, to strengthen the President's hand in the war against terrorism. In his conclusion Dean suggests that we recall that this is a war, not a peace-keeping mission. If we are to provide it with the gravity of war, both Congress and the President have obligations. Included in those obligations are military tribunals, which provide a historically viable and reasonable way to try non-citizen enemy combatants.

In another paper, Dean (2001b) argues that the criminal justice system is inappropriate for trying terrorists. Two criminal trials for terrorists indicted in the 1993 World Trade Center bombing were long and expensive. The first trial lasted five months and had 207 witnesses, while the second was eight months and had 200 witnesses. This, Dean argues, is inefficient. Moreover, witnesses at these trials are at risk of revenge from other terrorists. Jurors also may live in fear of retribution. Finally, the criminal justice system is designed to err on the side of letting the guilty go free. However, when the danger posed by terrorists is great—with possible outcomes involving mass killings and hundreds of millions of dollars—"we can no longer afford procedures that err so heavily on the side of freeing the guilty. Protection of society and the lives of thousands of potential victims becomes paramount" (Dean, 2001b).

Dean's (2001b) argument carries several assumptions that are probably not valid. His views of the criminal justice system are idealized and do not reflect a practicing reality in which there is a very high likelihood of a finding of guilt. There certainly is not a "heavy err" on the side of freeing the guilty as Dean suggests. Indeed, a finding of guilt is so commonplace via guilty pleas at arraignment that it is difficult to imagine a greater frequency of guilty outcomes produced by members of a military tribunal that actually *tried* all cases. Moreover, witness and juror identity can be protected and routinely is in special cases.

Finally, in the event that an individual is seen as a potential community danger, the use of indefinite detentions have been carried out by the criminal justice system, though civil libertarians are sharply critical of them. For example, sexual predators have been held beyond the end of their sentences out of public fears that they will recommit sexual acts, even though the evidence is clear that they do not have a high recidivism rate. So there are court precedents for indefinite holdings of individuals past the end of their sentences.

Though supporting military tribunals, Dean expressed concern over how they were advocated by the executive branch. Most concerns about military tribunals, Dean noted, stemmed from the administration's failure to communicate its aims clearly. Issues concerning the tribunals were being raised because of the administration's penchant for secrecy, and because of the Attorney General's seeming lack of knowledge about the operational details of the tribunals. Dean noted that Attorney General Ashcroft, providing testimony before the Senate Judiciary Committee on December 6, 2001, provided "not a scintilla of documentation for his conclusion about the President's authority." Nor was he clear on a point of uncertainty raised by many observers: Was the Administration going to suspend the writ of *habeas corpus*? From this, Dean concluded that the principal problem with the tribunals was not the core idea, but the way in which the idea was being communicated to the public by the administration (Dean, 2001c).

Also supportive of tribunals, Addicott (2001) observes that the use of military tribunals is consistent with the way in which the war on terrorism is being addressed by the administration. Both the U.S. and the North Atlantic Treaty Organization (NATO) characterized the events of 9/11 as an "armed attack" on the United States, and NATO for the first time invoked its collective self-defense clause. This clause framed the attack as equivalent to an act of war under international law. From these decisions, the war on terror has been legally couched in "law of war" terminology, even though the aggressor was not a state. The U.N. Security Council Resolution 1368 was received by the U.S. as a "very strong statement of support," and it recognized the U.S.' "inherent right of individual and collective self-defense in accordance with the Charter." The resolution also emphasized that states supporting terror groups would be held accountable. The resolution hence provided the U.S. and its allies the authority to respond with military force in self-defense if a state that harbored or supported terrorists refused to cooperate in bringing them to justice. Individuals captured in this conflict are thus appropriately tried under tribunals.

Military tribunals, Addicott (2002) continued, derive their legitimacy from Articles I and II of the Constitution:

> Respectively, Congress has the power to "define and punish . . . offenses against the Laws of Nations" and the President is the "Commander in Chief of the Army and Navy." Furthermore, Congress has specifically provided for the use of military commissions in Article 21 of the Uniform Code of Military Justice (Addicott, 2001:4).

It is generally accepted that citizens cannot be tried by tribunals. The decision *Ex Parte* Milligan (1866) ruled that the use of tribunals to try citizens who were not actual belligerents was unconstitutional as long as civilian courts were working. Historically the legal question has been whether military tribunals can be used to prosecute non-citizen belligerents for offenses in violation of the rules of war. As previously mentioned, *Ex Parte* Quirin (1942) provides tribunals with the jurisdiction to try offenses against the law of war. Moreover, in its January 2002 report on the legal use of military tribunals, the ABA Task Force on Terrorism and Law "found that the terror attacks of September 11, 2001, were arguably violations of the law of war that would justify the use of military tribunals to prosecute accused terrorists" (Addicot, 2002:5). (See Figure 8.1.)

The compelling issue, Addicott suggested, was not whether tribunals were legal in the current case but how they would operate. What standards of fairness will be used? What kind of evidence would be permitted? And what post-trial remedies would be permitted? He concluded that the rules of procedure presented by the Secretary of Defense, were adequate to guarantee the essential fairness of the proceedings in all regards.

Tribe: A Critique of the Tribunals

Lawrence Tribe, a constitutional lawyer and scholar, rebuked the use of tribunals in the war on terror. In a presentation before the Senate Judiciary Committee on December 6, 2001, he argued for a different way to think about terrorism. The principal issue facing the nation was not between liberty and security.

> It is properly to achieve freedom from the terrorism of all fanatics, foreign or domestic, who would challenge the living fabric of our society, including the constitutional compact that unites and gives it purpose (Tribe, 2001:3).

Tribe is presenting a view of liberty that is part of the cultural "fabric" available to U.S. persons, including immigrants and visa entrants. Our unique cultural identity, framed by the Constitution and given texture by the freedoms worked out in court processes, is what liberty is all about. Identity as a free person—this means that individuals have a body of lawful protections from governmental intrusion—is a large part of what government is responsible for. And this cultural/legal identity is what makes America uniquely what it is. And it is this cultural fabric, which provides our core identity as Americans, that we must protect the most. This is what we are fighting for in the war on terrorism. Hence, the proper response to terrorism is

> . . . a steadfast refusal to succumb to any attempt to force upon us a will, and a way of life, that offend the freedoms at our country's core (2001:2).

The military tribunals are a threat to these freedoms. As stated, they are a direct threat to 20 million resident aliens in the United States. One of the central problems with the presidential order is that it's definition of terrorism is so broad that it could include almost any behavior. How many people have contributed, for example, to the Irish Republican Army? Many people involved with the African National Congress, who supported sanctions against South Africa, could be accused of having as their aim adverse effects in United States foreign policy. Further confounding the definition of terrorist is that the President, through the Attorney General, has discretion to determine who fits the definition. This unreviewable decision places tremendous powers of life and death into the administration's hands. Moreover, the definition of terrorist is vague and indefinite, providing the Attorney General, vis-à-vis the authority of the Executive, wide latitude in determining who is subject to a tribunal. It is this open-ended latitude to place U.S. persons in tribunals that is an affront to our U.S. cultural and legal identity.

Also disturbing is the blending of separate Constitutional authorities. The executive branch is:

> . . . lawgiver as well as law enforcer and law interpreter and applier, leaving to the executive branch the specification, by rules promulgated as it goes along, of what might constitute terrorism or a terrorist group, what would amount to aiding and abetting, or harboring such terrorism or such a group, and a host of other specifics left to the imagination of the fearful observer (2001:7).

Citing *Reid v. Covert* (1957), Tribe notes that this "blending of the executive, legislative, and judicial powers in one person or even in one branch of government is ordinarily regarded as the very acme of absolutism" (2001:7).

Tribe reminds us that we have effectively used the criminal courts to try members of Al Qaeda who bombed the World Trade Center. He fears that we will use the military courts in order to compensate for the failure of the intelligence communities to track terrorists. Using the courts to convict individuals with weak evidentiary standards is simply political cover for the executive's failure to anticipate terrorism. This is compounded by the secrecy associated with the government's actions. Efforts to cover the evidentiary trail or to hide the identity of individuals important to the case can easily become a cover, "whether deliberate or not, for ineptly unreliable or otherwise unconscionable behavior by the executive . . ." (2001:10).

Tribe argues that Congress should endeavor to tighten and clarify just who may be brought before tribunal, and on what charges. This, however, is not what the military order creating the tribunals did. It dramatically expanded the role of tribunals to include "'any and all offenses triable by military commission,' sec4(a), not just those that offend the laws of war . . ." (2001:12). Congress needs to establish some form of tribunal to assess the President's "threshold assertion of military jurisdiction" (2001:13), and then establish an expedited *habeas corpus* review in an Article III (of the Constitution) court.

Two observations should be made. First, Tribe is not arguing that tribunals should not be used. He is arguing that we insure that fundamental notions of fair play be incorporated into them. Elements of fair play were not in the original military order, but some elements were incorporated into the tribunals in the subsequent March 21 procedures announced by the Secretary of Defense. However, the essential looseness of the definition of terrorism, and the wide ranging authority of the President in determining who could be considered terrorist, remains a central issue and is not addressable through changes in tribunal procedures. Second, he argues that the distinction is not between liberty and security. However, the elements with which he builds his position are elements concerning legal definitions of the individual, which are not distinguishable from liberty. In the end, the argument is between liberty and security, only with liberty defined as a part of the constitutional goods available to American citizens, and acted out on a day to day basis by the body of laws that create an individual as an entity distinct from the state.

Other Concerns Regarding Tribunals

Critics of tribunals have raised additional concerns:

1. Stating that the Geneva convention should not apply to the Afghan Taliban is nonsense, many critics contend. The argument that Taliban soldiers were not subject to the Geneva Convention is based on the principle that the convention requires that soldiers have a 'fixed distinctive sign.' The Taliban did not. However, the rule is to distinguish combatants from civilians, and the Taliban did not attempt to hide among the civilian population, but fought as military units (Neier, 2002). The Taliban lacked the financial resources to have regular uniforms, but in all ways they acted as a military unit; and finally, it is somewhat hypocritical for us to prosecute the Taliban when it was the U.S. that declared war on them, not vice versa.

2. If the U.S. refuses to grant the Taliban some protection under international codes, what is to protect U.S. troops if they are in turn captured by the Taliban? More generally, if we fail to demonstrate some respect for international codes of fairness in the treatment of prisoners, what will happen in other countries in which we have troops placed? During the Vietnam war, the U.S. at first refused to grant the Vietcong prisoner of war status. This policy was changed when the Vietcong began to take American prisoners (Glaberson, 2001).

3. The U.S. has often criticized other countries for their use of military tribunals. However, if we use tribunals, we legitimate the use of tribunals by other countries. 'If we argue that it (military tribunals) is legal, we are arguing that other sovereigns—Lybia, Syria, Iraq, Cuba—could also have tribunals,' said Alfred R. Rubin, a former Pentagon lawyer who is a professor at the Fletcher School of Law and Diplomacy at Tufts University (Glaberson, 2001).

    The U.S. State Department, for instance, issues an annual Country Reports on Human Rights Practices in which it evaluates countries on the extent to which they guarantee a 'fair public trial.' The State Department expressed concern over 11 countries where tribunals or other uses of the judicial process to suppress dissent and eliminate opposition were used, including Burma, China, Colombia, Egypt, and Malaysia. Human Rights Watch (2001b) observed that the Military Order issued by the President did not include many of the rights that are used to assess the fairness of these other countries' trials. It worried that the "text of the order may become a model for governments seeking a legal cloak for political repression" (2001:1).

The following additional concerns were noted by the Jurist (2001), in an open letter to Chairman Patrick Leahy of the Senate Judiciary Committee.

4. The tribunals undermine the tradition of the Separation of Powers. Congress has the power to define and punish offenses against the law of nations, but that authority was shifted to the Secretary of Defense by the Military Order.

5. The order was not consistent with either Constitutional or international standards of due process. It permitted indefinite detention, secret trials, and no appeals.

6. The text of the order violated treaty obligations. (It should be observed that treaty obligations override national law.) "The International Covenant on Civil and Political Rights was ratified by the U.S. in 1992, and obligates State Parties to protect the due process rights of all persons subject to any criminal proceeding" (2001:2).

7. The successful prosecution of terrorists can take place in the courts, as it has in the past. A public airing of the facts in a criminal trial has been successful in the convictions of international terrorists.

8. The attacks of 9/11 did not stop the functioning of any of America's institutions. The presidential decree should not be permitted to now stop the functioning of one of them, the civilian court system.

The courts have provided conflicting signals with regard to the rights of prisoners held at Guantanamo. On January 8, 2003, the Fourth Circuit Court of Appeals, in *Hamdi v. Rumsfeld*, ruled favorably with regard to Government detentions at Guantanamo. It stated that "judicial review does not disappear during wartime, but the review of battlefield captures in overseas conflicts is a highly deferential one" (Brown, 2003). This decision was taken as a sweeping victory for the administration's right to hold individuals indefinitely, without recourse to American courts, at the discretion of the President.

Two decisions in December, 2003, however, challenged the President's authority. The Ninth Circuit Court of Appeals ruled on December 18 that Al Qaeda and Taliban detainees have a right to federal courts. They stated that:

> We cannot simply accept the government's position that the Executive branch possess the unchecked authority to imprison indefinitely any persons, foreign citizens included, on territory under the jurisdiction and control of the U.S. without permitting such prisoners recourse of any kind to any judicial forum, or even access to counsel, regardless of the length or manner of their confinement (Sullivan, 2003).

In a separate decision, the Second Circuit Court of Appeals, on December 19, rejected the President's argument that he had constitutional authority as Commander in Chief to decide who is an enemy of the U.S. The two assenting judges stated that "Presidential authority does not exist in a vacuum" (Lane, 2003:1).

The appellate court decisions were appealed to the Supreme Court, and on June 29, 2004, the Supreme Court issued rulings on *Hamdi v. Rumsfeld* (03-6696). In what may be the most far-reaching decision concerning presidential authority since 1952, when President Truman tried to seize steel mills for the Korean War effort, the Court declared that the President did not have the authority to lock up those indefinitely whom he considered enemy combatants. While recognizing the President's wartime authority to seize individuals considered potentially threatening, the justices ruled that all persons in U.S. custody, whether American or foreign, have the right to challenge the bias for holding them. In *Hamdi v. Rumsfeld* (03-6696), Justice Scalia reaffirmed the principle of *habeas corpus*, stating that:

> The very core of liberty secured by our Anglo-Saxon system of separated powers has been the freedom from indefinite imprisonment at the will of the executive . . . The practice of arbitrary imprisonment . . . in all ages is one of the favorite and most formidable instruments of tyranny (*The Idaho Statesman*, 2004:7).

This decision meant that non-U.S. detainees at Guantanamo Bay could use the U.S. courts to contest their captivity. Procedural details such as standard of proof and applicable court were returned to lower courts to resolve. The case did not apply to foreign detainees held elsewhere, hence affected only a component of America's international prison system. And in the case of *Rumsfeld v. Padilla* (03-1027), the court turned back the case on the technicality that the petition had been filed in the wrong court.

The court's decision is far-reaching. It has overturned the authority of the U.S. to hold individuals indefinitely. The full implications of the decision will not be resolved for many years, as it becomes a monolithic feature of the legal landscape of the war on terrorism.

Coercive Interrogation and Torture

In the war against terrorism, the most important information available may be intelligence. But how does one gain intelligence against an enemy who fights in an environment in which he or she is indistinguishable from the citizenry, whose acts are often directed against citizens, and whose consequences may involve large-scale mortality? Information on suspects is hard to develop. There are no geographic front lines to map. Yet the danger is very real. The enemy could be anywhere, and the threat may be immediate.

In the U.S. criminal justice system, the purposes of interrogation are ostensibly to find information regarding the details of a crime. In such circumstances, interrogation seeks information and confession. However, in anti-terror assessment, interrogation sometimes has an added dimension— the identification of an immediate security threat which the interrogator believes the detainee has information about but does not want to provide. In such circumstances, some people argue that interrogators should consider a tool offensive to traditional democratic practices—coercive interrogation, or, in the vernacular, torture. The relationship between interrogation, torture, and ethics is discussed in Figure 8.3 below.

Figure 8.3
Excerpts from "A Nasty Business"

> Security forces face special challenges from the threat of terrorism. How does one obtain information about an enemy who is indistinguishable from the civilian populace? He argues that:
>
> > military forces must learn to acquire intelligence by methods markedly different from those to which they are accustomed. The most "actionable," and therefore effective, information in this environment is discerned not from orders of battle, visual satellite transmissions of opposing force positions, or intercepted signals but from human intelligence mostly gathered from the indigenous population. The police, specifically trained to interact with the public, typically have better access than the military to what are called human intelligence sources. Indeed, good police work depends on informers, undercover agents, and the apprehension and interrogation of terrorists, who provide the additional information critical to destroying terrorist organizations.
>
> Hoffman describes a conversation he had with a Sri Lankan army officer in charge of fighting the Liberation Tigers of Tamil Eelam (LTTE). The LTTE are known for their professionalism and ruthlessness. He gives the agent the pseudonym "Thomas."
>
> > 'By going through the process of laws,' Thomas patiently explained, as a parent or a teacher might speak to a bright but uncomprehending child, 'you cannot fight terrorism.' Terrorism, he believed,

Figure 8.3, *continued*

could be fought only by thoroughly 'terrorizing' the terrorists—that is, inflicting on them the same pain that they inflict on the innocent.

(He gave) me an example of the split-second decisions he was called on to make. At the time (he cited), Colombo was on 'code red' emergency status, because of intelligence that the LTTE was planning to embark on a campaign of bombing public gathering places and other civilian targets. Thomas's unit had apprehended three terrorists who, it was suspected, had recently planted somewhere in the city a bomb that was then ticking away, the minutes counting down to catastrophe. The three men were brought before Thomas. He asked them where the bomb was. The terrorists—highly dedicated and steeled to resist interrogation—remained silent. Thomas asked the question again, advising them that if they did not tell him what he wanted to know, he would kill them. They were unmoved. So Thomas took his pistol from his belt, pointed it at the forehead of one of them, and shot him dead. The other two, he said, talked immediately; the bomb, which had been placed in a crowded railway station and set to explode during the evening rush hour, was found and defused, and countless lives were saved. On other occasions, Thomas said, similarly recalcitrant terrorists were brought before him. It was not surprising, he said, that they initially refused to talk; they were schooled to withstand harsh questioning and coercive pressure. No matter: a few drops of gasoline flicked into a plastic bag that is then placed over a terrorist's head and cinched tight around his neck with a web belt very quickly prompts a full explanation of the details of any planned attack.

Hoffman noted that the conversation had an 'unsettling relevance' since the 9/11 attacks. A part of that relevance was how the distinction between moral good and bad becomes less clear.

'There are not good people and bad people,' he told me, 'only good circumstances and bad circumstances. Sometimes in bad circumstances good people have to do bad things. I have done bad things, but these were in bad circumstances. I have no doubt that this was the right thing to do.' In the quest for timely, 'actionable' intelligence will the United States, too, have to do bad things—by resorting to measures that we would never have contemplated in a less exigent situation?

Source: Adapted from Bruce Hoffman, "A Nasty Business." *Atlantic Monthly*, January, 2002:49-52.

Torture is a highly controversial form of interrogation. Those who advocate its use argue that some circumstances are so compelling that intelligence must be obtained at any cost. Those who argue against it contend that the ethics violate human rights standards. Its use has such polarizing effects on groups so interrogated and divisive effects among one's supporters that the backlash against it more than offsets any potential gains.

In civilized societies, torture is widely viewed as a throwback to barbarism, and associated with the behavior of a government out of control. Yet, in the war against terrorism, many people have asked if torture, in extreme circumstances, has its place.

Israel has in the past used methods of interrogation that fall within the UN definition of torture. Prior to 1999, Israel's General Security Services set standards for methods of interrogation called "moderate physical pressure" and "increased physical pressure." These interrogation methods included "subjecting detainees to sleep deprivation, prolonged shackling in painful positions, hooding with filthy sacks, being forced to squat like a frog, and violent shaking" (CINJust, 2001). One widely cited method was called "shabeh," in which a suspect was bent over backwards on a chair, hands and legs shackled beneath. One suspect, who was later released without charges, claimed to have been kept in that position for the better part of three months (Kessel, 1999).

In May of 1997 these interrogation methods were found to be torture under the UN *Convention Against Torture*. In September, 1999, the Israeli Supreme Court banned the use of these interrogation techniques. However, the court concluded that the state had a right to defend itself. It left open the question of what to do in a "ticking bomb" case, a situation in which a terrorist refused to provide information necessary to locate a bomb that was about to kill hundreds of civilians.

The United Nations (1997) defines torture in Article 1 in the *Convention Against Torture* as follows:

> For the purposes of this Convention, torture means any act by which severe pain or suffering, whether physical or mental, is intentionally inflicted on a person for such purposes as obtaining from him or a third person information or a confession, punishing him for an act he or a third person has committed or is suspected of having committed, or intimidating or coercing him or a third person, or for any reason based on discrimination of any kind, when such pain or suffering is inflicted by or at the instigation of or with the consent or acquiescence of a public official or other person acting in an official capacity. It does not include pain or suffering arising only from, inherent in or incidental to lawful sanctions.

Dershowitz (2002) has extended the ticking bomb case to the United States. American police, he argues, would undoubtedly use the "time-tested technique for loosening tongues" in a ticking bomb case, whatever the UN Convention stated. The question is whether torture will be held to democratic standards of accountability or whether it will be carried out "below the radar screen."

He suggests that torture should be permitted, but only with the issuance of a "torture warrant" by a judge. The warrant would have to contain (1) absolute need to obtain immediate information to save lives, (2) probable cause that the suspect had such information, and (3) the suspect was unwilling to reveal such information. The suspect would be given immunity from prosecution for information elicited, and the warrant would be limited to nonlethal means.

He notes that such a policy might legitimate torture as a policing tool. However, he counters that the only way it can be controlled is to bring torture under the highly visible accountability of a judge. Only in this way could torture be monitored and limited.

Delattre (1994) observed that there are times when, as an interrogator, he might be tempted to employ physical coercion against suspects. Should he do so, however, he would call for a full inquiry. Moreover, he views it as a violation of the public trust, and would resign from his current assignment "to make clear that no one who has violated the standards of a position of authority should continue in it" (Delattre, 1994:213). He expresses deep concern about the morality of the act. "Some actions," he noted, "are not just morally hazardous, but are morally suicidal" (Delattre, 1994:214).

Accusations of torture against the United States have emerged in the war on terror. Accusers have focused on the mistreatment and deaths of some detainees in Afghanistan, and on the highly visible and much-documented abuse at Abu Ghraib in Iraq, discussed at the end of this chapter. Another form of torture may be a consequence of "rendition." "Rendition" means that a suspect is deported extralegally from one country to another, outside of the United States, because there is insufficient evidence to try him in the United States. The use of rendition focuses on the movement of suspected terrorists to places where they are beyond the jurisdiction of U.S. law and hence unprotected by due process. Figure 8.4 discusses rendition, interrogation, and concerns of torture of terrorist suspects held in secret overseas locations.

Is there any evidence that prisoners under rendition have been tortured? On September 26, 2002, a Syrian-born Canadian, Maher Arar, was seized by immigration officials at Kennedy International Airport. He was on his way home to Canada after visiting his wife's family in Tunisia. He denied any connection to terrorists, nor was he accused of any crimes. After several days of interrogation, he was put on a plane and flown to Washington D.C. From there, he was delivered to Syrian interrogators in Jordan. This was legal, the government claimed, because he had been born in Syria, even though he had not been there in 16 years and was traveling under a Canadian passport.

Arar was locked in an underground cell "the size of a grave," 3 feet wide, 6 feet long, and 7 feet high. He was then questioned repeatedly under torture for the following 10 months. He was released when it became clear that he had no terrorist ties. How was Arar linked to terrorism? A computer generated association had noted that his mother's cousin had been a member of the Muslim Brotherhood nine years earlier. And the lease on his apartment had been witnessed by a Syrian born Canadian who was thought to know another Egyptian born Canadian who was allegedly mentioned in an Al Qaeda document.

Today, he is free, though he has chronic nightmares. He has lost 40 pounds and walks with a pronounced limp (Pyle, 2004).

Figure 8.4
Interrogations and Accusations of Torture of Overseas Prisoners

Al Qaeda operatives and Taliban commanders are held at the U.S. occupied Bagram Air Base in Afghanistan. For their potential intelligence, they may be the prizes of the war. Those who give up their information are provided with basic comforts. Those who do not are turned over to foreign intelligence services through a process called rendering.

Lower-level detainees are handed by the CIA to foreign intelligence services by the CIA, particularly Jordan, Egypt, and Morocco. These are referred to as "extraordinary renditions" and the detainees are often handed over with a list of questions to be answered.

One official involved in the rendering of prisoners was quoted as stating:

We don't kick the (expletive) out of them. We send them to other countries so they can kick the (expletive) out of them.

Another, the then head of the CIA Counter-terrorist Center, offered:

This is a highly classified area, but I have to say that all you need to know: There was a before 9/11, and there was an after 9/11. After 9/11, the gloves came off.

Officials have responded by stating that renditions are not for purposes of torture and other aggressive forms of interrogation, but because the countries are culturally suitable for the captives. They involve interrogators who speak the dialect of the detainees and can more effectively use shame and familial reputation to extract information. And the Bush administration denies any allegations of torture as the result of its rendition policy. The former CIA inspector general stated that the organization doesn't do or support torture. However, in practice, some officials noted, a narrow definition of knowing about torture is used. As one observed, "If we're not there in the room, who is to say?" One detainee, Abu Zubaida, was shot in the stomach during his capture. At the beginning of his interrogation, selective painkillers were used to encourage cooperation.

The countries used for rendition have bad civil liberties records. Jordan, for example, was criticized in the State department's 2001 report for using torture methods such as sleep deprivation, beatings on soles of feet, prolonged suspensions with ropes in contorted positions, and use of family members to induce talk. Morocco has a similar history of the use of torture during interrogation, noted in the same state department report.

Figure 8.4, *continued*

> Other means of violence are associated with interrogations. According to those who have witnessed treatment of detainees at Bagram,
>
> Captives are often 'softened up' by M.P.s and U.S. Army special forces who beat them and confine them to tiny rooms. The alleged terrorists are commonly blindfolded and thrown into walls, bound in painful positions, subjected to loud noises and deprived of sleep. The tone of intimidation and fear is the beginning, they said, of a process of piercing a prisoner's resistance.
>
> As one administration appointee observed, "we may kick them around a little bit in the adrenaline of the immediate aftermath."
> Independent verification of the condition of detainees is not obtainable. Overseas interrogation facilities are not accessible to outsiders and to other government agencies. Prisoner conditions and treatment is not monitored by such organizations as the Red Cross, nor do prisoners have access to legal counsel. In a word, they have disappeared off the face of the earth.

Source: Adapted from Priest, Dana and Barton Gellman, "U S. Decries Abuse but Defends Interrogations " *Washington Post*, December 26, 2002.

Allegations have also been made that Afghan prisoners were beaten to death at Bagram Air Force Base in Afghanistan. According to a military pathologist's report, one prisoner, a 22-year-old farmer and part-time taxi driver, died from "blunt force injuries to lower extremities complicating coronary artery disease." The death certificate, signed by Major Elizabeth Rouse, indicated that the man died from "homicide." The other death being investigated was that of Mullah Habibullah, who died of a pulmonary embolism, a blood clot in the lung. Prisoners at the base have also claimed that detainees are "chained to the ceiling, shackled so tightly that the blood flow stops, kept naked and hooded and kicked to keep them awake for days on end" (Guardian Newspapers, 2003). The commander of coalition forces stated that interrogation techniques were "adapted," and that, "They are in accordance with what is generally accepted as interrogation techniques," and would be changed if needed. He denied that prisoners were chained to the ceiling.

The Case of Khalid Sheikh Mohammed

On Saturday, March 1, 2003, Khalid Sheikh Mohammed was captured in Pakistan by a joint American and Pakistani force. His capture represented an important break in the counter-terrorist campaign in Pakistan and Afghanistan because Mohammed was widely believed to be the mastermind of the September 11 terrorist attacks against the United States. As noted by Senator Pat Roberts of Kansas, Chairman of the Senate Intelligence Committee, "This is a giant step backward for the Al Qaeda. Now their operations commander is simply out of operations" (Lumpkin, 2003c). On Monday March 3, he was flown to Bagram AFB in Afghanistan.

As important as the decommissioning of an officer of Al Qaeda, Mohammed's arrest represented a significant intelligence opportunity. He was widely viewed as the third in the Al Qaeda chain of command and as personally close to bin Laden. He might know where bin Laden was. And he was implicated in many past terrorist campaigns and might hold a great deal of information about future operations and their personnel. However, his capture made headlines, and whatever information he carried was likely to deteriorate rapidly as Al Qaeda operatives developed contingencies to allow for the information he carried. Pressure was on the intelligence community to use interrogative techniques to acquire information, and to do so rapidly. What options were available to achieve useful results?

Bravin and Fields interviewed several individuals regarding Mohammed and the treatment of prisoners generally. According to military interrogators, their prisoners

> . . . can be lied to, screamed at and shown falsified documents in the hopes that they might unwittingly confirm certain pieces of information. They can also play on their prisoner's phobias, such as fear of rats or dogs, or disguise themselves as interrogators from a country known to use torture or threaten to send the prisoner to such a place. Prisoners can be stripped, forcibly shaved and deprived of religious items and toiletries (Bravin & Fields, 2003).

The U.S., Bravin and Fields (2003:B1) note, recognizes the United Nations Convention against Torture, which was ratified by the Senate in 1994. The Convention prohibits the causing "severe pain or suffering, whether physical or mental, and transferring other prisoners to countries that may practice torture." The central problem with the treaty is that it lacks an enforcement mechanism. No provision is provided to review whether the Convention is followed by signatories. Also, what constitutes "severe" suffering is open to interpretation. The convention seems to permit pain and suffering, up to a point. U.S. officials state that they are even authorized to use "a little bit of smacky-face," or as one intelligence official put it, "some al-Qaeda just need some extra encouragement" (Bravin & Fields, 2003:B9).

Further, interrogators will ensure that Mohammed is located in a place where he will not have access to rights such as the Miranda Warning. This, the agent said, is not for the purposes of prosecution, but "for intelligence. God only knows what they're going to do with him. You go to some other country that'll let us pistol whip this guy" (Bravin & Fields, 2003:B9).

How has Mohammed ultimately been treated? This is a question for which an answer may never be known. In the war on terror, the United States has intentionally established a pattern of treatment of prisoners that minimizes access of the press and the public, and is beyond the reach of legal protections. And interrogators and intelligence officers complacently justify the use of violence even while claiming that it is not carried out. We enter an era in which the use of force and violence against peoples by the U.S. government is secretive and beyond accountability, behind closed doors. Secrecy is justified in terms of the ability to gain potential intelligence about future crimes and avoid divulging counter-terrorism practices to other terrorists. In important ways, the moral character of the American government is up for grabs, and the contenders are those who can justify such behaviors, and those who cannot.

Torture, Morality, and Effectiveness

Torture

Torture can be morally framed as a means-versus-ends conflict. Is some information so vital, so valuable, that we should consider torture even if it is morally reprehensible? In the preceding discussion, coercive interrogation is supported as an essential tool under conditions of imminent threat of large-scale violence against civilians. But how valid is this argument? This argument may be guilty of the logic of false concreteness. It assumes that torture will get the information we want if we can get around our queasiness at the deliberate infliction of on a suspect.

Below, the use of torture is scaled against two criteria. One criteria is that of human rights—is it morally acceptable? The second is effectiveness—does it work?

Morality

The question of moral acceptability does not provide easy answers. Those who take a utilitarian approach can justify the use of torture in the face of an immediate threat. In Figure 8.3 above, "Thomas" was able to justify the use of torture because of the extraordinary security threats posed by the Tamil Tigers, the lack of alternative ways to acquire information, and his assertion that torture had indeed been successful in uncovering imminent threats to the public safety.

From the "means" perspective of ethical formalism, torture is unacceptable. The easy willingness to flay the human flesh in the pursuit of information is inconsistent with all doctrines of human rights. The 1997 U.N. *Convention Against Torture*, cited above, rejects torture under any circumstances.

The use of torture has implications for one's perceived moral identity. When we use torture, it tells us as much about ourselves as about the people we use it against. As one agent put it, it redefines who we are. The core issue—who is the "bad guy" and who is the "good guy"—becomes muddy when the "good guys" carry out the same acts that make the "bad guys" bad.

Torture can mobilize one's enemies, justifying their violent resistance to the evil of an enemy who uses torture. In the example of interrogation carried out at Abu Ghraib, incidents of torture have provided a justification for violence against the U.S. The policy implication of this is that interrogations must be carefully documented, preferably by videotaping, to disprove torture accusations. The absence of adequate interrogative oversight is as potentially damning as the actual use of torture on prisoners. It is crucial as well that administrators do not create an environment that encourages mistreatment in the name of the ends justifying the means, when gathering intelligence about the enemy. And finally, it is important that those who work with detainees are adequately trained and prepared for their work. In the infamous Abu Ghraib incident discussed next, all these elements were missing.

Effectiveness

The effectiveness of torture argument is based on a straightforward logic—individuals, fearing for their personal harm, will provide whatever information they can in order to avoid harm. But in practice, that notion is difficult to sustain, for several reasons.

First, can we believe the unprovable assertions of those who use torture that it has prevented additional terrorist activity? Such assertions may be made as an appeal to avoid prosecution by the World Court. Carmi Gillon, head of GSS in Israel, was charged by Amnesty International with violations of the UN charter against terrorism, who appealed to Denmark to take Gillon into custody. As part of his response, Gillon argued that his interrogation techniques could have prevented the August 1995 suicide bus bombings in Jerusalem that killed four people and wounded 80. However, this argument was rejected in court.

Second, we see in those who use coercive interrogation techniques a tendency to generalize torture to a general information-gathering process. Torture becomes a lazy interrogator's way to short-circuit more difficult, but typically more effective, information-gathering investigative processes. Figure 8.4 above shows that torture was used, not for imminent threats, but for general information gathering.

Third, there is a certain illogic to the argument that torture is effective. It is reasonable to conclude that a person facing torture will tell his interrogators anything to avoid torture. As an intelligence source put it, a tortured prisoner is "not only going to tell you he is al-Qaeda, he's going to tell you he was the other guy on the grassy knoll" in Dallas where President

Kennedy was killed in 1963 (Diamond, Lucy & Willing, 2003). Torture is likely to be marvelously effective at producing results but ineffective in producing valid results. The central logical problem with torture, beyond moral issues, is that it presupposes knowledge on the part of the suspect when the actual presence of knowledge is unknown. This is an illogical presupposition, because the point of torture is to find unknown knowledge.

Fourth, the use of threats as part of an interrogation scheme may create a security threat where there is, in fact, none. Suspect A, fearing torture, may turn in Suspect B and concoct a story that Suspect B is an imminent threat to public safety. Suspect B is then arrested, and the testimony of Suspect A becomes evidence for the prosecution's case against Suspect B. This kind of interrogation scheme is sometimes used by federal prosecutors in the United States who interview individuals arrested for suspected drug crimes, and then offer leniency in exchange for testimony implicating other drug suspects. Indeed, in many cases, suspects are ultimately convicted from such testimony where no drugs have been found (Walker, 1994), a circumstance analogous to interrogations in which a detainee fabricates an imminent threat to mitigate punishment or avoid torture.

Fifth, the use of interrogation as a stand alone tool has a known history of wrongful outcomes in the practice of the American criminal justice system (Sheck, Neufeld & Dwyer, 2001). In 1993, Governor George H. Ryan of Illinois, citing the inability of the Illinois legislature to reform practices after the state of Illinois exonerated 8 prisoners wrongly convicted of murder, commuted the sentence of all inmates on death row to life in prison. "The Illinois capital punishment system is broken," he observed, "and I must act" (*New York Times*, 2003). Police interrogation tactics were implicated in many of these cases of individuals, found guilty in court, later found to be truly innocent because of DNA testing. If police misconduct and aggressive interrogation—what some of the truly innocent later called torture—result in wrongful conviction in the relatively transparent criminal justice system practices in the U.S., in which individuals have due process protections, is it reasonable to hope that mistreatment to acquire intelligence and convictions will be less likely in counter-terrorism cases where such transparency and due process is nonexistent? The answer is clearly no, and stands as a brute challenge to the effectiveness, if not the ethics, of coercive interrogation and the implicit sanctioning of torture.

Torture at Abu Ghraib

In late February 2004, a report was completed by Major General Antonio Taguba. The report was devastating. It found that, between October and December of 2003, numerous instances of "sadistic, blatant, and wanton criminal abuses" had been carried out against detainees by the 372nd MP

Company at Abu Ghraib. These abuses included pouring phosphoric acid on detainees, threatening male detainees with rape, sodomizing a detainee with a chemical light and perhaps a broomstick, and using military dogs to threaten and bite detainees. Detailed witness statements and photographs were available to document the charges (Hersch, 2004).

A central element of the interrogation practices was sexual humiliation. It was believed that prisoners who were sexually humiliated would be too shamed to return to their families. By photographing prisoners so interrogated, and showing the photographs to other prisoners, the other prisoners would be more likely to provide critically needed intelligence. Consequently, techniques included nakedness around females, forced masturbation and sodomization, and the piling of naked men on top of each other in the form of a pyramid. Some photographs showed dead Iraqis, and concerns have been raised over whether they were killed during interrogation. One Iraqi, who voluntarily turned himself in to coalition forces, General Mowhoush, died after being shoved head first into a sleeping bag and then questioned, while being rolled repeatedly from his back to his stomach.

Subsequent investigations have uncovered a pattern of command decisionmaking associated with the mistreatment of prisoners and a link to Guantanamo. Hersch (2004) contended that the ongoing insurgency in Iraq during the American occupation was highly successful, and the outcome of the war was at risk. In part, this was because human intelligence was poor or lacking. The solution was to get tough with detainees. The Iraqi prison system would be "Gitmoized," by which was meant that it would become more focused on interrogation like that at Guantanamo Bay. Major General Geoffrey Miller went to Iraq from Guantanamo Bay in the summer of 2003 to recommend improvements for intelligence training. Teams from Guantanamo Bay were subsequently sent to Abu Ghraib for 90-day tours at the end of 2003, the period of the worst reported abuses of prisoners.

Three forces were in play at Abu Ghraib that contributed to the torture and abuse of prisoners. First, the members of the MP Company who committed the acts were not trained in prison control and had no experience in such tasks. Secondly, an administrative climate across the chain of command encouraged coercive interrogation practices. Prisoners in Iraq, unlike those at Guantanamo Bay, were protected by Geneva Convention rights. However, these were frequently overlooked in practice. Moreover, an August 1, 2002, memo prepared by Alberto Gonzalez, Counsel to the President, argued that the Geneva Convention only prohibited the most extreme acts of torture, and did not include "cruel, inhuman, or degrading treatment or punishment." Violations of the convention could be justified for necessity or self-defense, such as the war against "Al Qaeda and its allies" (U.S. Department of Justice, 2002). And, as we have previously discussed, Secretary Rumsfeld had argued that the interrogation was a higher priority than due process, justifying the holding of detainees at Guantanamo Bay. Rumsfeld had personally held a prisoner in Abu Ghraib secretly as a "ghost detainee" so that the Red Cross would not know of his presence. (The Red Cross is the organization primarily responsible for ensuring that the Geneva Convention is enforced.) In sum, an administrative climate had emerged that justified the use of harsh techniques, torture, humiliation, and investigations into homicide during interrogation.

Third, in the myriad of problems at Abu Ghraib, we see the reach of Guantanamo. The techniques for interrogation, its legal justification, some of its personnel, and the core logic—ends justify the means—derive from practices and arguments developed and refined at Guantanamo, and transported to Iraq from the officers who developed and used them at Guantanamo. Many will justify the use of torture as a means to end the Iraqi insurgency. Others will express profound concerns over the mistreatment of prisoners, and will draw the parallel between the United States' and Saddam Hussein's use of Abu Ghraib for torture. Certainly, the damage internationally to the legitimacy of the war is immense and perhaps, to some extent, irreparable. In Abu Ghraib we see in play one of the central dilemmas of the war on terrorism: If we justify setting asides principles of due process and fair play in the conduct of the war on terrorism, then what constraints on our moral behavior do we have?

Conclusion

Guantanamo is at the center of a firestorm of criticism over the way in which people are treated in the war on terror. The central logic underlying the use of Guantanamo as a place to hold suspected terrorists—provide the opportunity to carry out interrogations and hold suspects indefinitely, and carry out military tribunals in the absence of U.S. court relief—has been troubling to many observers of the U.S. and its counter-terrorism efforts. A top United Kingdom judge, Law Lord Johan Steyn characterized the detentions as "a monstrous failure of justice" because its primary purpose was "to put them (prisoners) beyond the rule of law" (CNN.com, 2003a). These are strong, rhetorical statements, and reveal the depth of the criticism that Guantanamo has generated.

The government has generally retreated from some of the more controversial aspects of the Guantanamo detentions. A few prisoners have been released. It has attempted to add some due process protections to prospective tribunals. In November of 2003, it announced that two Australians held at Guantanamo would not receive the death penalty if convicted (Mintz, 2003c). It is negotiating with the United Kingdom over its citizens held at Guantanamo as well, and has suspended cases against two British terror suspects held at Guantanamo (Semple, 2003).

The controversies over Guantanamo are not only international, but are increasingly sparking debate in the U.S. courts. The three appellate court cases discussed in this chapter suggest that the U.S. government may face court imposed limits to its authority. And three retired military officers and former WWII prisoners of war submitted friend-of-the-court briefs on behalf of detainees at Guantanamo, saying the failure to recognize Geneva Convention rules would provide other nations with an excuse to do the same, endangering American soldiers captured in the future (*Arizona Daily Star,* 2003). What is clear is that, however this growing controversy is resolved, it is one of the central areas of contestation in the war on terror. That contestation is, as the second court of appeals noted, more than whether prisoners are justly treated in Guantanamo. It goes to the core of the war on terrorism—should it be treated as a war or as a crime control problem? And that question is likely to be contested, among a large variety of groups and nations, for quite a long time.

CHAPTER 9

Reflections on the War on Terror: Critiques and Ethics

The declaration of a war on terror has emerged as the principal political response of the United States to the 9/11 attacks. This book has considered many aspects of that response, its political, legal, and moral complexity. It is not a comfortable chapter for those who are wholly supportive of the government's behavior, nor is it intended to be. It is written with the recognition that any governmental response on the scale of war will inevitably have many consequences, some anticipated and some unexpected. Our purpose in this chapter is to reflect on the controversies that characterize important elements of the war on terror, with the hope that, after reflection, we can adjust our strategies and move forward.

This chapter considers three aspects of U.S. response. The first aspect is the treatment of 9/11 detainees. Three reports are discussed here concerning the way in which detainees were treated after 9/11. The second is the secrecy with which the government has carried out the war on terrorism. A critique by Paul McMasters is presented in this section. Ethical issues are the third aspect considered in this chapter. Two perspectives are presented for the ethical consideration of the war on terror: the fit of "just war theory" to the counter-terrorism response to 9/11, and means-ends conflicts in the war on terror.

Treatment of Detainees

In May 2003 Amnesty International published its annual report, in which it was sharply critical of the way in which the U.S. treated individuals swept up in the post 9/11 furor. This report was followed in June 2003 by an analysis proffered by the Inspector General of the Justice Department, and then a report from the Migration Policy Institute three weeks later. These three reports are reviewed below.

The Amnesty International Report

In the 2003 report titled "Counter-terrorism and Human Rights," issued in May, Amnesty International (AI) challenged the U.S. for the way in which it was carrying out its "War on Terrorism"(Amnesty International, 2003b). AI noted four areas it viewed as inconsistent with human rights standards: detentions outside the U.S., military commissions, abuses in Afghanistan and Yemen, and detentions in the U.S. after the September 11 attacks.

Detentions Outside the U.S.

Three aspects of extra-territorial detention were troubling:

1. AI expressed concern that foreign nationals held in Guantanamo Bay, Cuba, were being held without charges, access to courts, or access to their relatives. The U.S., though seizing them during armed conflict, had refused to grant them prisoner of war status and thus did not recognize international rights granted under the Geneva Convention.

    Detainees' conditions were of particular concern, AI noted. During the flight to the U.S., detainees were "handcuffed, shackled, made to wear mittens, surgical masks and ear muffs, and were effectively blindfolded by the use of taped-over ski goggles. They also had their beards and heads shaved" (2003:1). Housing at Camp X-Ray was a temporary facility of small wire mesh cells, exposed to the elements, and lit continuously by powerful arc lighting. Prisoners were shackled whenever taken out of cells, and were granted almost no exercise time. The more permanent prison, Camp Delta, was built and prisoners were relocated there. However, its cells were smaller than those at Camp X-Ray, and some prisoners were held in them for 24 hours a day.

2. Some suspected members of Al Qaeda were held in U.S. custody at unknown locations outside the U.S. Like those in Guantanamo, their legal status was not clarified, and they were not provided rights under international law including rights to contact their families or access to outside representatives. Some of these were transferred to third countries, and their fate was unknown.

3. Two U.S. nationals were held in incommunicado detention. These individuals, Yaser Esam Hamdi had surrendered to the Northern Alliance in Afghanistan in 2001, and was transferred from Guantanamo Bay to Virginia. Jose Padilla was arrested in Chicago on a material witness charge in May 2002 on suspicion of involvement in a conspiracy to detonate a "dirty bomb." On June 9, 2002, he was transferred to U.S. military custody without notice to his attorney.

Military Commissions

The Department of Defense released operating procedures for the trials of non-U.S. nationals in March 2002. AI has challenged these commissions because they have the power to impose the death penalty and lack fundamental standards associated with fair trials.

Abuses by U.S. Forces in Afghanistan and Yemen

These charges constitute allegations of ill treatment of civilians and detainees. The following allegations were made.

1. In Uruzgan province in Afghanistan, U.S. Special Forces killed at least 16 villagers. Some of their bodies were discovered "with their hands tied behind their backs." Twenty-seven villagers were taken into custody where they were kicked, beaten and punched by U.S. soldiers. All were later released.

2. At Bagram AFB, the Washington Post alleged that the CIA were operating "stress and duress" techniques, including prolonged kneeling and standing, hooding, blindfolding, sleep deprivation and 24-hour lighting.

3. In Yemen, six men were killed in "extrajudicial" executions when their car was attacked by a missile launched by a Predator drone aircraft controlled by the CIA. One of these men was a U.S. citizen.

Detentions in the U.S.

1. About 1,200 foreign nationals were arrested during investigations following the September 11 attacks. Many were held under an interim rule that permitted extended holdings without charges. Some were in custody for months awaiting clearance by the government, even after being granted bail by judges or being issued voluntary deportation orders. Detainees also reported ill treatment, verbal and physical abuse, prolonged solitary confinement, and heavy shackling for court appearances. By the end of 2002, most detainees had been

released or were charged with crimes unrelated to the September 11 attacks. In December 2002 the Justice Department reported that only six of the 765 people detained on immigration charges in the above sweeps remained in custody and 500 had been deported; 134 others had been arrested on federal criminal charges and 99 convicted.

2.   A federal order required males over 16 from designated Muslim and Arab countries and North Korea to register with the Immigration and Naturalization Service. During the registration process, many who complied were detained for alleged visa irregularities. Some were subjected to conditions such as handcuffs and leg shackles, held in cold cells with inadequate clothing and blankets, and some were reportedly moved around so that their lawyers could not contact them. Some individuals who had a legitimate claim to lawful status faced deportation proceedings.

Irene Kahn, the Secretary General of Amnesty International, viewed these security issues in an international context in which the rollback of human rights and expansion of governmental control were increasingly justified in the name of counter-terrorism security (Amnesty International, 2003c). The outcome, she argued, was greater insecurity, not increased security.

Our fears were once again confirmed over the past year (2002) as the drive for security gained greater momentum around the world. A combination of forces sought to roll back the human rights gains of the past five decades in the name of security and "counter-terrorism." But the restrictions on liberty have not necessarily led to increased dividends on safety. Greater emphasis on security, far from making the world a safer place, has made it more dangerous by curtailing human rights and undermining the rule of international law; by shielding governments from scrutiny; by deepening divisions among people of different faiths and origins; and by diverting attention from festering conflicts and other sources of insecurity (Amnesty International, 2003c:1).

During this period, Kahn observed, governments have elected to ignore or undermine the collective system of security represented by international law.

Draconian measures—by democratic as well as autocratic governments—to intrude and intercept, to arrest and detain suspects without trial and to deport people with no regard for their fate, weakened human rights protection of individuals as well as respect for the standards of international law (Amnesty International, 2003c:1).

The U.S. did not escape criticism. By detaining prisoners in defiance of international law, it "undermined its own moral authority to speak out against human rights violations in other parts of the world." "Human rights," she concluded,

> must be upheld at all times, including times of danger and insecurity. They restrain governments from actions that harm and provide the standards for accountability. They empower people and give them the power to choose, to challenge and to shape their own destiny. They provide the framework for a constructive dialogue between governments and peoples. If the quest for a safer world is to succeed, human rights must lie at its heart (Amnesty International, 2003c:3).

The domination of a crime control way of thinking characterizes all aspects of Guantanamo. This can be seen in the comments of one of the commanders, on the policy not to allow any reporter within 200 meters of the prisoners or have more than a glance at the prisoners:

> "We're trying to prevent future guests, if you will, from understanding what's happening down here," says Lieutenant Colonel Dennis Fink, spokesman for Joint Task Force 170, the interrogation task force that periodically grills the Guantanamo prisoners about Sept. 11 and other terrorist activities. "We don't want them to know what the process is about so they can prepare and train. We don't want them to know what we know and what we don't know. We don't want them to know who's here. All these factors only contribute to the terrorists" (Knox, 2002:2).

Colonel Fink's way of thinking reveals the extent to which a crime control perspective dominates all considerations of counter-terrorism. It encapsulates a steely logic that views any due process notion or fair play concern as a threat to security interests. What is different in this view is that it legitimizes a way of thinking that views due process not simply as adversarial, but as a fundamental threat to security interests. Put simply, due process is an enemy of the state. This way of thinking is equally revealed in the refusal to provide POW status for the detainees. POW status would permit detainees to refuse interrogations, and require their release at the end of hostilities.

Many organizations have argued on behalf of the prisoners held at Guantanamo. The Inter-American Commission on Human Rights, an agency of the Organization of American States, asked the U.S. in 2002 to ascertain the legal status of all detainees. It argued that the detainees, because they have not been provided a formal status, should be treated as POWs until they can receive a formal status before a competent tribunal. It noted that "such measures were appropriate and necessary so that the detainees were afforded the legal protections commensurate with the status that they were found to possess, which in no case may fall below the minimum standards of non-derogable rights." Moreover, the commission noted that "OAS members such as the United States were subject to an international legal obligation to comply with such precautionary measures" (Weissbrodt, Fitzpatrick & Newman, 2002). The response of the U.S. was that the OAS had no jurisdiction in the matter.

The September 11 Detainees: A Report of the Inspector General, Department of Justice

Within a few weeks of the publication of the AI report, Inspector General Glenn Fine of the Justice Department released a report on immigrants detained after the September 11 attacks (September 11 Detainees, 2003). A total of 762 immigrants were jailed shortly after the attacks, none of whom were ultimately charged as terrorists.

Perhaps most important about this report is the light it shed on one of the areas in which the government has sought to restrict information—details of the actual administrative processing of detainees. The figure below, adapted from the *New York Times*, is a statistical profile of characteristics of the detainees.

Figure 9.1 shows that nearly three-fourths of the detainees were from Pakistan. Also, the majority of detainees were arrested in New York. The greatest number of arrests were made in the first week following the attacks, suggesting that decisions about who to arrest were not systematically formulated, but occurred in and was affected by the emotional climate of the attacks.

Figure 9.1
Detainees, Profiled

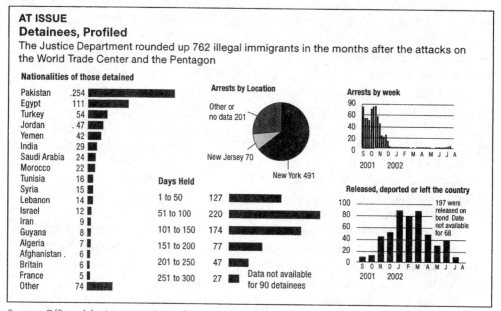

Source: Office of the Inspector General Justice Department.

Mirroring the AI report, Fine noted that many detainees were placed in highly restrictive 23-hour lock-down confinement, limited to one phone call a week, and were in handcuffs, leg irons, and chains when they moved outside their cells. Moreover, because of a blackout of communications, many relatives were told that family members were not arrested when they were. Furthermore, charges were delayed because of the indefinite time period permitted the Justice Department in bringing charges under the extraordinary circumstance clause in the USA PATRIOT Act. Some inmates were not notified of charges for a month.

One of the factors associated with the slow processing of detainees was a policy shift that occurred shortly after the September 11 attacks. Authority to make decisions about when and if detainees should be released was shifted from the Immigration and Naturalization Service to the FBI. The policy, though unannounced, was nevertheless cleared by the Justice Department. Because of it, anyone picked up was held regardless of the strength of the evidence and was presumed to be a terrorist until cleared by the FBI. As Lichtblau (2003:A1, A25) summarized the findings,

> Had it not been for the attacks, "most if not all" of the arrests would probably never have been pursued, the report said. Some illegal immigrants were picked up at random traffic stops, others because of anonymous tips that they were Muslims with erratic schedules, officials said. . . . A Muslim man, for instance, was arrested when an acquaintance wrote to officials that the man had made "anti-American statements." The statements "were very general and did not involve threats of violence or suggest any direct connection to terrorism," the report found, but the man had overstayed his visa and was held. Although the bureau's New York office and the Central Intelligence Agency cleared the man of any terrorist connections by mid-November 2001, F.B.I. headquarters did not clear him for release from incarceration until more than three months later because of an "administrative oversight," the report said (Lichtblau, 2003).

The report concluded with an acknowledgment of the chaotic circumstances surrounding the detainee's connections to terrorism. This chaos explained some of the problems; however, it did not explain them all. The report's conclusion contained the following observations (September 11 Detainees, 2003:195-198):

1. The way in which the FBI classified cases had large long-term unforseen consequences. It instituted a blanket "no-bond" policy that, when combined with the slowness of the clearance rate, resulted in long-term detention of individuals who had no connections to terrorism.

2. Aliens were held for clearance investigations even after they had received final orders for removal or voluntary departure. The legality of these clearance investigations in this circumstance, again under the "no-bond" policy, was never assessed.

3. Detainees were held under the highest security available. However, because of the slowness of the clearance rate, they were held in such conditions for lengthy periods. Timely clearance checks should have been carried out for individuals held under such harsh security conditions.

4. Some confinement conditions were unduly harsh. Many detainees had illuminated cells 24 hours a day. Metropolitan Detention Center (MDC) staff also failed to inform detainees about the process for filing complaints in a timely way.

5. Detainees at MDC were also provided with inconsistent information on telephone access, preventing them from getting legal counsel in a timely way. Earlier, the report noted that MDC staff would ask detainees, "Are you OK?" This was understood by the staff to be shorthand for, "Do you want to place a legal telephone call this week?"

FBI director Mueller responded to some of these concerns on June 12, 2003, at the first nationwide meeting of the membership of the American Civil Liberties Union. He observed that the bureau's handling of detainees had to be considered in the context of the times. There were concerns that other terrorists might be in the United States, and that in the days and months ahead, the U.S. would be again susceptible to attack. However, he acknowledged that there was a need for clear and consistent criteria for determining whether a detainee is a threat. He also noted the need for more FBI manpower and improvements in communication between agencies in order to more quickly clear detainees (CNN.com, 2003b).

The Migration Policy Institute Report

In 2003, the Migration Policy Institute (MPI) issued a report on the effects of post-9/11 security measures on immigration and civil liberty (Chisti et al., 2003). The findings were a sharp rebuke of many of the immigration measures taken by the government. The central problem, the MPI assessed, was at the strategic level:

Al-Qaeda's hijackers were carefully chosen to avoid detection: all but two were educated young men from middle-class families with no criminal records and no known connection to terrorism. To apprehend such individuals before they attack requires a laser-like focus on the gathering, sharing, and analysis of intelligence, working hand-in-glove with well-targeted criminal and immigration law enforcement.

Instead, the government conducted roundups of individuals based on their national origin and religion. These roundups failed to locate terrorists and damaged one of our great potential assets in the war on terrorism: the communities of Arab- and Muslim-Americans (Migration Policy Institute, 2003:7).

The use of categoric indicators of national origin rather than "individualized suspicion or intelligence-driven criteria" (2003:3) was the central problem with the war on terror. It created the illusion that we were actively "doing something" about terrorism. Al Qaeda, the authors argued, had already adapted to this by using "clean" operatives who could pass through immigration controls. The programs implemented post-9/11 suffered from poor planning, contradictory objectives, and ethnic focus. The report interviewed 406 of the detainees and identified the following specific concerns:

1. One-third of the post-9/11 detainees picked up in immigration sweeps were from Egypt and Pakistan. There was no good reason for this disproportionate ethnic selection.

2. Of the detainees the authors could find out about, 46 percent had been in the U.S. for more than six years, and almost one-half had family relationships in the United States. In other words, about half the detainees had significant family ties in the U.S., unlike the hijackers.

3. Many detainees were apprehended because of profiling by ordinary citizens. These calls were often based on ethnicity or appearance. Law enforcement selectively followed up on these for persons with Arab or Muslim backgrounds.

4. More than one-half the sample of detainees were held for more than five weeks, and "almost 9 percent were detained more than 9 months before being released or repatriated" (2003:13).

5. Many detainees suffered "exceptionally harsh treatment" (2003:13). There were problems in notifying and communicating with family members and lawyers. Many were held for excessive periods prior to being charged, had excessively high bond or were not given bond. Fifty-two percent were on FBI hold, which meant that they were held, even for weeks or months, after having been ordered removed from the U.S.

6. Due process protections were seriously compromised for the detainees. The use of the material witness statute allowed the government to hold individuals without charges for long periods in harsh conditions, effectively resulting in preventive detention, constitutionally impermissible.

7.   The voluntary interview program created substantial problems with Muslim and Arab communities. The program rapidly became one of immigration enforcement, which worked against the FBI's efforts to gather intelligence from members of these communities.

8.   The absconder immigration enforcement measure is a legitimate and useful tool for counter-terrorism. However, after 9/11, the program was changed to be nationality-specific, a strategy that had "marginal security benefits" (2003:13).

9.   The NSEERS program was poorly planned and did not achieve its objectives. Its goals were contradictory—gathering information about non-immigrants and deporting those with immigration violations. "Many non-immigrants have rightly feared they will be detained or deported if they attempt to comply, so they have not registered" (2003:14).

This report challenged all aspects of the war on terrorism. Its central indictment was that immigration measures have been used as a proxy for counter-terrorism and law enforcement. A consequence of such measures was that the U.S. had not in fact become safer. If anything, the federal strategy of immigration enforcement had closed off important areas of communications and information, the cornerstones of police investigation. And, according to this report, the only good tools to actually deal with terrorism are investigation and intelligence.

The report also provided substantive recommendations to correct problems in current counter-terrorism matters. Below is a brief summary of those recommendations.

Congressional Oversight. The powers of the executive branch have greatly expanded. They need to be monitored. Current sunset provisions in the USA PATRIOT Act should be retained and congressional committees need to assert their oversight role in evaluating how immigration provisions are being used. The FISA court's permission for surveillance where intelligence is a "purpose" needs to be changed back to its original wording, a "significant purpose."

Information Sharing and Analysis. The unification and automation of government watch lists is an urgent need. The FBI needs to be more open in allowing other organizations to review its intelligence. Clear procedures for placing individuals on and off watch lists need to be developed. Risk assessments of visa applicants need to dig deeper than "mere citizenship in a country where Al Qaeda or other terrorist organizations have a presence" (2003:15).

Due Process. In all areas, due process needs to be reasserted and protected. Closed hearings should be approved only on a case-to-case basis. Detention is "the most onerous power of the states," and should not be used as an investigatory or preventive tool unless a charge is brought. The "automatic stay" rule, allowing immigration authorities to stay an immigration judge's decision to order a non citizen's release, should be rescinded. Individuals should be immediately released after a determination of their cases. And the material witness statute should not be used to circumvent established criminal procedures.

Law Enforcement. Several recommendations were aimed at law enforcement programs. The approval of terrorism investigations needed to be returned to headquarters so that appropriate oversight could be placed on investigators to correspond to their increased powers. Law enforcement activity needed to mend fences with immigrant communities and be careful not to alienate important sources of intelligence. Nationality-specific programs should be ended and follow up reporting should be terminated. Narrow restrictions should apply to future non-immigration registration programs. State and federal police should not affirmatively enforce federal immigration law.

National Unity. A variety of policy changes should be made on behalf of national unity. An independent national commission should be established to address the challenges to unity posed by 9/11 and subsequent actions. Widespread bans on Islamic charities should be reexamined. Government agencies should assess housing and employment discrimination against Muslims, Arabs, and South Asians. Muslim communities themselves must take a more active role in promoting democratic values overseas. And Muslim leaders should denounce terrorism, just as non-Muslim religious leaders should denounce intolerance of Muslims.

Foreign Policy. The impact of immigration policies on foreign policy in combating terrorism should be weighed. Immigration policy is today heavily enforcement oriented, which gives propaganda advantages to terrorists. Immigration policy should not undermine the comparative advantage of the U.S., which is "openness to the world and to people of all nationalities and cultures" (2003:19). It should instead promote cultural exchange, education, and economic activities that promote the national interest.

Secrecy and Governmental Access

One of the concerns of many observers of the government has been the secrecy with which the government carries out counter-terrorism. Citizens are losing the ability to access governmental information to find out what it is doing, and inadvertently undermine democratic notions of government.

The logic behind governmental secrecy is straightforward—advocates argue that secrecy enables the government to keep terrorists uninformed concerning counter-terror measures. Secrecy aids the government in finding and apprehending terrorists when they do not know what the government is doing. Critics, however, see a different pattern in governmental secrecy. They express a concern that government is using the veil of counter-terrorism to act with impunity in counter-terrorism efforts. According to this point of view, a critical element of democracy is access to information regarding what the government is about.

McMasters and Access to the Government, Post-9/11

Paul McMasters, a 30-year journalist, is the Freedom Forum Ombudsman. In an address to the National Press Club (televised on C-SPAN) in May, 2003, Paul McMasters argued that access to the government was one of the "casualties" in the war on terrorism (McMasters, 2003). The U.S. government, he argued, had failed to recognize that access to government information was important to the survival of democratic institutions in the U.S.

"It is openness that defines our particular brand of democracy as unique and exemplary," he said. "It is access that measures the true dimensions of our freedom."

In times of national crisis, when immediate action seems imperative, access to government can be neglected, as it has been in the current post-9/11 crisis. McMasters noted several impediments to the free exchange of information in the government's response to the events of September 11, 2001.

1.   The government had issued warnings to the American people and to the press to be careful of what they said.

2.   The number of White House security briefings to Congress was reduced, as were the number of members who were permitted to attend the briefings.

3.   A shadow government was established to act in the absence of the government in the event of a catastrophic attack. Importantly, Congress (and the American people) learned of the existence of a shadow government, not from the White House but from a report in the Washington Post.

4   The USA PATRIOT Act was enacted hastily, granting law enforcement unprecedented powers, without extensive discussion or debate It transferred large quantities of court authority to the executive branch, and provided minimal oversight.

5   The Justice Department has maintained secrecy regarding the identities and locations of persons detained for investigation.

6. The Defense Department has maintained a similar silence regarding detainees from the war in Afghanistan.

7. The Homeland Security Act exempted businesses considered "critical infrastructure" from the obligation to disclose of information, as required under the Freedom of Information Act.

8. Several other actions protected the government from disclosure, including several that had nothing to do with terrorism. A DEA analyst in Atlanta, for instance, was the first government employee ever to be charged and imprisoned for giving unclassified information to the press.

These actions have fundamentally changed the rules as to what information is and is not available to the public. New vague terminology such as "sensitive but unclassified" and "critical energy infrastructure information," along with memos from the Attorney General and the White House Chief of Staff, have led most federal officials to be more cautious about releasing information to the public, the press, and even to other federal agencies. Yet, it is not clear that such measures are warranted. It is legitimate to ask if they are, but the process for asking is itself increasingly obscure.

Without access, McMasters noted, citizens and legislatures cannot monitor how policies are carried out. Neither can officials be held accountable for abuses of authority when those abuses are protected by an administrative code of silence. The Constitution, McMasters observed, contains a system of checks and balances designed to protect citizens from abusive power. However, in the broad transition to executive power, post-9/11, those checks and balances have been sharply curtailed. And Congress, the courts, and the press have failed to assert democratic rights to access, but instead have been complacent in the face of the U.S. administration's actions.

He concludes with the admonition about what life will mean to citizens absent access to governmental information:

> Of course security and privacy are important. But so is meaningful and timely access to information. Without it, in the end, all we may have left is the privacy of the suspected criminal and the security of the fearful hostage.

Ethics in the War on Terrorism

In this third section we consider ethical issues regarding the war on terrorism. Perhaps more than anything else, the way in which we formulate ethics tells us about the values that make us what we are. It is through the ethics we bring to the world around us that we are known and judged as a people. In the sections below, we will review two ethics appropriate to the war on terrorism. The first, concerning means-ends conflicts and the "noble cause," was developed to study police ethics and is used here to provide insight into the legal prosecution of the war. The second, called just war theory, is suited for thinking about the terrorism conflict in the language of war.

Means/Ends Conflicts in the War On Terrorism

One of the central moral dilemmas in the war on terrorism is the conflict between good ends that agents pursue, finding terrorists before they carry out some vile deed, and good means, which refers to the extent that agents should be held accountable to the laws of due process, international notions of fair play, and to agency protocols. The "good ends" argument is persuasive. It is that the potential ends of successful terrorism are so horrific that no laws should stand in the way of counter-terror efforts. The ends argument is described by the ethics of utilitarianism. Utilitarianism means that good is determined by the consequences of our actions. If our behavior produces more good than harm, it is morally right. In the U.S. criminal justice system, utilitarianism is acted out in terms of justice system efficiency in the prosecution of suspected criminals, and sometimes justifies illegal police behavior and prosecutors' misdeeds in efforts to apprehend and imprison criminals.

In the war on terrorism, utilitarianism argues for a forceful response to terrorism. If some of the legal rules of conventional society have to be set aside for the duration, then we should consider whether a greater good will come from aggressively attacking terrorism than the inevitable harm of prosecuting those who are factually innocent. It also suggests that we can justify fighting terrorism with the same "dirty" means the terrorists use. In figure 8.3, for example, torture was justified because it could prevent a greater harm—the mass killing of civilians. Also, in the incidents at Abu Ghraib, we learned that, once we justify the need for coercive interrogation, we can become surpisingly brutal.

Smith (2003:116-117) describes a utilitarian position in the following statement:

> In the real world, the best intelligence often comes from the worst sorts of people. That is the very reason why they know what they do and are willing to sell out their friends for money. Congress recently has put onerous demands on the nation's intelligence gathering apparatus by disallowing fraternization with certain unsavory types, but still expecting the same quality of information. The problem with this situation is illustrated by the old Texas saying, "When you wrestle with a hog you both get dirty, but the hog likes it." International terrorism is a dirty business. To come to grips with it, one sometimes must get dirty, too. The United States either has to learn to like it or be willing to pay for those who do.

Critics of this view contend that, if we resort to the same tactics that terrorists use, then we are no different from them. This ethical view is grounded in the notion that democracy, to work, requires respect for law and due process in all its practices. Ethical arguments advocating the importance of means are called "ethical formalism." This means that our behavior is the basis for deciding the rightness and wrongness of our acts, independent of their consequences (Pollock, 1998). In democratic societies, ethical formalism is practiced by providing citizens with an identity independent of the state, and requiring the state to carry out clearly stated procedures before taking away citizens' rights. These procedures are embodied internally in the U.S. in the Bill of Rights, through which the legal identity of citizens is created and maintained. Internationally, due process is embodied in international treaties such as the Geneva Convention, which guarantees prisoner rights.

Chomsky presents a means argument to challenge contemporary antiterrorism efforts. He contends that the U.S. government has a moral responsibility to treat non-citizens as it treats its own citizens. In the film *Brothers and Others* (2003), Chomsky stated his position as follows:

> The question of the right way to deal with terrorism is a serious question. However, if we want to be serious about it, we have to at least satisfy the most elementary of moral truisms; namely, if something is wrong for others, it is wrong for us, and if it is right for us, it is right for others.

> I mean, it's a famous definition of a hypocrite in the gospels. The hypocrite, Jesus says, is the person who will not apply to himself the standards he applies to others. Okay, so, unless we concede that we are total hypocrites and we don't even reach elementary moral standards, we will agree—in fact, we will insist—that whatever we say is the right way to deal with others is the right way to deal with us.

> Okay, that's elementary. Incidentally, once we have established that, we can throw out 100 percent, literally, of all commentary on this topic (treatment of aliens), 'cause it doesn't rise to that minimal moral level.

Ends and the Dirty Harry Problem

Police in the U.S., a number of observers have noted, tend to be committed to the good end. The ethics most applicable to police issues are those having to do with their belief in doing good for society. This commitment to society, variously described in terms of the "Dirty Harry problem" or the "Noble Cause," carries the notion that police are morally committed to doing something about "bad guys." This moral commitment is a good end. However, the noble cause is corrupted when police use illegal means, violating the law in order to achieve the good end.

Klockars (1980) argued that police feel that they must sometimes use dirty means in order to achieve good ends. He cites a famous example, what is called the "Dirty Harry problem," to make this point. In an incident acted out in the movie *Dirty Harry*, a police officer faced a dilemma. He sought the good end—to save the life of an innocent victim of a kidnapping. The means he used were bad—he extorted a confession from the suspect using third-degree tactics. His dilemma—the Dirty Harry problem—is whether his behavior was justified in order to save the life of the victim. The Dirty Harry problem is stated as follows: Is it acceptable to use bad means in order to achieve an unquestionably good end?

Caldero and Crank (2005) reframed the ends-means conflict in terms of the "Noble Cause." Taking the term from Delattre (1996), they defined the noble cause as "a profound moral commitment to make the world a safer place to live." Put simply, it is "getting bad guys off the street" (1996:35). When police officers are asked about why they entered police work, some variant of the noble cause usually characterizes their answer, for example, "I believed in it," "I wanted to contribute to society," "I wanted to do something important with my life" (1996:34-35).

Both of the writings described above reveal a "good ends" orientation on the part of the police. And because of that orientation, police are vulnerable to what Crank and Caldero call the "corruption of noble cause." This means that, when police face an ethical dilemma of the Dirty Harry kind, they are vulnerable to seeking the good end even if they "stretch" the law or violate department policy in order to do so.

Crank (2003a) suggested that noble cause problems exist in varying degrees throughout the criminal justice system (See also Pollock, 2004). Prosecutors in particular wield tremendous authority but have only limited oversight and little accountability for ethical misbehavior, and consequently are vulnerable to the temptations of noble cause corruption. For instance, a series of articles on prosecutorial misconduct published by the *Chicago Tribune* cited 381 cases in which a homicide conviction was later overturned because prosecutors concealed evidence suggesting innocence or presented evidence they knew to be false (Armstrong & Possley, 1999).

Those that carry out the war on terrorism are also faced with the temptations of noble cause corruption. The pressures they face to avoid another 9/11magnitude of terrorist incident are intense. And the USA PATRIOT Act, the FISA court, and detention practices provided by Presidential orders provide for a great deal of secrecy in carrying out the war. In the absence of all but minimal and cursory oversight, can we assume that those who prosecute the war will act in good faith? Yes we can, but we must get our ethics straight and understand what "good faith" means. Their faith is likely to be doing something about bad guys, not following the niceties of legal or constitutional standard. To think otherwise is to fail to understand government's willingness to use power in the name of self-protection. The corruption of noble cause can occur in the war on terrorism in several ways:

1. Prosecutors, in their zeal, will arrange for guilty pleas for individuals suspected of terrorism. These pleas may occur independently of whether the individual is truly guilty. In the current era, prosecutors face a great deal of pressure to prosecute terrorist-related suspects, and suspects know that their chances in court are not good. There is the chance that individuals will plead guilty, not from guilt, but from fears that they will face extremely lengthy sentences or death from hostile juries if they do not plead. There is also a concern that they will give prosecutors what they "want to hear" in exchange for preferred treatment. This concern was identified in the previous chapter, in the obtaining of guilty pleas from the "Lackawanna 6," who feared being sent to Guantanamo Bay.

2. Federal agents may decide that it is morally acceptable to use tools that are of questionable legality, given what they perceive to be the magnitude of the terrorist threat. They, for example, might pass on to prosecutors selective intelligence about legal wrongdoing when the prosecutors cannot make a case for terrorism in spite of their suspicions.

3. Legislators, responding to public fears, may turn a blind eye to any abuses of legal authority by agents of the government. They may reason that it is far better to prosecute an innocent person, or to inadvertently arrest or hold someone without evidence, than to allow a terrorist to carry out an act of extensive lethality.

4. Judges may be more willing to let federal agents and prosecutors carry cases forward on minimal, secret, or questionable evidence.

5. Public opinion polls have consistently shown high support for strong governmental actions in the war on terrorism. There is little evidence that the public is concerned with the way in which immigrants have been treated in the war on terrorism, in spite of widespread evidence that immigration interdiction strategies have provided no help on the war and the repeatedly cited questionable seizure, and sometimes abuse, of immigrants.

All of these examples represent instances in which a good—doing something about terrorism—is sought by an individual or group. But they also represent an arbitrary or covert challenge to democratic processes, in which constitutionally protected rights might be "set aside" to do something about terrorism. This does not mean that the commitment to the good end will inevitably overwhelm respect for law and constitutional standards. This does mean that the pressures for the good ends are powerful and those responsible for carrying out counter-terrorism must be vigilant about their use of power.

Prosecutors and police face tremendous pressures to locate and act against suspected terrorists. The public, judges, legislators, and the government all create pressures to find evidence and achieve convictions in the war on terrorism. In such a climate, it is reasonable to suspect that noble cause corruption will be pervasive across the legal system. We are reminded of Caldero's caution to police executives: For those who are not particularly concerned about the corruption of noble cause, he noted with regard to officers in the war on drugs:

> We underpin anti-drug police tactics with a simple morality. Good. Bad. Good cop. Bad drug user. One value system against another. We hire for this . . . His morally good ends determine his means. He has to learn how to avoid getting caught (Caldero & Crank, 2005).

Substitute "terrorist" for "drug user" and the dilemma is clear. This uncomfortable view of police work applies with equal vigor to the war on terrorism. It is simply unreasonable to expect that police and prosecutors are going to act within the constraints of due process law in efforts to carry out the war. Substantial pressures are pushing them the other way—to avoid getting caught doing what they "know" to be right, winning the war on terrorism.

Moreover, police and prosecutors are likely to find these pressures echoed within agencies. In their study of police violations of law to enforce narcotic laws, Manning and Redlinger (1977) described two kinds of pressures: department pressures to violate laws to enforce narcotics laws, and pressures to obstruct justice. Pressures to violate laws include aspirations for promotion and salary, administrative directives, and self-esteem. Pressures to obstruct justice include the protection of informants, the creation of informants through threats of prosecution, and the suppression of information on cases pursued by other officers.

We see in Manning and Redlinger's discussion of police counter-narcotics a variety of organizational pressures that likely find their equivalents in the war on terrorism. Moreover, we can anticipate that these pressures will be substantially greater in the war on terrorism, where the stakes are much higher. In sum, police and prosecutors are likely to feel a great deal of pressure to commit noble cause corruption. One must keep in mind that noble cause corruption does not come about from an absence of moral commitment—it comes from a great deal of moral commitment. It is a commitment to utilitarianism, a belief in the rightness of the good end.

The central problem with a utilitarian commitment to good ends is its undemocratic implications. Alderson (1998) observed that utilitarianism is interpreted by the police in terms of increased police authority in order to preserve order. An over-concern for utilitarianism, for the good end, can lead to quite undemocratic behaviors. Justice systems live in an uneasy relationship with democracies, and under some circumstances can lead to the destabilization of democracies.

Yet, the most powerful pressures for the corruption of democratic process in the war on terror may come, not from the police and prosecutors, but from the American public. Though powerful advocacy groups resist the siren song of a "no-holds-barred" fight against terrorism in which all tactics are justified, large segments of the American public does not. For many citizens, the issue is not whether the State acts to protect constitutional standards in the war on terror. It is whether they are safe from terrorist threats. The actions of the government reflect the desires of the public, and part of that desire may be to not know what the state is doing.

"Just War" and the War on Terrorism

An ethic particularly suited to the military and to issues of international security is called "just war." Much has been written in an attempt to identify the circumstances in which one country can justly use military fore against another. At the core of the "just war" doctrine is the notion of self-defense. One country has a right to protect itself from imminent destruction by another country. "Just war" theory is an attempt to identify the basis and limitations of permissible self-defense. Views on "just war" are presented below.

"Just War" and Catholicism

Because by nature the notion of "just war" is moral, the first consideration of "just war" will be taken from a moral doctrine—that presented by the Catholic Church. (Catholic Answers, 2003). The "Catholic Answers" discussion is quoted and paraphrased below.

There are two sets of criteria for just war doctrine, the reasons for going to war, and the actions taken after one is engaged in war. Figure 9.2 presents the conditions that apply to reasons for going to war:

Figure 9.2
Just Force: Paragraph 2309 of the Catechism of the Catholic Church

---

The strict conditions for legitimate defense by military force require rigorous consideration. The gravity of such a decision makes it subject to rigorous conditions of moral legitimacy. At one and the same time:

1. The damage inflicted by the aggressor on the nation or community of nations must be lasting, grave, and certain.

2. All other means of putting an end to it must have been shown to be impractical or ineffective.

3. There must be serious prospects of success.

4. The use of arms must not produce evils and disorders graver than the evil to be eliminated. The power of modern means of destruction weighs very heavily in evaluating this condition.

These are the traditional elements enumerated in what is called the "just war" doctrine. The evaluation of these conditions for moral legitimacy belongs to those who have responsibility for the common good.

Source: Catholic Answers, 2003 "Catholic Answers to Just War Doctrine," page 2.

The four elements are discussed below.

Lasting, Grave, and Certain Damage. This means that war can only be fought to counter aggression. Moreover, an aggression that is temporary or mild is inadequate to qualify. The effects must be foreseen to be lasting and grave. This means that "it is not necessary for the aggressor to strike first. A moral certainty that the aggression will occur is sufficient" (2003:1). Such certainty can include the amassing of troops or munitions for war. Further, because an aggressor can attack from a substantial distance with little warning, one should identify a potential aggressor early to determine if he is a morally certain danger.

Other Means Practical or Ineffective. This means that war is a course of last resort. Other practical means of stopping the aggressor must first be used. These can include diplomacy, economic sanctions, blockades, quarantines, covert actions, and small-scale raids. All of these do not have to be carried out; what is important is that rigorous consideration shows them to be insufficient.

Prospects of Success. It is impossible to have certainty that the outcome will be successful. History is replete with examples of super-powers losing wars to small countries. There simply must be a substantial possibility of success.

Greater Evils. The damage that is created by a conflict must be taken into consideration. Given the widespread availability of weapons of mass destruction, it is possible that a nation could use excessive force to stop an aggressor. One must also consider the collateral damage caused in terms of civilian casualties, destabilization of neighboring countries, harmful changes in international alliances, and economic problems.

The evaluation of the conditions for legitimate defense belongs "to the prudential judgment of those who have responsibility for the common good" (2003:4). In nation states, this means the government. The public, the doctrine notes, must be ready to trust its leaders to make the right decision. This is because the government is privy to information that is not publicly available. The public, nevertheless, has a voice. Through public debate, the public helps leaders make decisions.

Once a decision is made to go to war, a second set of issues emerge. These have to do with how the war is carried out. A commonplace danger during war is that of brutality against individuals who are not engaged in the conflict. According to the doctrine:

> Non-combatants, wounded soldiers, and prisoners must be respected and treated humanely. Actions deliberately contrary to the law of nations and to its universal principles are crimes, as are orders that command such actions (2003:5).

Also, weapons of mass destruction create particular moral challenges. An act of war that is aimed at the indiscriminate destruction of cities or "vast areas with their inhabitants is a crime against God and man . . ." (2003:5). This principle requires that strenuous efforts be employed to avoid harm to innocents. It does not mean that no innocents will be harmed, a result impossible to guarantee.

The law of "double effect" is employed with regard to harm to citizens. According to this law, it is permissible to employ an action which has two effects, one of which is good and one of which is evil. The following conditions have to be met. (1) The act should not be in itself evil, for example, the intentional killing of civilians. (2) The evil must not be an end in itself but a means to accomplish a good effect. This can include the killing of captured combatants. (3) The evil effect must not outweigh the good effect. This includes the foreseen consequences of the war. For example, this might include the targeting of civilian areas in order to kill suspected militants. Only if these three conditions are met can an action be taken that will cause harm to citizens or other damage.

Cook's "Just War"

Dr. Martin Cook, of the U.S. Army War College, applied the "just war" doctrine to the war on terrorism (Cook, 2001). He noted, like the Catholic doctrine above, that the "just war" tradition has two different assessments of the use of military force. The first, called *jus ad bellum* and defined as the right of justice toward war, assesses the circumstances that justify a military response. The agents against whom we wage war are those responsible for funding and directing the activities of the hijackers. If they are identified to a moral certainty they can be targeted. However, how about those who harbor terrorists, in this case, the Taliban? He stated that:

> The justification for attacking them (the Taliban) has two aspects: first, it holds them accountable for activities which they knew, or should have known, were being conducted in their territories and did nothing to stop; second, it serves as a deterrent to motivate other states and sponsors to be more vigilant and aware of the activities of groups on their soil (2003:2).

Cook proposes applying a legal standard to the Taliban, the government in Afghanistan that provided the stamp of approval for the actions of Al Qaeda: that of the "reasonable person." The question, he asserts, is not whether the Taliban had specific knowledge that attacks were being carried out under their watch, but whether a reasonable person in those circumstances would have known. Hence it is not a question of what they did know, but what they ought to have known.

Legitimate targets of U.S. military action also include those actively preparing to carry out attacks against U.S. citizens and forces. Again using a legal analogy, he suggests that all who fall within the standard for criminal conspiracy are legitimate targets. Criminal conspiracy means the shared intent to carry out a criminal act, combined with evidence that concrete steps have been taken to carry out the act. In this instance, criminal conspiracy would include those who possessed information about the contemplated attack, and those who supplied weapons, training, funding, or safe harbor.

The second criteria, *jus in bello,* is defined as the right conduct of military operations. The two key concerns are discrimination and proportionality. Discrimination refers to the use of force against others. Attacks must have a strong likelihood of success, and damage to innocent persons and targets must be minimal. Proportionality refers to the balance between the damage done and the value of the military targets. He notes, for example, that one is not justified obliterating an entire town for a small cell of terrorists.

Two other considerations are important. First, "military necessity permits actions that might otherwise be ethically questionable." However, this is not a justification for military convenience, which he argued is ethically unacceptable in and of itself. Second is the enemy tactic of deliberately locating military operations amid civilian populations, using the latter as human shields. In this context the principle of "double effect" permits attack, because the killing of innocents is not purposeful but an unavoidable byproduct of "legitimate military action."

Finally, he addresses the moral status of Al Qaeda. He states that the individuals who carried out the terrorist attacks are in no sense "soldiers," and consequently are not entitled to any war convention protections. This justifies the imprisonment of Al Qaeda combatants in Guantanamo without legal recourse. Moreover, for effectiveness purposes, it would be undesirable to carry out criminal proceedings which provide for due process. As long as they act under civilian cover, the best response is swift elimination. However, should they organize into military units, their legal status as combatants would have to be reconsidered.

Limits to the Ethics of "Just War"

In practice, "just war" terminology can be slippery. Lichtenberg (2001) notes that the issue of proportionality excludes very little in the way of retaliation. Proportionality requires that we weigh means against ends. When a country is attacked and its survival seems to be in question, the principle of proportionality appears to rule out only "purposeless or wanton violence" (2001:6). Virtually anything else can be done to justify survival, including the mass killing of civilians if it is seen as serving the greater good of protecting the homeland.

More important, she argues, is the issue of noncombatant immunity, whose core idea is that during war civilians cannot be targeted. Two principles underlie this notion, the principle of threat and the principle of the reduction of carnage. First, in the war in Afghanistan, President Bush stated that low civilian casualties were central to war efforts. This decision was, in part, strategic, because it aimed at winning public opinion in the Muslim world. Beneath this was a moral consideration—it was morally wrong to kill noncombatants.

But who are noncombatants? Some soldiers are unwilling conscripts and are basically innocent. Some noncombatants are heavily involved in the war effort. The issue is not one of moral guilt of those waging war against us, but their threateningness. For instance, a 10-year-old child may carry no moral guilt when it aims an automatic weapon at American troops, but he nevertheless poses an imminent threat to life. Second, discussing George Mavrodes, she suggests that there is not so much a moral difference between combatants and noncombatants as a "pragmatic calculation that in the long run less carnage and destruction will result if we limit battle to a circumscribed class of people" (2001:7). The problem is that civilians will always be killed in war, and how can we justify this? She returns to the doctrine of double effect discussed above.

According to the doctrine of double effect, killing civilians intentionally is never permitted. However, anticipating that civilians may be killed during a military operation is not prohibited. Discussing Walzer (1984), she states that it is inadequate to simply not intend the deaths of civilians. There must be a positive commitment to save lives, even if this means risking soldiers' lives. "It's not enough not to try to kill civilians; you have to try *not* to kill them [italics in original]." That is, our soldiers have to take risks to protect their civilians. In practice though, it is difficult to justify why the lives of "our" troops are worth less than the lives of "their" civilians.

Greetham's (2003) criticisms of notions that war can be just or "fair" are sharper. Consider the *jus ad bellum*, justice toward war. He states that citizens are always told by their governments that any war they are about to fight involves imminent threats. Describing Nazi Germany, Greetham notes that:

> Lurid tales were retold of supposed Jewish sexual crimes and 'ritual murders.' The notorious forgery known as the Protocols of the Elders of Zion was used by the most fanatical followers of Hitler to whip up fears of an international Jewish conspiracy that would sweep like a rapacious pestilence not just across Germany and Europe, but across all civilization (2003:5).

Greetham's point is that "just war" in practice is not much more than the way a government rationalizes its behavior in order to maintain legitimacy before its citizens and in the community of nations.

In actuality, wars are rarely fought over ultimate threats to values and cultural survival. At a pragmatic level, governments often present an imminent threat argument to take the moral high ground. For example, the Vietnam War was justified in terms of the "better dead than red" belief which, when coupled with the domino theory—that communists could knock over the countries in Southeast Asia like dominos without U.S. intervention—was deemed to present an immediate threat to the U.S. and allow for a "just war" response. However, the publication of documents such as the Pentagon Papers (a classified study, commissioned by the U.S. Defense Department, of the Vietnam War) revealed a pattern of U.S. involvement in Vietnam dating to President Truman; the covert war had, in fact, been planned well before the American public was notified (Pentagon Papers, 2004).

Even WWII, famously known as the "good war," presented ethical problems in "just war" theory. For example, the cities of Hiroshima and Nagasaki in Japan and Dresden in Germany were bombed precisely because they were civilian. Dresden was targeted in 1945, even though it was clear from late 1940 that Germany would be unable to gain air superiority over England, and that, after three million German soldiers were relocated to the Russian front in 1941, no invasion of Britain would be forthcoming. And the Catholic doctrine discussed above condemned the nuclear bombing of Nagasaki and Hiroshima as a clear moral violation of principles regarding how a just war is conducted, *jus in bello*, because civilian targets were deliberately selected for mass destruction. Many people argue that the bombing of these civilian targets was *just*, because it served a larger purpose—it hastened the end of the Second World War and saved thousands of American lives. However, a crucial element of just war theory was not present. At this point on both fronts, in Germany and Japan, the threat of invasion simply did not exist (Greetham, 2003).

Moreover, Greetham argues, the bombings had a barbaric long-term postwar consequence. They legitimized the use of terror as a weapon among terrorists and governments alike.

> the real significance of the Allies' use of terror lies in the fact that it legitimized what has now become a standard strategy in postwar diplomacy for terrorists and governments alike. In the nuclear age exploiting the insecurity of ordinary people through terror has become an indispensable part of defense policies (2003:7).

These sharp criticisms of WWII are recognizably controversial. They are not included as a criticism of the war, though perhaps it is fitting that all war is closely examined and relentlessly critiqued. The point is that "just war" ideals often collapse in the face of sustained long-term conflict and mass killings. At some point in conflicts involving mass casualties, the grievance of loss and hatred of the enemy overwhelm sentiments of moral fairness, and both sides easily justify using any tactics that hurt the enemy, be it the enemy's military or civilian population.

Conclusion

This chapter has provided a variety of perspectives on the war on terrorism. For the most part, these perspectives have been critical. This is purposeful. We believe that at the core of successful democratic process is the unrelenting desire of the public to be informed. The war is controversial, and this chapter summarized central controversies about the war. However, we emphasize that being informed does not necessarily mean disagreeing with the actions of the government. What being informed means is understanding the full range of complexity of the decisions made by the government. Some perspectives presented herein, Cook's interpretation of "just war," for instance, were critical but supportive.

However, the perspectives presented herein reveal another important dynamic of the war. The first two main sections of this chapter were taken from reports published or presented two years after the 9/11 attacks launched the war on terror. Seen from this view, they represent perspectives that look at the first two years in hindsight. That they are critical and challenge fundamental aspects of the war suggests that the contestedness of the war is not diminishing. If anything, at this juncture, people and groups seem to be taking sides and marshaling their arguments. We also noted this phenomenon with regard to the actions of appellate courts in the previous chapter. Hence, as the war continues, at least at this juncture, its central controversies are stabilizing around polar positions, that of liberty and freedom, and that of security and governmental secrecy. It may be unfortunate that the central debate in the war on terrorism took this form; certainly, many have argued that the war on terrorism need not have challenged constitutional protections but instead should have focused on preserving them in the face of adversity (see, e.g., Gilmore, 2003). But it is the central debate in the war on terrorism today, and it shows no signs of abatement.

Imagining Terrorism, Governing a Free Society

In response to 9/11, the U.S. embarked on a series of fundamental changes in the name of counter-terrorism. It launched a "war against terrorism" and is waging wars against the Taliban and Al Qaeda in Afghanistan, a second against terrorists generally, and is in the midst of the occupation of Iraq, justified in part by its claim that Iraq had terrorist connections to Al Qaeda. It established quasi-military courts that operate with rules different from traditional military jurisprudence. It placed terrorist suspects in locations beyond the reach of federal courts to prohibit their access to traditional legal protections. The citizenry became conditioned to routine color-coded terrorist alerts and ways of responding to those alerts.

A variety of laws have been enacted that permit local and federal police to dramatically expand surveillance of criminal and terrorist behavior, and legislation permits the use of that evidence in court actions against suspects, absent criminal behavior. We have put in place a Department of Homeland Security that reorganizes large sections of government to deal with terrorism and elevated its importance to the cabinet level. In parallel military developments, we created the eighth military command, USNORTHCOM. This creates a worldwide military unified command that includes the United States. Its effects on *posse comitatus* are yet unclear, though the government has sought to leave all first-response roles to civilian populations. USNORTHCOM seeks a role in which military is in a superordinate and coordinating role. We seek out immigrants on the basis of their religious, organizational, and national affiliations, secretly imprison them and sometimes deport them, without the provision of access to legal counsel.

All of these changes have been carried out under the advocacy of the U.S. administration, with the overwhelming support of the legislative branch and with little judicial resistance. Public opinion polls through 2003 consistently show that the majority of Americans are in favor of these changes. One can reasonably conclude from this level of support that the changes instituted over the past few years and described throughout the book are going to be with us for the long haul. At some level, they resonate with a shift in the American psyche, a shift that elevates fears of personal security over support for individual rights. In conclusion, we present a way to think about the long-term consequences of these changes.

The Hauntings of Great Enterprises

It has been famously observed that the elements that comprise the foundation of great enterprises haunt them throughout their histories. The founding of the U.S. exemplifies this notion; the republic was established with strong democratic elements, and the core constitutional identity of the U.S., grounded in enlightenment ideas of governance, has sustained it and continues to drive enduring features of its political culture. At the same time, slavery was permitted in the Union, a decision with a harsh long-term impact on the Union. Today, at the beginning of the twenty-first century and more than 200 years after the founding of the United States, economic and criminological issues pertaining to African-Americans are among America's most trenchant and unresolved problems.

The events of 9/11 initiated a great enterprise. That enterprise was a "war on terrorism" that led to fundamental changes in policy regarding international security, practices and laws regarding internal security and policing, restructuring of the President's Cabinet and expansion of in military command to encompass the U.S., and a re-thinking of the relationship between rights, privacy, and security. Today, we can look at the founding elements of the war on terrorism and begin to consider what will endure.

Three features of the war on terrorism, embedded in its foundation, are important to understanding it. First, 9/11 caused a great deal of grief, and coupled with fear of additional terrorist attacks, grief and fear have become institutionalized in American life. The second is that terrorism is a contested concept, and because of this the war on terrorism is polarizing both within the U.S. and between the U.S. and other nations, and there is no way to bring the war to a close through declaration of victory or defeat. The third is that the war has marked a threshold change in the relationship between crime control and due process, in which crime control, represented by security interests and acted out as administrative decisionmaking, takes precedence over due process. Each is discussed below.

The Institutionalization of Grief and Fear

For many people, the grief caused by the tragic events on 9/11 seems to endure without relief. The second anniversary of 9/11 was marked with solemn ceremonies across the United States. Memorial events were held at the Pentagon, and at Arlington National Cemetery where 125 of those killed at the Pentagon were buried. In New York, the Mayor led a ceremony described by Barron (2003:1):

> 'Today, again we are a city that mourns,' Mayor Michael R. Bloomberg said at Ground Zero, the 16-acre site where the trade center stood until September 11, 2001. In 10 terse sentences, Mr. Bloomberg introduced and thanked the children helping in the ceremony. 'Their world is still in the making,' he said. 'As the mayor, and a father, I hope it will be a wise and just world.'

A ceremony was also held in Shanksville, Pennsylvania, where United Airlines Flight 93, one of the four hijacked airlines in 9/11, crashed. The flight crashed shortly after passengers called relatives on their cell phones to tell them they were going to storm the cockpit.

The White House actively participated in 9/11 remembrance ceremonies. President Bush held a moment of silence at 8:46 a.m., the time at which the first hijacked plane struck the North Tower. The president also attended a prayer service in St. John's Church across from the White House, and Vice President Cheney attended an interfaith service in memory of the 84 Port Authority of New York and New Jersey workers who were killed on 9/11.

Barron observed that one of the notable features of the ceremonies was that the emotions associated with 9/11 had not diminished. One of Barron's interviewees referred to a "paralysis of grief" that affected many of those tied to the events of 9/11, and expressed hope that the ceremonies of the second anniversary might begin the process of moving forward. Another noted that they were a "little bit further in the grieving process . . . but it's still pretty much the same."

The sustenance of emotions associated with the war on terror is, to an extent, a social structural phenomena built into the ceremonies held this year. In the ceremony held at "Ground Zero," the children of the victims were selected to read the victims names. As Barron continued,

> It fell to the children to read the victims' names—children as young as 7, children as old as 35, children who were two years younger chronologically and far younger emotionally on the morning their worlds changed. Yesterday, they read from an alphabetized list—at times tearily, at times awkwardly as they stumbled over names they had trouble pronouncing, at times haltingly as they added their own postscripts (Barron, 2003:1).

This ceremony and those like it serve as generational transmitters of the emotions associated with the loss of life on 9/11. The children are reminded of the grief of the passing of their relatives. The grief of initial emotions is in this way sustained as a central element of the war on terrorism.

Anecdotal information presented in a newspaper column, however respected, does not carry the representativeness of random sampling. Public opinion polls, however, have shown that citizens continued to be worried about terrorism. Two years after the attacks, the economy had replaced terrorism as the public's top priority, according to a PEW poll taken between July 14 and August 5 (Lester, 2003). Fifty eight percent of those polled worried there would soon be another terrorist attack. And three-fourths indicated that they accepted that acts of terrorism would be part of life in the future. These numbers represent a drop in the overall public prioritizing of terrorism, which had equaled in importance the economy. However, as the pollsters noted, "The fear factor lingers two years later—a much greater percentage of people than just prior to the attacks see this as a more dangerous world" (Lester, 2003).

The sustenance of fear and grief suggest that America, a country young in its nation-state history, may be learning what many older countries have experienced—that bitterness and enmity are passed by families through generations and tend to endure. The history of the Balkans and of the Middle East suggests that such sentiments can endure for centuries. Indeed, as noted in Chapter 2, many in the Middle East view the current conflicts involving themselves, the U.S., and Israel as extensions of the conflicts associated with the Crusades of the Middle Ages. The focus on grief and fear is sustained by the war on terrorism. Because the war on terrorism has become the central focus of the Bush administration, it serves as a constant reminder of the grief and tragedy of 9/11.

The War on Terror: Warring Against a Contested Concept

This book has identified many different dimensions in which the war on terrorism is contested. Their continued contention two years after the initiation of the war provides insight into what issues will endure. In this section, we look at those enduring elements of conflict in the war on terrorism.

The Occupation of Iraq

"This fence is here for your protection" reads the sign posted in front of the barbed-wire fence. "Do not approach or try to cross, or you will be shot" (Filkins, 2003:3).

This sign was posted by American troops on a fence surrounding the town of Abu Hishma in Iraq. The fence's purpose was to seal off the town and to protect American troops. Yet, the sign is symbolic of the enormous ambiguity in the war on a contested concept like terrorism. Who is a friend of the U.S.? Who is the enemy? Is the U.S., as some have suggested and as implied by the sign, fighting a war against a quasimilitary tactic? What has to be done to win the war, and how will the U.S. know when it has won?

At the two-year point, the war on terrorism was being carried out in many different countries, with Iraq in the foreground of the war. The United States, like it or not, had chosen to become embedded in world affairs in a profoundly militaristic and political way. The U.S. had elected to place itself in the center of an aggressive war on terror, and its reputation had suffered for this. A poll carried out as part of the Pew Global Attitudes Project showed that overall views of the U.S. had dropped from a favorability rating of 52 percent in the summer of 2002 to 34 percent in the summer of 2003 (Bernstein, 2003).

The occupation of Iraq has become the front in the war on terrorism. And like the notion of terrorism itself, the occupation is hotly contested. In the current era, one can discern five conflicting views regarding the war on terrorism as carried out in Iraq. On September 12, 2003, President Bush announced that "Iraq is now the central front on the war on terror" (Stout, 2003b). This view is shared widely by those in the Bush administration, and the view that the U.S. is safer with the leadership of Iraq deposed has substantial public support. Supporters of the President argued that the potential for terrorism against the U.S. was ever-present under Hussein, and his threat had to be dealt with at some point.

A second view is highly skeptical that the war in Iraq is related to counter-terrorism efforts. To many scholars, the statement regarding the centrality of Iraq in the war on terrorism was surprising given the absence of evidence of mutual support between the two groups. Moreover, there was a history of well-known hostilities between Islamic Al Qaeda and Iraq, a secular state under Saddam Hussein. The war in Iraq, from this view, is exacerbating tensions in the Middle East and increasing the ability of terrorists to recruit new members. A third perspective suggests that the President was using 9/11 to justify an increasingly expensive and lethal military adventure. The occupation of Iraq, according to this view, as a pretext for acquiring their oil. Fourth, some argue that, whether or not Iraq was a terrorist threat prior to the military occupation of Iraq, it was certainly a threat after the occupation simply because the U.S. had moved large numbers of vulnerable American soldiers into the country and terrorists now had the means and access to attack the United States directly. Fifth, some observers indicated a concern that the war on terrorism in Afghanistan was being neglected, and the Taliban, who provided support for Al Qaeda, was regrouping and trying to regain control in parts of Afghanistan.

The presence of these divergent views reveals the way in which central elements of the war on terrorism, including the language used to describe it, is contested. Each view carries with it a complete narrative, and that narrative contains a way of thinking about what is going on with regard to terrorism and international security efforts, and justifications for those actions.

In the long term, the determination of which group is right will be acted out on the great stage of the Middle East, where factors beyond the control of the U.S. may ultimately determine the success or failure of our military ventures in that region.

Surveillance

The expansion of surveillance, discussed in Chapter 4, has been a source of controversy. Executive pressures to increase surveillance characterized the two-year mark. On September 10, 2003, the eve of the second anniversary of 9/11, President Bush called for a "significant expansion of law enforcement practices under the USA PATRIOT Act" (Sanger, 2003). This call came shortly after Attorney General Ashcroft carried out a national tour in which he sought to quell fears about the USA PATRIOT Act. The President called for expansion in three areas, (1) permitting law enforcement agencies to issue "administrative subpoenas" in terrorism cases without the approval of judges of grand juries, (2) holding suspected terrorists without bail, and (3) expanded death penalties for terror-related crimes. The first of these, subpoena power, would enable agents to obtain subpoenas without the approval of the FISA court. This would enable agents to demand private records of individuals and to compel testimony (Lichtblau, 2003). This act would increase the reach of the government into individual's private records absent even the limited oversight provided by the FISA court. Yet, the notion of a broader act extending the USA PATRIOT Act has been enormously controversial. At the current time, the PATRIOT II ACT, Israel noted, "is dead. For now" (Israel, 2003) The Anti Terrorism Tools Enhancement Act (HR-3037, S-1606), also called the Victory Act, is suffering from the severe criticism of PATRIOT I.

The Department of Homeland Security

In some casese, the war on terrorism has not had a direct impact on Americans' lives. However, it has had an impact in its efforts to reassure the public that the U.S. is doing all it can to stop terrorism so that Americans will be safe. Chapter 5 looked at the way in which counter-terrorism affected Americans' daily lives, focusing particularly on the Department of Homeland Security. In its public pronouncements, the DHS affects on the lives of Americans by making them feel more secure. At the two-year mark, the Bush administration continued to consolidate the DHS, yet the final shape and activity of the department remains to be seen. The color-coded terrorism alert system, widely criticized, was revamped to make terror alerts more difficult to impose. Under the new revisions, the "elevated," or yellow, threat level would only be raised if "there is credible, detailed evidence of an imminent terrorist attack on American soil" (Shenon, 2003). This change came in response to congressional concerns that the existing system had confused the public and was vague in detailing terrorist threats.

Concerns over air transportation continue. The key issues raised by Michael Boyd, in his airline security analysis in Figure 5.4—weak airline security, random screening, and problems with the TSA bureaucracy—were stated just prior to the second anniversary of 9/11 and for some that overall security has not improved much. Yet, the presence of security is much more visible in the daily lives of airline commuters and users. An area highly contested at the second anniversary is the rights of the airlines to obtain personal information about individuals as part of the routine security process. And the airlines suffer from financial problems that were preexisting but exacerbated by 9/11 and its economic effects on the airline industry. That the government is acting forcefully to control airline security is not debatable. What is debatable is whether it is acting effectively, And this can only be answered in the long term. Yet, at the 9/11 second anniversary, there were no additional incidents that resulted in successful acts of terror against the airline industry. Overall, the DHS has received little criticism, and most of what it has received has been in the spirit of recommendations for increased bureaucratic rigor. At least at this juncture, the DHS has been a widely accepted, generally uncontested development in the war on terror.

Immigrants and Visitors to the U.S.

If one is either Muslim, Middle-Eastern, an immigrant, or visiting the U.S. on a visa, the war on terrorism has had a considerable effect. Chapters 6 and 7 looked at the treatment of aliens in the U.S. after 9/11. As discussed in the critiques of government's treatment of aliens in Chapter 9, agencies within the government as well as independent "watchdogs" such as Amnesty International have cited what they consider to be excesses, mistreatment, and brutality. The government can be described as apologetic of these excesses but steadfast in its belief that it has acted appropriately in the face of potential terror threats posed by aliens entering the U.S. In assessing the political status of immigrants, one might best describe their status as participants in an administrative nondemocratic regime. Because most due process venues have been coopted by the administration in favor of administrative process, and because the courts have been reluctant to challenge this process of administrative cooptation, immigrants and visa holders who are identified as potential terrorists (which, it should be recalled, can be done through their associations, through their conversations, and through their donations to Islamic charities) as individuals who may know something (material witnesses), or individuals who have violated some term of their visa, do not have access to court relief until after administrative prerogatives are satisfied, and then only at the convenience of the justice department. They lack the key element that creates democracy: No legal space is created that provides a body of rights protecting individuals from government. They have fewer rights than convicted criminals, who maintain a thin but important veneer of *habeas corpus* rights, the rights to appeal their sentences.

Treatment of Foreign Detainees

As of the second anniversary of 9/11, the government was expanding its tracking system for immigrants and other aliens. A new system, called the *United States Visitor and Immigrant Status Indicator Technology* (US-VISIT) will require all visitors to the U.S. to have their fingerprints and photographs scanned at points of entry. Also employed will be facial and iris scans, to be checked in the future against databases of criminal and terrorist suspects. To support the program, the Secretary of Border and Transportation Asa Hutchinson announced the future hiring of 11,700 inspectors, hundreds of border patrol agents, and the creation of an Office of Compliance to manage information about visas and visa holders (Jachimowicz, 2003).

Chapter 8 discussed the treatment of foreign prisoners in the war against terrorism. This discussion focused on the use of the facility at Guantanamo Bay, a facility that, because it is outside the jurisdiction of U.S. courts, enabled the administration to avoid due process issues in the treatment of prisoners. Secretary of Defense Rumsfeld has indicated his intention to hold trials at Guantanamo Bay, and has instituted a limited right to legal counsel for those to be tried. As more information is acquired about prisoners at Guantanamo Bay, it has become apparent that many prisoners played bit parts in the global war on terror, and some seemed to be there only because they were in the wrong place at the wrong time. Interestingly, prisoners taken from the war against Iraq have not been housed at Guantanamo Bay, though Iraq is now considered the center of U.S. counter-terrorism.

Trials, when they occur, can place the U.S. in an awkward dilemma. Under immense international and internal pressure to have a degree of openness in its procedures, trials may reveal weaknesses in the Administration's case. If openness is avoided, the U.S. will be seen as arbitrary and in violation of fundamental human rights by much of the world, a view that would delegitimize any U.S. claim as an advocate of human rights.

The Core Concept: A War on Terrorism?

Chapter 9 presented critiques of the war on terrorism. The critiques suggest that fundamental notions of the way in which the war is being carried out remain in dispute. The ethical perspectives present a more complex picture. The ethics derived from "just war" perspective seem to dovetail closely with the war on terrorism. Yet concerns were also noted that what constitutes "just war" is determined by the winners in retrospect. At the two-year point, in the week of December 5-12, two raids on suspected guerillas by Americans resulted in the deaths of 6 and 9 Afghani children respectively. The U.S. government states that it seeks to avoid civilian casualties. Yet, because we are at war with a contested concept, we continue in military actions in Afghanistan long after the Taliban were routed and Al Qaeda was decimated and deprived of its bases. We see in this continued military action one of the central problems with a war against a contested concept—there is no way to tell when victory occurs.

The noble cause ethics are also controversial. It is clear that the administration takes a noble cause view of the war on terrorism, and its unremitting focus on the ends—do something about terrorism—are uncomfortable for those who believe in the rightness of good conduct, whether it is in terms of due process or international treaties governing the treatment of prisoners. Yet, a commitment to the noble cause itself carries the central danger that noble means—in this case, a commitment to democratic process internally and international conventions in the international setting—are abandoned. Again here, we see the problem of a war against a contested concept. Because the U.S. cannot determine what constitutes victory, its battle against terrorism is unremitting. As Soros (2003:4) noted ". . . it (the war on terrorism) may bring about a permanent state of war. Terrorists will never disappear."

In the critiques, we found that the central element of the war on terrorism—its disputed and contested identity as a war—were the most intensely focused. This suggests that the future of counter-terrorism—all other things being equal—will be marked by the contestedness that characterized its inception.

The Elevation of Crime Control over Due Process

> U.S. citizens classified as "enemy combatants" should gain access to attorneys only after they have disclosed everything they know about terrorist operations, federal law officials said Tuesday. Three senior Justice Department officials, briefing reporters on condition of anonymity, outlined the policy for the first time and said it is the proper way to balance national security and constitutional protections for people in government custody as part of the war on terror. One of the officials said the goal never has been to deny counsel, only to delay it until interrogations are finished (*Port St. Lucie News*, 2003).

This quote embodies the principle of elevating crime control over due process. One of the far-reaching changes in the war on terrorism was the elevation of crime control over due process. This change was attributable to two factors: (1) long-term trends in criminal justice policy, and (2) labeling counter-terrorism as a war, thus justifying a military view of the conduct of those officials engaged in the war, whether they are military personnel dealing with foreign combatants or civilian prosecutors dealing with U.S. citizens. The confluence of these two trends is to change the relationship between due process and crime control, in a manner that prioritizes crime control and permits due process only after crime control issues are resolved. They may be resolved through intelligence gathering, through administrative protocols, through seizure as a material witness, or due process may even be postponed indefinitely, as in the case of prisoners at Guantanamo Bay. But however crime control issues are resolved, due process—that critical and singular guarantor of American freedom—is increasingly postponed or placed in a subordinate relationship to crime control.

After 9/11, U.S. citizens learned to *imagine* terrorism. We learned to fear every unknown for its terrorist implications. We changed practices of international diplomacy to self-protective unilateralism, coercive "us versus them" diplomacy, and a principle of "preemptive war" based, not on an actual risk assessment, but on our fears of future or potential danger. And we expanded internal security into the potential for danger, focusing on patterns of association, communications that carried critical views of U.S. policy, unordinary behaviors, birthplace, language and accent, and skin color as markers of potential threat. These, rather than actual criminal or harmful behavior, became the "dots" that the government "connected" as it surveilled immigrants, visa holders, and increasingly, criminal suspects and controversial citizens. Why those dots? It may be sheer convenience. It is easier to find out information about associational activity and birthplace, for example, than actual criminal activity. Consequently, if associational activity or birthplace can be criminalized as terrorism, made to look suspect, or in some way triggers a surveillant response, it can be easily confused as doing something about terrorism.

That anti-terror legislation is constituted in terms of civil liberty restrictions is itself a turn of events that might have occurred differently. There are other ways to conceive of anti-terrorism strategy. For example, strategy could be organized around international diplomacy aimed at the amelioration of conflict and the use of foreign aid to improve the life-quality of those groups from whom terrorists are recruited. Instead of launching into a maze of anti-terrorism strategies, research could assess the effectiveness of proposed strategies, research which is already quite plentiful, and often negative. We might develop strategy directly and systematically from those demonstrable loopholes in anti-terror coverage that have been shown to fail badly, instead of trying to anticipate every conceivable contingency. We might have focused on reducing the capacity for privacy in mass public spaces, locating our defensive efforts specifically on those areas where terrorism is most likely to occur. We might have viewed individual rights as that element of American identity most important to preserve, and selected a variety of anti-terror tactics designed to protect those rights. Instead, we located the drive for self-protection in the diminishment of due process and individual rights. We have selected a way of fighting terrorism that carries the potential to undermine fundamental democratic institutions. As Griset and Mahan (2003:282) summarize the thrust of legislation, "how vigorously can a democracy fight terrorism and remain a democracy?"

If thinking about terrorism post-9/11 in terms of asserting crime control over individual rights sounds like a dramatic departure from a history of democratic support for due process, it is not. To the contrary, it represents a continuation of existing justice system trends. Current anti-terror strategies, conceived of in terms of diminution of civil rights and due process protections, derive from historical trends already present in local and national criminal justice policy. Because crime control has been so politically marketable, Democrats and Republicans alike have advocated harsh reforms aimed at "getting tough on criminals." Concerns over individual rights throughout this period have taken a back seat to creating the appearance of punitiveness through legislation, through the expansion of administrative authority to intercede in counter-terror and anti-drug activity, and through the expansion of surveillance activity, particularly under the 1996-2000 Clinton administration and 2000-2004 Bush administration. Seen in this way, the war on terrorism intensified already existing themes in electoral politics, themes which viewed crime control in terms of "taking the handcuffs off the police" and aptly contextualized by Gordon (1991) with her book titled *The Justice Juggernaut: Fighting Street Crime, Controlling Citizens.*

Two years after 9/11, the U.S. witnessed the increasing normalization of counter-terrorism laws for crime fighting. A study by the General Accounting Office found that 75 percent of the terrorism investigations undertaken by the Justice Department after 9/11 were "wrongly labeled." Many of them dealt with common crimes (Lichtblau, 2003). However, the Justice Department has taken an aggressive posture toward the new laws made available under the counter-terrorism umbrella. One official noted that:

> 'There are many provisions in the PATRIOT Act that can be used in the general criminal law,' Mark Corallo, a department spokesman, said. 'And I think any reasonable person would agree that we have an obligation to do everything we can do to protect the lives and liberties from attack, whether it's from terrorists or garden variety criminals' (Lichtblau, 2003).

Examples cited by officials include a love-sick woman who planted threatening notes aboard a Hawaiian-bound cruise boat to try to return home to her boyfriend, a drug distributor, a 4-time killer, an identity thief, and a fugitive who fled on the eve of a trial with a fake passport. These individuals were prosecuted using expanded authority to track private internet communications under the USA PATRIOT Act, or in the case of the love-sick woman, the use of the act for threats of terrorism against mass transportation.

By 2004 the use of terrorism laws in the prosecution of ordinary crime continued to expand. A deputy chief for legal policy in the Justice Department's asset forfeiture and money laundering section, Stefan Castella, noted that the USA PATRIOT Act contained many elements that were on prosecutors' wish lists for years. A spokesman for the National Association of Criminal Defense Attorneys complained that the Justice Department was conducting seminars on how to stretch the wiretapping laws beyond terrorism cases (cnn.com, 2003c).

Several examples of the uses of counter-terrorism legislation for ordinary crimes are emerging. A North Carolina prosecutor charged a man, Martin Miller, with the violation of a state law barring the manufacture of chemical weapons. The man, accused of running a methamphetamine lab, used a law that defined chemical weapons of mass destruction as any substance that had the capability to cause death or serious injury. In another instance, a provision of the USA PATRIOT Act was used to recover 4.5 million from telemarketers who had been accused of deceiving elderly U.S. citizens into thinking they had won the Canadian lottery (Cnn.com, 2003c). In a third example, participants and the sponsor of an anti-war forum in Iowa on November 15, 2003, received subpoenas to appear before a federal grand jury. The forum, called "Stop the Occupation! Bring the Iowa Guard Home" and attended by 21 people, was the object of federal prosecutorial interest. The subpoena asked for "all requests for use of a room, all documents indicating the purpose and intended participants in the meeting, and all documents or recordings which would identify person that actually attended the meeting" (Davey, 2004).

Accompanying this expanded use of counter-terrorism legislation is the sharing of intelligence for cases that can be labeled as both criminal and terrorist. In the process of intelligence gathering, the distinction between criminal and intelligence investigations is administratively erased: both are now handled under the same classification number, and both criminal and intelligence investigators work together on the same squads (Eggen, 2003). Given the wide mandate that permits a case to be labeled as terrorist, Eggen noted that this creates an opportunity to funnel all cases into "the intelligence mode. It's an end run around the Fourth Amendment," protecting individuals from unreasonable searches. It also permitted the gathering of secret evidence. In this way, the government could designate an individual a potential terrorist threat, develop information through the intelligence and criminal investigation, conduct extended and covert surveillance operations on the individual, and then use the accumulated information to bring forth criminal charges. Hence, the counter-terror legislation is increasingly being used, not against foreign operatives, but against American citizens suspected of criminal activity.

Though the elevation of crime control over due process flows from existing trends, 9/11 created a threshold effect. The threshold has been approached incrementally, but passing it has been dramatic. That change is the relationship between liberty and security, according to which many and increasing aspects of crime control, whether conceived as violent criminality, sexual predatorship, terrorism, or a war on drugs, trumps due process protections. Yet it is the body of laws that constitute due process that carves out a legal identity of individuals in the American political system. Without a body of due process laws, a legal notion of an individual existing outside government authority does not exist. Such a legal identity as an individual no longer exists for visa holders, and immigrants; it has been coopted by administrative processing carried out at the discretion of the executive. It has been partially coopted for criminal suspects, for whom the war on terrorism provides the collection of intelligence and information if the administration claims that terrorism is a part of the investigation, a claim that the administration is not under any legal obligation, except cursory and secret FISA court review, to substantiate. And it is increasingly coopted for U.S.-born citizens, who are under increasingly wider surveillance at the borders when they travel, in airports, in any investigation once it is determined that terrorism is associated with the investigation, during routine screening for air travel, and by neighbors as encouraged by the government.

If the elements that make up the foundations of great enterprises tend to haunt them throughout their histories, then two elements of the war on terror will always be in conflict—the widespread public perception of the need to do something, and fundamental disagreement as to what that something is. The contention that marked the early days of the war was diminished by a large public outpouring of grief, and that grief will always be viewed historically as a justification for counter-terrorist action. And, in a sense, our continued grief sustains and justifies for many people continued militaristic action. Yet through time, though we are in some ways frozen in a "paralysis of grief," we disagree with increasing intensity as to the appropriate way to deal with the 9/11 attacks.

For now, we will move forward, seeking a notion of national identity reconstituted to include the grief and fears of 9/11. How we adapt to our newfound fear is still evolving. The greatest enemy of our newfound fear today is democracy, a force that pushes us ever toward openness of view and respect for others. Those themes that are contested—the issues of war or police action, governmental secrecy, due process and fair play, treatment of aliens, and a healthy distrust of government—are at the core of American politics and culture, and will not disappear readily. The hopes of democracy and the fears that drive national security are countervailing forces that are embedded in our many interpretations of 9/11. The way these forces play out against each other, sometimes in harmony and sometimes in conflict, will likely mark the enterprise of justice in the United States for many years to come.

Bibliography

Abrams, Jim (2001) "Bush Tightens Air Security, But Changes Will Take Time" *Arizona Daily Star,* November 20 http.//www.azstarnet.com/attackindepth/1120airsecurity.html

Addicott, Jeffrey (2002) "Military Tribunals Are Constitutional" *Jurist.* http.//jurist.law.pitt.edu/forum/forumnew51.php

Ahmad, Eqbal (1998) "Terrorism. Theirs and Ours" In R. Howard and R Sawyer (eds.) *Terrorism and Counter-Terrorism: Understanding the New Security Environment*, pp. 46-53. Guilford, CT McGraw-Hill.

AILA.org (2002) "AILA Urges House Members to Vote to Suspend Funding for NSEERS American Immigration Lawyers Association," May 30. http.//www.aila.org/

Akbarpour, Susan (2001) "Reaction to Bush Snitch Visa Proposal" *Iran Today*, December 7 http.//www.ncmonline.com/content/ncm/2001/dec/1207snitch.html

al-Zawahiri, Ayman, (2001) "Knights Under the Prophet's Banner, as printed in al-Sharq al-Awsat, 2 Dec; in Benjamin, Daniel and Steven Simon (2002) *The Age of Sacred Terror* New York, NY Random House: 102

ALA (2002) See American Library Association, 2002

Alderson, John (1998) *Principled Policing*. Winchester Waterside Press

Alonso-Salvidar (2003) "U S to End Immigrant Registration Program." *Los Angeles Times*, December 2

American Bar Association (2002) "September 11 and the Constitution" Videotaped Panel presentation. American Bar Association C-SPAN.

American Bar Association (2001). "ABA Leadership Statement of Robert E Hirshon President, American Bar Association November 9, 2001" ABA Network http.//www.abanet.org/leadership/justice_department.html.

American Civil Liberties Union (2003). "The Rights of Immigrants—ACLU Position Paper" http.//www/aclu.org/ImmigrantsRights.htm

American Civil Liberties Union Freedom Network (2002) "Rights Groups Urge Secret Appeals Court to Reject Ashcroft's Radical Bid for Broadly Expanded Powers to Spy on U S Citizens" September 20 http://archive.aclu.org/issues/privacy/FISA_feature.html

American Library Association (2002) "The USA PATRIOT Act in the Library" http.//www.ala.org/

Amnesty International (2003) "U.S · 'Operation Liberty Shield' An Attack on Asylum-Seekers' Rights " http://www.web.amnesty.org/web/web.nsf/print/usa-270303-action-eng.

Amnesty International (2003b) "USA." In Report 2003, 'Counter-Terrorism' and Human Rights http://web.amnesty.org/web/web.nsf/prit/usa-summary-eng

Amnesty International (2003c). "Security for Whom? A Human Rights Response. A Message from Irene Khan, Amnesty International's Secretary General." http://web.amnesty.org/web/web.nsf/print/message-eng.

Arena, Kelli (2003). "FBI Intensifies Investigations of Hezbollah, Hamas " http://www.cnn.com/2003/LAW/05/08/fbi.hezbollah.hamas/. May 8.

Arizona Daily Star (2003). "Guantanamo Opposition on the Rise." October 10 http://www.cgi.azstarnet.com/.

Armstrong, Ken and Maurice Possley (1999). "The Verdict: Dishonor." *Chicago Tribune* January 8.

Associated Press (2004). "Pentagon Eases Terror Tribunal Rules " *New York Times*, February 5. http://www.nytimes.com/aponline/AP-lawyers-tribunals.html.

Associated Press (2003). "Three Israelis Suffocate in Sealed Room " http://www.nytimes.com/a..../AP-Israel-Iraq-Suffocations.htm.

Associated Press (2003b) "Post-9/11 Interviews Faulted " MSNBC News. http://www.msnbc.com/news/9/11759.asp?cp1=1.

Associated Press (2002) "Non-U.S. Students Jailed over Class Load " *CNN Student News*. December 27.

Associated Press (2001a) "Bush Vows Victory in the 'First War' of the 21st Century" *Decatur Daily* http://www.deaturdaily.com/decaturdaily/news/010903/war.html.

Associated Press (2001b). "Oregon Won't Interview Foreigners." *New York Times on the Web* November 29 http://www.nytimes.com/aponline/AP-attacks-intrerviews.html.

Audsley, D. (1985). "Posse Comitatus. An Extremist Tax Protest Group " *TVI Journal*, 6(1) 13-16

Baker, Bonnie (1989). "The Origins of Posse Comitatus." http://www.airpower.maxwell.af.mil/airchronicles/cc/baker1.html

Baker, Mark (2003). "Afghanistan: Kabul's Entry into ICC Hailed by Rights Groups." February 10, 03 http://www.rferl.org/nca/features/2003/02/110022003153509.asp

Baltimore Sun (2003) "U.S. Prison Population Largest in World." June 1

Barron, James (2003). "Another 9/11, and the Nation Mourns Again " *New York Times,* September 12 http://www.nytimes.com/2003/9/12/nyregion/12TOWE.html

BBC News (2002a). "Mass Arrests of Muslims in LA " 19 December http://news.bbc.co.uk/1/hi/world/americas/2589317.stm.

BBC News (2002b). "Life in a Guantanamo Cell " February 7. http://news.bbc.co.uk/1/hi/world/americas/1766037.stm

Benjamin, Daniel and Steven Simon (2002). *The Age of Sacred Terror.* New York, NY: Random House.

Berkowitz, Bruce (2003) "Terrorists' Talk Why All That Chatter Doesn't Tell Us Much." *New York Times,* February 16 http://www.nytimes.com/.

Bernstein, Richard (2003). "Foreign Views of U.S. Darker Since Sept. 11 " New York, September 11

Bill of Rights Defense Committee (2002) "Local Resolution to Protect Civil Liberties." Detroit City Council, December 6 http://www.bordc.org/Detroit-res.htm.

Binder, Guyora, and Robert Weisburg (2000) *Literary Criticisms of Law* Princeton, NJ: Princeton University Press.

Blumenfeld, Laura (2003) "Former Aid Takes Aim at War on Terror." June 16 http://www. washingtonpost.com/

Boston Bar Association (2002). "BBA Individual Rights and Responsibilities Section Newsletter." http://www.bostonbar.org/sc/in/nl_0202.html.

Bravin, Jess and Gary Fields (2003). "How Do U S. Interrogators Make a Captured Terrorist Talk?" *The Wall Street Journal*, March 4:B1, B9.

Brookings Forum (2002) "Homeland Security: The White House Plan Explained and Examined." The Brookings Institution September 4

Brothers and Others (2003) Worldlink Special

Brown, Deborah (2003). "Appeals Court Upholds Detention of 'Enemy Combatant'." January 9. United States Mission to the European Mission. http://www.useu.be/Terrorism/ USResponse/Jan0903RulingEnemyCombattent.html

Brownfeld, Peter (2003) "Legislative Battle Predicted for PATRIOT II " http://www.foxnews. com October 11.

Brzezinski, Zbigniew (1993) *Out of Control: Global Turmoil on the Eve of the Twenty-First Century* New York, NY: Charles Scribner's Sons

Burke, Jason (2003) "Powell Doesn't Know Who He Is Up Against " *The Observer.* Sunday, February 9 http://www.observer.co.uk.html/

Butterfield, Fox (2001) "Police Are Split on Questioning of Mideast Men " *New York Times on the Web,* November 29 http://www.nytimes.com/2001/11/22/national/22POLI.html

Caldero, Michael and John Crank (2005). *Police Ethics: The Corruption of Noble Cause,* Second Edition. Newark, NJ: Matthew Bender.

Cantlupe, Joe (2002) "No Takers on Ashcroft Offer to Terrorist Tipsters " *The San Diego Tribune.* http://www.signonsandiego.com/news/nation/terror/20020201 -9999_1n1inform.html.

Carroll, Misty (2003) "NSEERS Funding Suspended by Senate Budget Bill " *Immigration News* http://www.usvisanews.com/memo2012/html.

Catholic Answers (2003) "Catholic Answers Guide to Just War Doctrine." http://www.catholic. com/library/Just_War_Doctrine_1.asp

CDI Terrorism Project (2003). "CDI Fact Sheet: Transportation Security Agency (TSA)." January 21 http://www.cdi.org/terrorism/tsa-pr.cfm

Center for Defense Information (2002). "POSSE COMITATUS: Caution Is Necessary." August 6 http://www.cdi.org/terrorism/pcomitatus.cfm.

Chisti, Muzaffer, Doris Meissner, Demetrios Papademetriou, Jay Peterzell, Michael Wishnie, and Stephen Yale-Loehr (2003) *America's Challenge: Domestic Security, Civil Liberties, and National Unity After September 11.* Migration Policy Institute http://www. migrationpolicy.org/

Chua, Amy (2003) *World on Fire* New York, NY. Doubleday.

CINJust (2001) "Amnesty International on Torture in Israel." http://www.cin.org/archives/cinjust/200108/0047.html.

Click10.com (2003) "Three Men Detained After Terror Tip." September 13 http://www.click10.com/mia/news/stories/news-166587720020913-050912.html

CNN com (2003a). "Top UK Judge Slams Guantanamo" November 26. http.//www.cnn.com/2003/WORLD/europe/11/25/guantanamo.judge/index.html.

CNN.com (2003b). "Mueller Defends FBI at Civil Liberties Meeting." June 13 http://cnn.law.printthis.cl...cpt/?action=cpt&expire=-1&urlID=6608647&fb=Y&partnerID=201.

CNN Com (2003c). "Anti-Terror Laws Increasingly Used Against Common Criminals" September 15 http.//www.cnn.com/2003/LAW/09/14/anti.terror.laws.ap/index.html

CNN.com (2002a). "Is Airport Security Moving in the Right Direction?" July 3. http.//www.cnn.com/ALLPOLITICS/07/03/cf.crossfire.

CNN.com (2002b). "U S. Prepares Cuba Base for Afghan Prisoners" http.//edition.cnn.com/2002/01/06/ret.guantanamo.prisoners/index.html?related

CNN.com (2002c) "Shackled Detainees Arrive at Guantanamo." January 11 http.//edition.cnn.com/2002/WORLD/asiapcf/central/01/11/ret.detainee.transfer/.

CNN com (2001). "ACLU's Lucas Guttentag: Immigrants and Civil Liberties." October 17 http://www.cnn.com/2001/COMMUNITY/10/17/guttentag.

Cole, David and James Dempsey (2002). *Terrorism and the Constitution.* New York, NY The Free Press

Cook, Martin L (2001) "Ethical Issues in Counter-Terrorism Warfare." September. http.//ethics.sandiego.edu/Resources/PhilForum/Terrorism/Cook.html.

Coser, Lewis (1956). *The Functions of Social Conflict* New York, NY The Free Press.

Council on American-Islamic Relations (2002). "New 'Voluntary' Interviews Create Perception of Profiling. March 20. http://www.ccmep.org/hotnews2/newvoluntary032002.html.

Council on Foreign Relations (2003). "Military Tribunals." Terrorism: Q & A http://www.terrorismanswers.com/responses/tribunals_print.html.

Cox, Stephen (2003) "Engage in Military Retaliation Against Terrorists" In *The Terrorist Attack on America: Current Controversies,* pp. 132-138. Farmington Hills, MI. Greenhaven Press

Crank, John (2003). "Crime and Justice in the Context of Resource Scarcity." *Crime, Law and Social Change,* 31(1).

Crank, John (2003) *Imagining Justice.* Cincinnati, OH: Anderson Publishing Co.

Davey, Monica (2004) "An Anti-War Forum in Iowa Brings Federal Subpoenas" February 10 http.//www.nytimes.com/2004/02/10/national/10PROT.html

Dean, John (2001a). "Military Tribunals A Long and Mostly Honorable History" FindLaw December 7 http://writ.findlaw.com/dean/20011207.html.

Dean, John (2001b) "Appropriate Justice for Terrorists: Using Military Tribunals Rather Than Criminal Courts." FindLaw. September 28 http.//writ.findlaw.com/dean/20010928.html.

Dean, John (2001c) "A Matter of Justice: Ashcroft's Appalling Failure to Explain Military Tribunals" *Truthout.* http://www.truthout.org/docs_01/12.25D.Dean.Justice.htm.

DeBono, Norman (2003) "Spooked Americans Stuck on Duct Tape from London." *The London Free Press News*, February 14. http://www.canoe.ca/LondonNews/lf.lf-02-14-0002.html.

Defense Threat Reduction Agency (2003) "Mission." http://www.dtra.mil/about/ab_mission.html.

Delattre, Edwin (1994). *Character and Cops: Ethics in Policing,* Second Edition. Washington, DC: The AEI Press

Department of Justice (2001). Interim Rule: Prevention of Acts of Terrorism and Violence. Bureau of Prisons 28 CFR Parts 500 and 5001.

Department of Justice (2002). "Attorney General's Remarks Implementation of NSEERS, Niagara Falls, New York, November 7, 2002." http://www.usdoj.gov/ag/speeches/2002/110702agremarksneseers_niagarafalls.htm.

Dershowitz, Alan (2002). "Let America Take Its Cues from Israel Regarding Torture" http://www.jewishworldview.com/0102/torture/asp.

Detroit Free Press (2002) "Terror War Hits Home . . Strange Bedfellows." November 12. http://foi.missouri.edu/terrorandcivillib/terrorwar.html.

Diamond, John, Toni Lucy, and Richard Willing (2003). "Interrogation Is Tough but Not Torture." *USA Today*, March 6:4a.

Dinh, Viet (2003). "Security and Privacy in the United States." Invited panel presentation. Annual meetings of the American Bar Association

Dirks, Tim (2003). *Modern Times.* Review (1936) http://www.filmsite.org/mode.html.

Donn, Jeff (2003). "Terrorist Threat Puts Fallout Shelters Back in Vogue." Associated Press http://multimedia.belointeractive.com/attack/news/1207 fallout.html.

Dorf, Michael (2002) "What Is An 'Unlawful Combatant,' and Why It Matters. The Status of Detained Al Qaeda and Taliban fighters." January 23. FindLaw's Legal Commentary. http://writ.findlaw.com/dorf/20020123.html

Dyson, William (2005). *Terrorism: An Investigator's Handbook*, Second Edition. Newark, NJ: Matthew Bender.

EFF (2001) see Electronic Frontiers Foundation, 2001

Eggen, Dan (2002). "Interrogations to Begin Soon for Illegal Mideastern Aliens." *Washington Post.* http://www-tech.mit.edu/V122/N2/war_deport_2.2w.html.

Eggen, Dan (2003a) "Plan for Counterterrorism Database Unveiled." *Washington Post,* September 17:A02.

Eggen, Dan (2003b). "Tapes Show Abuse of 9/11 Detainees." *Washington Post,* December 19. A01.

Electronic Frontiers Foundation (2001) "Analysis of the Provisions of the USA PATRIOT Act that Relate to Online Activities" October 31 http://www.eff.org/Privacy/Surveillance/Terrorism_militias/20011031_eff_usa_PATRIOT_analysis.html

Eller, Jack (1999) *From Culture to Ethnicity to Conflict: An Anthropological Perspective on International Ethnic Conflict.* Ann Arbor, MI University of Michigan Press.

Environmental Measurements Laboratory (2003), "EML's Mission Statement" http.//www.eml.doe.gov/about/mission/.

FAA News (2002). "Fact Sheet: Aircraft Security Accomplishments Since Sept 1" Federal Aviation Administration September 5 http://www1.faa.gov/index/cfm/apa/1064/AAA53E5 E-018C-4775-8725C5311FFB9F3D

The Federalist Society (2001) "Monitoring Attorney-Client Communications of Designated Federal Prisoners" National Security White Papers. http://www.fed-soc org/Publications/Terrorism/attorneyclient.html

Federal Emergency Management Agency (2003). "Are You Ready?"

Fessenden, Ford and Michael Moss (2002) "Going Electronic, Denver Reveals Long-Term Surveillance New York Times. December 21. http://www/nytimes.com/2002/12/21/technology/21PRIV/html

Filkins, Dexter (2003) "Tough New Tactics by U.S Tighten Grip on Iraq Towns." New York Times, December 7 http.//www.nytimes.com/2003/12/07/international/middleeast/07TACT.html

Fish, Mike (2001) "Many Warnings Over Airport Security Preceded Terrorist Attacks" http://www.cnn.com/SPECIALS/2001/trade.center/flight.risk/stories/part2.main bar.html

Foreign Intelligence Surveillance Court (2002) Memorandum Opinion of the Foreign Intelligence Surveillance Court, Rejecting and Revising Justice Department Intelligence Sharing Procedures May 17

Foucault, Michel (1995). Discipline & Punish: The Birth of the Prison, Second Edition. New York, NY Vintage Books

Fraser, James and Ian Fulton (1984) Terrorism Counteraction FC 100-37 Fort Leavenworth, KS. U S Army Command and General Staff College

Friedman, Thomas (2000). The Lexus and the Olive Tree: Understanding Globalization. New York, NY Anchor Books.

Gall, Carlotta and Neil Lewis (2003) "Inmates Released from Guantanamo Tell Tales of Despair" New York Times, June 17 http://www.nytimes.com

Gallie, W. (1956) "Essentially Contested Concepts" Proceedings of the Philosophical Society, 51:157-198

Ganor, Boaz (2002) "Defining Terrorism. Is One Man's Terrorist Another Man's Freedom Fighter?" Police Practice and Research: An International Journal, 3(4) 287-305

Gilmore, James (2003) The Advisory Panel to Assess Domestic Response Capabilities for Terrorism Involving Weapons of Mass Destruction Fifth Annual Report to the President and Congress The Rand Corporation http.//www.rand.org/nsrd/terrpanel.

Glaberson, William (2001) "Critic's Attack on Tribunals Turns to Law Among Nations" New York Times, December 26 http:/www.nytimes.com/2001/12/26/national/26LAW.html

Greetham, Bryan (2003) "Terrorism and the Collapse of Moral Authority." http.//ethics.sandiego.edu/Resources/PhilForum/Terrorism/Greetham.html.

Griset, Pamala and Sue Mahan (2003) Terrorism in Perspective. Thousand Oaks, CA Sage

Gross, Benjamin (2003). "New Report Analyzes Recent Middle East Immigration." International Immigration Programs, 15 August http://usinfo.state.gov/topical/global/immigration/02081502.html.

Gordon, Diana (1991) *The Justice Juggernaut:Fighting Street Crime, Controlling Citizens*. New Brunswick and London Rutgers University Press

Guardian Newspapers (2003) "Afghan Prisoners Beaten to Death at U.S Military Interrogation Base." http://www.buzzle.co.uk/editorials/text3-6-2003-36813.asp.

Habermas Jurgen (1994) "Struggles for Recognition in the Democratic Constitutional State." In A Guttman (ed.) *Multiculturalism: Examining the Politics of Recognition*, pp. 107-148. Princeton, NJ: Princeton University Press.

Hernandez, Eugene, Brian Brooks, and Wendy Mitchell (2002) "Visa Denials for NYC Cultural Events Continue with Cuban Artist Unable to Attend Film Premiere." *Indiewire,* October 10. http://www.indiewire.com/biz/biz_021010_briefs.html.

Hersch, Seymour (2004) "The Grey Zone " *The New Yorker* http://www.newyorker.com/printable/?fact/040524fa_fact

Hobsbawn, Eric (1994) *The Age of Extremes: The Short 20th Century, 1914-1991*. London, Michael Joseph

Hoffman, Bruce (2003). "Terrorism Defined." In R. Howard and R Sawyer (eds.) *Terrorism and Counter-Terrorism: Understanding the New Security Environment,* pp 2-53 Guilford, CT: McGraw-Hill/Dushkin

Hoffman, Bruce (2002). "A Nasty Business." *Atlantic Monthly,* January:49-52.

Homer-Dixon, Thomas (1999) *Environment, Scarcity, and Violence* Princeton, NJ: Princeton University Press

Homer-Dixon, Thomas (1994) "Environmental Scarcities and Violent Conflict " *International Security,* 19-1:5-40

Human Rights Watch (2001). "Letter to Attorney General John Ashcroft." September 28. http://www.hrw.org/press/2001/09/ashcroft0928-ltr.htm

Human Rights Watch (2001b) "Fact Sheet: Past U S. Criticism of Military Tribunals " November 28. http://www.hrw.org/press/2001/tribunals1128.htm.

Huntington, Samuel (1996) *The Clash of Civilizations and the Remaking of World Order* New York, NY: Simon & Schuster.

IIMCR (2001) See Institute for International Mediation and Conflict Resolution, 2003.

Illinois Coalition for Immigrant and Refugee Rights (2003). "Fact Sheet: Immigrant Fairness Restoration Act (S 955) http://www.icirr.org/newsandaction/IFRA%20Fact%20Sheet.htm

Immigration com (2003) Immigration com-S Visa Query Answered Here http://www.immigration.com/faq/svisa.html.

Immigrationlinks.com (2001). "Interim Rule Granting INS 48 Hours, or More, to Detain Alien Without Filing Immigration Charges." September 20 http://www.immigrationlinks.com/news/news1114.htm.

Infocon (2002). "New Security Department Reinforces USNORTHCOM Mission " November 27 http://www.mail-archive.com/infocon@infowarrior.org/msg00338.html

Institute for International Mediation and Conflict Resolution (2001). World Conflict & Human Rights Map, 2001 Washington, DC. A J Jongman.

International Information Programs (2001). "Transcript: Bush Welcomes Kenyan and Ethiopian Leaders to White House" State Department Information Page. http://usinfo.state.gov/regional/af/security/a2120501.htm.

Israel, Michael (2003) "Washington Report, 108th Congress." 20.4 December 8.

Israeli Defense Front (2003) "Protected Spaces" Homeland Command. http://www.idf.il/homefront/english/ie-index05.stm.

Jachimowicz, Maia (2003). "Comprehensive Visitor Tracking System Moves Forward" *Migration Information Source*, June 1.

Jachimowicz, Maia and Ramal McKay (2003). "'Special Registration' Program." Migration Informaiton Source. Http.//www.migrationinformation.org/USfocus/display.cfm?ID-116.

Johnson, Chalmers (2000). *Blowback: The Costs and Consequences of American Empire*. New York, NY: Henry Holt Co.

Jurist (2001) "Law Professors Oppose Military Tribunals for Terrorists." *Terrorism Law and Policy.* http://jurist.law.pitt.edu/terrorism/terrorismmilp,rof.php.

Kessel Jerrold (1999). "Israel Supreme Court Bans Interrogation Abuse of Palestinians." September 6. http://www.cnn.com/WORLD/meast/9909/06/israel.torture/.

Khouri, Rami (1991) "Collage of Comment: The Gulf War and the Mideast Peace; the Appeal of Saddam Hussein." *New Perspectives Quarterly,* 8, 56.

Huntington, Samuel (1996) *The Clash of Civilizations and the Remaking of World Order.* New York, NY Simon & Schuster

Klare, Michael (2001) *Resource Wars: The New Landscape of Global Conflict* New York, NY: Henry Holt and Company.

Klockars, Carl (1980) "The Dirty Harry Problem." *The Annals,* 45, 2:33-47.

Knox, Paul (2002). "War on Terror Ignites Battle Over Course of U.S. Justice." U S. Southern Command, September 5 http://www.foi.missouri.edu/terrorandcivillib/waronterror.html.

KOMO (2003) "Operation Liberty Shield Launched" http://www.komotv.com/news/print story.asp?id=23705

Kranich, Nancy (2002). "The Impact of the USA PATRIOT Act on Free Expression." http://www.fepproject.org/commentaries/PATRIOTact.com.

Kraska, Peter and Victor Kappeler (1997). "Militarizing American Police: The Rise and Normalization of Paramilitary Units." *Social Problems,* 44-1:101-117.

Lane, Charles (2003). "War on Terrorism's Legal Track Is Rejected" *Washington Post*, December 19 A22

Lawyers Committee for Human Rights (2003) Civil Liberties in the U.S. After 9/11. Chapter 3 http://www.lchr.org/us_law/loss/loss_ch3a.htm

Lee, Chisun (2003). "The Force Multipliers." *The Village Voice* http://www.villagevoice.com/issues/0309/lee.php.

Lee, R. (2002). New and Recent Wars & Conflicts in the World. The History Guy Website Retrieved 1/19/03 From http://www.historyguy.com/current_conflicts/index.htm.

Lester, Will (2003) "Terrorism Recedes as Top Political Issue, But Public Anxiety Remains High" *San Diego Union Tribune,* Signonsandiego com, September 4.

Lewis, Charles (2003). "The Assault on Liberty (continued). The Bush Administration Pushes to Expand the PATRIOT Act." Center for Public Integrity http://www.publicintegrity. org/report.aspx?aid=78&sid=200.

Lewis, Neil (2003). "Fate of Prisoners from Afghan War Remains Uncertain." *New York Times,* April 24 http://www.nytimes.com

Lewis, Neil and Eric Schmitt (2004) "Cuba Detentions May Last Years" *New York Times,* February 13. http://www.nytimes.com//2004/02/13/politics/13GITM.html.

Leibovich, Mark and Roxanne Roberts (2003). "Ready or Not? A Capital Question." http:// www.washingtonpost.com/ac2/wp-dyn/A59302-2003Feb11.

Lichtblau, Eric (2003) "U.S. Report Faults the Roundup of Illegal Aliens After 9/11." *New York Times,* Vol CLII, June 3, A1, A25

Lichtenberg, Judith (2001) "The Ehics of Retaliation" *Philosophy and Public Policy Quarterly,* 21(4)

Light, Paul (2002) "Assessing the Department of Homeland Security." Senate Committee on the Judiciary, Subcommittee on Technology, Terrorism and Government Information June 25 The Brookings Institution

Lumpkin, Beverly (2003a) "PATRIOT Act Redux." Halls of Justice. A Weekly Look Inside the Justice Department. Feb 21. http://abcnews.go.com/sections/us/HallsOfJustice/halls ofjustice.html.

Lumpkin, Beverly (2003b). "FISA Furor." Halls of Justice: A Weekly Look Inside the Justice Department Nov 22. http://abcnews.go.com/sections/us/HallsOfJustice/hallsof justice.html.

Lumpkin, John (2003c) "Interrogation Is a Race Against Time." *The Idaho Statesman,* 1.

MacIntyre, Alasdair (1988) *Whose Justice? Which Rationality?* Notre Dame, IN: University of Notre Dame Press

Malinowski, Tom (2002) "OAS Urges U.S. to Reverse Detainees Decision" Human Rights Watch. March 15. http://www.hrw.org/press/2002/03/oas031502.htm.

Mann, Charles (2002) "Homeland Insecurity." The Atlantic Online. September. http://www.the atlantic.com/issues/2002/09/mann.htm

Manning, Peter and Lawrence Redlinger (1977). "Invitational Edges of Corruption: Some Consequences of Narcotics Law Enforcement." In P. Rock (ed) *Drugs and Politics,* pp. 279-310. Rutgers, NJ: Society/Transaction Books.

Martin, Nancy (2004) "Grammy Nominees Denied U.S. Visas." *Miami Herald,* February 6. http://www.miami.com/mld/miamiherald/news/world/cuba/7887088.htm

Martin, Philip and Susan Martin (2001). "Immigration and Terrorism Policy Reform Challenges" October 8 http://migration.ucdavis.edu/ols/martin_oct2001.html

Martin, Philip and Jonas Widgren (2002) "International Migration: Facing the Challenge." *Population Bulletin,* 57-1

Marx, Gary (2002). "What's New About the 'New Surveillance?' Classifying for Change and Continuity" *Surveillance and Society,* 1(1):19-29.

McCaffrey, Shannon (2003) "U.S Says Terror Threat Was Fabricated" *The Mercury News,* February 14 http://www.bayarea.com/mld/mercurynews/news/politics/5185391.htm.

McGreevy, Patrick, Greg Krikorian, and Andrew Blankstein (2003). "LAX Steps Up Terror Security" *Los Angeles Times,* December 24.http://www.latimes.com/news/local/la-me-terror 24dec24,1,1191157.story?coll=la-home-headlines.

McMasters, Paul (2003). "Access to the Government." Presentation, National Press Club, C-Span, May.

Meek, James (2003a). "People That Law Forgot." *The Guardian,* December 3. http.//www.guardian.cc.uk.

Meek, James (2003a). "People That Law Forgot, Part 2." *The Guardian,* December 3. http://www.guardian.cc.uk.

Meserve, Jeanne (2003). "Duct Tape Sales Rise Amid Terror Fears." February 11. CNN: http.//cnn.usenews.

Meserve, Jeanne and Kathleen Koch (2003). "U.S. Intensifies 'Code Orange' Security Measures." CNN.com, December 24. http://www.cnn.com/2003/US/12/24/threat.level/index.html.

Migration Policy Institute (2003). "Chronology of Events Since September 11, 2001 Related to Immigration and National Security http://www.migrationinformation.org/USfocus/display.cfm?ID=116.

Miller, Greg (2002) "Many Held at Guatanamo Not Likely Terrorists" *Los Angeles Times,* December 22. http://www.latimes.com/news/nationworld/world/la-na-gitmo 22dec22.story?null

Miller, Sara and Seth Stern (2003). "Odd Bedfellows Fall in Line." *The Christian Science Monitor.* Http.//www.csmonitor.com/2003/1029/p16s01-usju.html.

Mintz, John (2003a). "FBI Worries About Revenge Terrorist Attacks" February 24: *The Idaho Statesman,* 4A.

Mintz, John (2003b). "U S Drops Search for 5 Middle Eastern Men" http./www.washington post.com/ac2/wp-dyn/A20400-2003Jan7.

Mintz, John (2003c). "Pentagon to Review Rules for Tribunals." November 26: *Washington Post,* A17

Moss, Michael (2003) "False Terrorism Tips to F.B.I. Uproot the Lives of Suspects." *New York Times,* June 19. http.//www.nytimes.com.

Mueller, Gerhard (2002). "The Nature, Definition, and Uses of Terrorism, and the Range of Rational Options to Deal with It" Presented at the annual meetings of the Academy of Criminal Justice Sciences.

Nadeem, Afzal (2003). "Gunmen Open Fire on Shiite Mosque in Pakistan, Killing 9." *The Idaho Statesman,* February 23:a13

National Communications System (2003) "Background and History." http.//www.ncs.gov/ncs/html/NCSHistoryBkgrd.html.

National Defense Council Foundation (2001) "World Conflict List 2001." Retrieved 1/20/03 From http://ndcf.org/Conflict_list/World2001/NDCFWorldConflictCount2001.htm

National Immigration Law Center (2002) In "Tracking Down 'Absconders' DOJ to Target Nationals of Countries Where al-Qaeda Is Active" *Immigration Rights Update,* 16(1) February 28. http://www.nilc.org/immlawpolicy/arrestedet/ad046.htm.

National Immigration Law Center (2001). "Justice Department Announces Plan to Interview 5,000 Men." *Immigration Rights Update,* 15(8): December 20. http.//www.nilc.org/immlawpolicy/arrestedet/ad040.htm

National Iranian American Council (2003). "Call for Compromise into INS Registration Heeded—Compromise on McCain Agreement." 2/15. http://www.payvand.com/news/03/feb/1072.html.

National Research Council (2001). "Terrorism: Perspectives from the Behavioral and Social Sciences" Washington, DC: The National Academies Press.

National Threat Initiative (2003). "Issues and Analysis: The Department of Homeland Security: Goals and Challenges" April. http://www.nti.org/e_research/e3_29b.html.

NBTA (2003). "Operation Liberty Shield: Statement by Homeland Security Secretary Tom Ridge." NBTA's Homeland Security Response. http://www.nbta.org/hsr/articles/threat_raised_htm.

Neier, Aryeh (2002). "The Military Tribunals on Trial." *The New York Review of Books,* 49(2). February 14. http:/www.nybooks.com/articles/15112

NewsMax com (2002). "Rumseld Chides Pro-Terrorist Complainers." NewsMax.com Wires, January 23. http://www.newsmax.com/archives./articles/2002/1/22/151910.html

New York Times (2003). "In Ryan's Words 'I Must Act.' http://www.nytimes.com/2003/01/11/na.../CND-RTEX.html.

Norris, Michele (2001). "Stopping Student Visas? Weaknesses Exposed in System of Tracking Foreign Students." abcNews.com, October 10. http://www.abcnews.go.com/sections/wnt/WorldNewsTonight/strike_studentvisas011010.html

Office of the Press Secretary (2001). "President Issues Military Order. Detention, Treatment, and Trial of Certain Non-Citizens in the War Against Terrorism." The White House http://www.whitehouse.gov/news/releases/2001/11/print/20011113-27.html

Packer, Herbert (1968). *The Limits of the Criminal Sanction.* California. Stanford University Press.

Pentagon Papers (2003) Encyclopedia Britannica. Encyclopedia Britannica Premium Service. 20 Aug. http://www.britannica.com/eb/article?eu=60597.

Peoples Daily Online (2002) "Iran Cries Foul Over U.S. Entry Restrictions." http://english.peopledaily.com.cn/

Pillar, Paul (2003a). "The Dimensions of Terrorism and Counter-Terrorism." In R Howard and R. Sawyer (eds.) *Terrorism and Counter-Terrorism: Understanding the New Security Environment,* pp. 24-45 Guilford, CT: McGraw-Hill/Dushkin.

Pillar, Paul (2003b). "Lessons and Futures" In P. Griset and S. Mahan (eds.) *Terrorism in Perspective,* pp. 205-302. Thousand Oaks, CA Sage Publications.

Pinsker, Lisa (2003) "Terrorism Puts Foreign Students in Spotlight." *Geotimes,* March. http://www.geotimes.org/mar03/NN_sevis.html

Pollock, Joycelyn (2004) *Ethics and Crime in Criminal Justice: Dilemmas and Decisions,* Fourth Edition. Belmont, CA West/Wadsworth.

Port St. Lucie News (2003). "Enemy Combatants Should Give Info First." December 17.A13.

Porter, Lawrence and Kate Randall (2002). "Bush Targets Middle Eastern Immigrants in New Police Dragnet." World Socialist Web Site http://www.wsws.org/articles/2002/feb2002/immi-f13_pr.shtml.

Powell, Michael (2002) "Domestic Spying Pressed" November 29. http.//www.washington post/com/ac2/wp-dyn/A51934-2002Nov28.htm.

Priest, Dana and Barton Gellman (2002) "U S. Decries Abuse but Defends Interrogations " *Washington Post,* December 26 A01. http.//www.washingtonpost.com/ac2/wp-dyn/A37943-2002Dec25.html.

Priest, Dana and Susan Schmidt (2003). "Weighing the Risks of Terror. Snippets and Threads Can Sway Threat Index." *Washington Post,* February 16. http://www.washington post.com.

Pugliese, Michael (2002). "Re: Mass Arrests of Muslims in California." 19 December. http://csf.colorado.edu/mail/psn/2002/msg02933.html

Pyle, Christopher (2004). "Torture by Proxy: How Immigration Threw a Traveler to the Wolves." *San Francisco Chronicle,* January 4. http.//www.sfgate.com.

Ramasastry, Anita (2003). "PATRIOT II, The Sequel. Why It's Even Scarier than the First PATRIOT Act " FindLaw. http.//writ.nres.findalw.com/ramasastry/20030217.html.

Ratnesar, Romesh (2003), "The State of Our Defense." *Time,* February 24

Regehr, R. (2001) "Armed Conflicts Report 2001 " Project Plowshares. Retrieved 1/20/03. http://www.ploughshares.ca/content/ACR/ACR00/ACR02-Introduction.html.

Ricks, Thomas and Peter Slevin (2003). "General Acknowledges Some U S. Personnel Already Are Inside Iraq." *The Idaho Statesman,* January 30:3

Rieder, J (1985). "Canarsi: The Jews and Italians of Brooklyn Against Liberalism." Cambridge, MA: Harvard University Press.

Risen, James sand Thom Shanker (2003). "Hussein Enters Post-9/11 Web of U S Prisons. *New York Times,* December 18.

Romano, Lois and David Fallis (2001) "Questions Swirl Around Men Held in Terror Probe " *Washington Post,* October 15. http://www.washingtonp...-dyn/articles/A59466-2001 Oct14.html.

Roth, Kenneth (2002). "U.S.: Growing Problem of Guantanamo Detainees." *Human Rights News.* http:/www.hrw.org/p;ress/2002/05/guantanamo.htm.

Rush, George (1994). *The Dictionary of Criminal Justice,* Fourth Edition USA· Dushkin Publishing Co

Sachs, Susan (2001) "The Despair Beneath the Arab World's Growing Rage " *New York Times,* October 14

Sanger, David (2003). "President Urging Wider U.S Powers in Terrorism Law." *New York Times,* September 11

Savage, David (2004) "Justices Bolster Rule of Law in the U.S " *The Idaho Statesman*, July 5:A1, A7

Semple, Kirk (2003). U.S. Suspends Case Against Two British Trror Suspects." *New York Times,* July 18. http://www.nytimes.com

September 11 Detainees (2003). "A Review of the Treatment of Aliens Held on Immigration Charges in Connection with the Investigation of the September 11 Attacks." Inspector General, Department of Justice. Washington, DC: Department of Justice.

Serrano, Richard and John Hendren (2002). "Rumsfeld Strongly Denies Mistreatment of Prisoners." *Los Angeles Times.* http://www.latimes.com/news/nationworld/nation/la-012302gitmo.story.

Sheck, Barry, Peter Neufeld, and Jim Dwyer (2001). *Actual Innocence.* New York, NY. Signet

Shenon, Philip (2003). "Lack of Attack Readiness Laid to Financing Delay by U.S." *New York Times,* February 13. http://www.nytimes.com/politics/13HOME.html.

Sinha, Vidushi (2003). "New Database Targets Student Visas " MSNBC. February 25. http://www.msnbc.com/news/877068.asp?cp1=1.

Smith, Lamar (2003) "Expanded Police Powers Are Needed to Ensure U.S. Security." In M. Williams (ed.) *The Terrorist Attack on America,* pp. 115-119. Current Controversies Series. New York, NY: Greenhaven Press

Soros, George (2003). "The Bubble of American Supremacy." *The Atlantic.* December. http://www.theatlantic.com.

Stalder, Felix (2003). "Opinion: Privacy Is Not the Antidote to Surveillance." *Surveillance and Society,* 1(1):120-124.

Stout, David (2003a). "U.S. Cuts Threat-Level Alert a Notch, from Orange to Yellow." *New York Times,* February 27.

Stout, David (2003b) "Bush Tells Returning Troops that Iraq Is Crucible in Fight on Terrorism." *New York Times,* September 12.

St. Petersburg Times (2001). "Snitch, and He'll Make You a Citizen " November 30. http://www.sptimes.com/News/113011/news_pf/Worldndnation/Snitch_and_he_ll_mak.shtml.

Sullivan, Laaura (2003). "2 Courts Reject Bush's Authority on Prisoners." December 18 http://www.sunspot.net/news/custom/attack/bal-padilla1218,0,445092.story?coll=bal-zattack-headlines.

Sullivan, Tim (2003). "INS deadline Passes Relatively Smoothly in Utah." *The Salt Lake Tribune.* http://www.sltrib.com/2003/Jan/01112003/Utah/19305.asp.

Sutton (2002). "Training for Terror False Alarm Trio Delayed." http://www.twincities.com/mld/twincities/4087326.htm.

Thal, Steven (2003). "IIRAIRA Reform: Immigration and Nationality Law." http://www.ilw.com/thal/iiraira,.htm.

Tien, Lee (2003) "Foreign Intelligence Surveillance Act " Electronic Frontier Foundation.

Tribe, Lawrence (2001) "Military Tribunals Undermine the Constitution." Testimony given before a senate subcommittee, December 6 http://www.counterpunch.org/ltribe1.html

Turk, Austin (2002) "Policing International Terrorism· Options " *Police Practice and Research: An International Journal,* 3(4):279-286.

Tussing, Bert and James Kievet (2003). "DOD, USNORTHCOM, and the Department of Homeland Security" Center for Strategic Leadership, U.S Army War College April Issue Paper. http://www.carlisle.army.mil/usacs/index.asp.

Tyler, Patrick (2003). "Overseer in Iraq Adapts Strategy as Hurdles Rise." *New York Times,* July 13 http://www.nytimes.com.

United Nations (1997). "Convention Against Torture and Other Cruel, Inhuman, or Degrading Treatment or Punishment." http://www.hrweb.org/legal/cat.html#Article%201.1.

United Press International (2002) "Report No Terror Link in LAX Shootings" *Newsmax Wires.* http://www.newsmax.com/82119.shtm.

U.S. Bureau of Customs and Border Protection (2003). "Welcome to Customs and Border Protection" http://www.cbp.gov/xp/cgov/toolbox/about/mission.

U.S. Department of Energy (2003), "Office of Energy and Assurance Mission Statement." http://www.mbe.doe.gov/budget/04budget/content/otherdef/ea.pdf

U.S. Department of Homeland Security (2002) "DHS Organization" http://www.dhs.gov/dhspublic/display?content=20

U.S. Department of Homeland Security (2003a): "Fact Sheet: Plum Island Animal Disease Center Transition" http://www.dhs.gov/dhspublic/display?theme=27, "Research and Technology" http://www.dhs.gov/dhspublic/theme_home5.jsp, "Under Secretary for Information Analysis and Infrastructure Protection. Frank Libuti.

U.S. Department of Homeland Security (2003b). "Press Briefing by Secretary Ridge" Press Room, February 14.

U.S. Maritime Administration (2002). Quarterly Report Number 64, July.

Usgovinfo (2002) "USNORTHCOM Provides Military Homeland Defense." October 4 http://www.usgovinfo.about.com/library/weekly/aanorthern.htm.

U.S. Department of Justice (2002) "Memorandum for Alberto R Gonzalez, Counsel to the President Re· Standards of Conduct for Interrogation Under 18 U.S.C Secs 2340-2340A" Washington, DC. Unpublished.

U.S Northern Command (2003). "News Room: Fact Sheets" http://www.USNORTHCOM.mil/index.cfm

Van Natta, Don and David Johnson (2003) "A Terror Lieutenant with a Deadly Past." *New York Times,* February 10 http://www.nytimes.com/2003/02/10/internati.../10TERR.html.

Van Bergen, Jennifer (2002). "Secret Court Decision Silently Overrules Provision of PATRIOT Act" Terrorism in the Age of Surveillance. http://www.ratical.org/ratville/CAH/FISAcourt.html

Walker, Samuel (1994). *Sense and Nonsense about Crime and Drugs: A Policy Guide,* Fifth Edition. New York, NY: McGraw-Hill.

Walzer, Michael (1994). "Comment." In A. Guttman (ed.) *Multiculturalism: Examining the Politics of Recognition,* pp. 99-103. Princeton, NJ· Princeton University Press

Walzer, Michael (1984) *Just and Unjust Wars* Harmondsworth. Penguin.

Washington Journal (2003) "Interview with Michael Boyd." August 8. C-SPAN

Washingtonpost com (2003). "Osama bin Laden Urges Attacks on the U S." htttp://www.washingtonpost/com/ac2/wp-dyn/A58869-2003Feb11.

Weaver, Mary Anne (1996) "Blowback." *The Atlantic Online.* http://www.theatlantic.com/issues/96may/blowback.htm.

Weissbrodt, David, Joan Fitzpatrick, and Frank Newman (2002). *International Human Rights: Law, Policy and Process,* Third Edition.

White House (2001a). "President Issues Military Order" http://www.whitehouse.gov/news/releases/2001/11/print/20011008.html.

White House (2001b). "President Establishes Office of Homeland Security." http://www.white house.gov/news/releases/2001/10/print/20011008.html.

White House (2003a): "First 100 Days of Homeland Security" http://www.whitehouse.gov/news/releases.

White House (2003b). "Fact Sheet: Operation Liberty Shield" http.//www.whitehouse.gov/news/releases/2003/03/print/20030317-9.html.

White, Jonathan R. (2002). *Terrorism: An Introduction,* Third Edition Stamford, CT: Thompson Learning.

Wilgoren, Jodi (2001) "Swept Up in a Dragnet, Hundreds Sit in Custody and Ask 'Why'?" *New York Times,* November 25. http://www.nytimes.com/2001/11/25/national/25DETA.html.

Wolf, Paul (2002) "FISA Court Decision." Terrorism in the Age of Surveillance. 2 September. http://www.ratical/org/ratville/CAH/FISAcourt.html.

Worldlink (2003). "Brothers and Others." Video. Worldlink Spotlight, April.

www.aclutx.org (2001). "Voluntary Interviews" American Civil Liberties Union of Texas. http://www.aclutx.org/ projects/police/lettervoluntaryinterviews120201.htm.

www.usembassy.si (2002). "Information About the New NSEERS Program." http.//www.us embassy.si/Consular/nseers.htm

Wu, Annie (2000) "The History of Airport Security." http://www.savvytraveler.org/show/features/2000/20000915/security.shtml.

Yancho, Carol (2001) "Hundreds in Michigan Asked to Submit to 'Terror Questioning'." CNN, November 28 http://www.cnn.allpolitics

Author Index

Subject Index